PRAISE FOR
LIKE SANDS THROUGH
THE HOURGLASS

"Bill Hayes was always a great singer, but who knew he would turn out to be such a terrific writer? He and his wife have given us an inside glimpse of what really goes on behind the scenes of a soap opera. It's so good someone should grab this book and turn it into a soap opera."
—Mel Brooks

"Bill and Susan Hayes have written such an interesting book and in such intimate style, it's like they're in the room talking to you—and they tell the truth. Read it. You'll have a wonderful time!"   —Sid Caesar

"It is very apparent that Bill and Susan love each other. What I did not expect is to fall in love with both of them, as you will when you read their book!"   —Carl Reiner

"Deeply personal, startlingly candid, touching, and hilarious. Above and beyond anything ever written about true-life love or the drama behind the scenes of daytime drama. *Like Sands Through the Hourglass* is a must read."   —Deidre Hall

"A true love story, told with complete honesty, about a joy for living, love for families and friends, and enthusiasm for their craft. What a wonderful lesson to cherish."   —Robert Clary

Like Sands

Through the Hourglass

BILL HAYES

and

SUSAN SEAFORTH HAYES

 NEW AMERICAN LIBRARY

New American Library
Published by New American Library, a division of
Penguin Group (USA) Inc., 375 Hudson Street,
New York, New York 10014, USA
Penguin Group (Canada), 90 Eglinton Avenue East, Suite 700, Toronto,
Ontario M4P 2Y3, Canada (a division of Pearson Penguin Canada Inc.)
Penguin Books Ltd., 80 Strand, London WC2R 0RL, England
Penguin Ireland, 25 St. Stephen's Green, Dublin 2,
Ireland (a division of Penguin Books Ltd.)
Penguin Group (Australia), 250 Camberwell Road, Camberwell, Victoria 3124,
Australia (a division of Pearson Australia Group Pty. Ltd.)
Penguin Books India Pvt. Ltd., 11 Community Centre, Panchsheel Park,
New Delhi - 110 017, India
Penguin Group (NZ), cnr Airborne and Rosedale Roads, Albany,
Auckland 1310, New Zealand (a division of Pearson New Zealand Ltd.)
Penguin Books (South Africa) (Pty.) Ltd., 24 Sturdee Avenue,
Rosebank, Johannesburg 2196, South Africa

Penguin Books Ltd., Registered Offices:
80 Strand, London WC2R 0RL, England

Published by New American Library, a division of Penguin Group (USA) Inc.
Previously published in a New American Library hardcover edition.

First New American Library Trade Paperback Printing, November 2006
10 9 8 7 6 5 4 3 2 1

 REGISTERD TRADEMARK—MARCA REGISTRADA

New American Library Trade Paperback ISBN: 0-451-22005-6

The Library of Congress has cataloged the hardcover edition of this title as follows:

Hayes, Bill.
    Like sands through the hourglass / Bill Hayes and Susan Seaforth Hayes.
      p.   cm.
    ISBN 0-451-21660-1
    1. Hayes, Bill. 2. Hayes, Susan Seaforth. 3. Television actors and actresses—United States—Biography.
4. Days of our lives (Television program) I. Hayes, Susan Seaforth. II. Title.
PN2287.H348A3   2005
791.45'028'092273—dc22   2005008536

Set in Bembo
Designed by Ginger Legato

Printed in the United States of America

To our parents,

who loved us always,

and our producers,

who loved us from time to time

Contents

Part Three

Part Four

Part One

I

The Day

BILL

"And, Bill," Macdonald Carey said in that great mellifluous bass voice, "this is our Susan Seaforth." (Bells.)

I stood up. "Susan," Mac went on, indicating me, "Bill Hayes. Playing Brent Douglas." (Balloons.)

This stunningly beautiful twenty-six-year-old brunette smiled that smile, took in my ruffled hair, mod bell-bottoms and flowered shirt, and, busily opening her script, said, "I know, I look like Denise Alexander, but she plays Susan and I play Julie. You'll get it straight." (Klieg lights.)

It was Monday, April 14, 1970, my fifteenth episode of *Days of our Lives*, and we were gathering for our one p.m. read-through and initial blocking in the *Days* Office, Stage 9, NBC, Burbank.

Director Wes Kenney called us to order, producer Jack Herzberg took out his stopwatch, secretary–script girl Helen Hall put a latex-rubber thimble on her index finger, and we proceeded to read through the script, which would be taped the following morning.

I couldn't keep my eyes off the girl. She and Frances Reid, who played Alice, read through one long scene together, and I was immediately captured by their acting competence and utter ease. With obvious understanding and effortlessness Susan and Frances read their fifteen-page scene, "emoting" just enough to show director Kenney what they felt head writer Bill Bell meant for them to play.

I kept sneaking peeks at the young lady across from me with brightly

3

colored yarn tied around her pigtails, a drapey blouse and slacks of some shiny material.

Moonstruck? Absolutely, but it would be a long time before my heart could admit it or take any definitive action.

We marked the timing cuts in our scripts, discussed meanings of words, noted discrepancies between today's script and yesterday's taping, all at a no-nonsense high speed, and then headed down the hall to another room, which was furnished only with a dozen plastic chairs.

There Wes Kenney blocked the scenes, describing basic scenery and where the cameras would be. "Bing, bing, bing, bing," I found, meant close-ups back and forth. I also learned that Susan Seaforth could listen to Wes giving directions, read her part, hear what other actors were whispering around the room, and make wry comments all at the same time. I was impressed.

We finished at three p.m., I received my seven a.m. call for the next day and—trying not to grin too broadly—followed those shiny slacks down the stairs and out into the parking lot.

SUSAN

A *new man*! The *DOOL* soap opera "family" was a small-cast affair in 1970. When a fresh face showed up at rehearsal it changed the dynamic of the whole room. The cast had taped that morning and was reading through the next day's material with muted energy. We were all so professional. It was all so familiar.

"Bill Hayes? Ah, yes, delighted." I nodded. Mac Carey seemed to know him well as he stylishly presented the new leading man to our little pod of performers.

I was a veteran of fifteen months on the show and at last in possession of a contract! "Seven years, starting at *twenty-five dollars over scale* per episode," my agent, Lew Deuser, had chortled. I'd been hanging in the dressing room doorway for weeks on end expecting to be fired and constantly hoping for approval from producer-director Wes Kenney. This contract, this job, was the best chance I'd ever had in twenty-two years of being an actress. I was deadly serious about the show, the character and, of course, myself.

Across the small room I noticed Hayes was carrying a leather-bound script cover with his name on it, and he was writing down his blocking in detail. Under the fluorescent lights he appeared untanned, unlined and strangely radiant. He was smiling, lively, and obviously tickled by the scenes. Such uncool delight was a contrast to our established cast. We were dramatic actors here, dealing with emotions, inner pain, and lots of subtext—that secret sorrow the audience knows all about that the characters bravely hide.

Hayes seemed to be enjoying himself. He was from the musical theater, of course. I eyed him over my pages (I'd never owned a script cover) and realized this was my childhood heartthrob, the blue-eyed, dark-haired Prince Charming type from NBC's *Your Show of Shows* of beloved memory.

He was wearing alarmingly lighthearted pants, striped cream and brown like saltwater taffy. His posterior in profile was adorable.

But Seaforth was nothing if not cool, glib and unmoved by such delights as charm and great looks. I'd seen him nine years before onstage, starring in the national company of *Bye Bye Birdie*. I had been ushering for a free seat in the top balcony that night. All I remembered of the show was Bill singing to a sad little girl onstage. When he danced with her his tap shoes were shining. At the number's end she had become a very happy girl indeed. Hayes was obviously from the lighthearted land of show business, so different from my world of daytime drama.

Rehearsals ended and I slipped into my little Toyota, the color and temperature of a baked potato in the Burbank sun. On the drive home to my mother's house in downtown Los Angeles I hummed Bill's song from *Birdie*: "Put on a happy face!" Well! A new man indeed! But, after all, just another actor. Who could take those taffy pants seriously? Not me!

2

The Days Before the Day

BILL

Here's how it happened.

In January 1970, I was playing a five-week run of Neil Simon's *Come Blow Your Horn* at the Thunderbird in Las Vegas, two shows a day, six days a week.

I had been divorced five months; my former wife, Mary, had moved on to another life, and I had custody of our underage children. Cathy, Tommy and Peggy were at that moment in Tucson, where I'd bought a house with my parents. But it had become evident to me that I needed to change my career completely so that I could be with them every night in order to be a stabilizing father to my children.

So, on my day off I flew over to have lunch with my Los Angeles agent, Sylvia Bloom. I told her, "I desperately need a job where I can be home every night to take care of my kids. I have to stop traveling. No more theater, no more nightclubs. And I need it right now." She promised she would get on it.

Then, during the last week of our run in Las Vegas, Sylvia called. "Bill, do you really want to take a job that will keep you in one place?"

"Yep."

"Do you care that the job might not pay very much?"

"Nope."

"Have you ever considered doing a daytime drama? A soap?"

"How much?"

"A hundred eighty-six dollars per half-hour episode."

"Ush!"

"Yes, I know, but if the character catches on you'd basically have a permanent job, and you might still go out and do theater jobs to make enough to get by."

I sighed. "Yeah, I guess you're right."

"Well, then," said Sylvia, "let me present your name, see what the reaction is. It couldn't hurt."

I was not eager to make such a move. In all my life I had never watched a TV soap, so I was (like many nonviewers) quick to ridicule the art form. In my mind, overemoted ham acting was "soap opera acting," stilted and clichéd writing was "soap opera writing." I just didn't know.

When she called back I was resigned to going along with whatever might happen. I figured what the heck, maybe I could even stand the shame of doing a soap for a year. Then, of course, I'd have to do something "worthwhile" to get my self-respect back.

Sylvia said, "I've arranged for you to have a meeting with executive producer Betty Corday [who had taken over the reins of *Days* following her husband Ted's death], head writer Bill Bell and producer-director Wes Kenney. I have the audition scene here; I'll send it to you today."

"Hey," I said, "I worked with Wes Kenney on *My True Story* in New York! Terrific director!"

She said, "So, you see? It can't be all bad, right?"

"Right. And when is this meeting?"

"The meeting is set for three thirty, Wednesday. Rehearsal Room Two, NBC, Burbank."

"You got it," I said, and started to hang up. "Oh, by the way, what's the name of this turkey?"

She laughed. "It's called *Days of our Lives*."

BILL GETS THE JOB

Days of our Lives, huh? Well, I thought, the days of my life had been a soap opera lately, so maybe I'd be able to relate to it. I received the audition scene and read it over. Surprisingly well written. The character was Brent Douglas, a con-man adventurer who obviously didn't care who he stepped on or over to get what he wanted, and I relished the idea of playing such a rogue. I studied the scene, two pages of quiet, sly seduction, and it wove its way into my brain very quickly.

At three p.m. on Wednesday, in the bare-walled *DOOL* office at NBC, I met Regina Gleason, who had just completed a two-year acting stint on the show. She'd played Kitty Horton, the contentious wife of Tommy Horton (John Lupton), and, though her character had been killed off, Regina seemed to have enjoyed the whole experience. She was to work with me in my audition scene and was a joltingly good actress. I thought, what a waste of good talent, working on a soap! I was, you see, not getting it at all.

We strolled down the midway, past Ben's (tacky commissary) Truck, to Rehearsal Room 2, where we did the scene for Bill Bell, Betty Corday and Wes Kenney, all of them intensely focused on what I was doing. Regina and I played the scene very realistically, striking sparks off each other in an understated but rather feral, sensuous way, and when we finished, our little audience sighed. Then they smiled broadly and said, "Mmmmm."

After the others left, Wes Kenney said, "That was terrific, Willie. And they all appreciated the fact that you memorized the scene. Can you come back to Studio Nine at twelve thirty tomorrow afternoon?"

I said, "Thanks for the kind words, H." His name is H. Wesley Kenney. "I'll be there."

The following day, I returned to Studio 9 at NBC. I could hear sounds coming from the big room where they were taping that day's episode.

Wes Kenney burst out through the door, shouted hello, and introduced me to very tall, very dark, very handsome Jed Allan, who'd been sitting across from me in the same gray waiting area. (Jed would be back, cast as Don Craig, eighteen months later.) Wes said, "We've narrowed it down to you two. We'd like you both to stand in the set and just let us look at you on camera."

So, feeling a little like meat hanging in a market, Jed and I stepped into the set, found some light, let the cameras look us up and down, and then Wes said over the PA system, "Thank you both. We'll be in touch with your agents in the morning."

The next morning I got the call from Sylvia. "Better start watching *Days of our Lives*, because they've offered you the part, and I told them you'd do it."

"Starting when?"

"Rehearsal one to three p.m., next Wednesday, February fourth. Taping seven a.m. to one p.m. the following day. They're mailing you your first script this morning."

It was nice to be wanted, I loved the idea of working in Los Angeles, and it was especially appealing to be cast as a roguish "heavy." It was for only $186 an episode, however, and, though Carrie, my eldest, was already married, with Billy in college and the other three kids having that old eating habit, I could see the money wasn't going to stretch very far.

What's more, this job offer was to work in a form of entertainment that was (in my untutored mind) of questionable value. So I dragged myself slowly over to the TV set and clicked it on just as Mac Carey was intoning, "This is Macdonald Carey, and these are the days of our lives."

Well, they've got Mac on their show, I thought. That's a point for their side. Macdonald Carey had guest-starred on *Your Show of Shows*, where I'd been a regular back in the early fifties, and we had performed back-to-back musicals at the Charlotte (NC) Summer Theatre in 1959, so we actually did know each other; and Mac had had quite a good career in radio, theater and films. It was impressive to realize he was now starring in a TV soap.

I watched three episodes (Friday, Monday and Tuesday) before flying back to Los Angeles, learned a jumble of character names—Mickey, Laura, Bill, Tommy, Sandy, Julie, Susan, Tom, Alice—and slowly began to figure out some of the relationships. Tommy's daughter was Sandy, Laura was married to Mickey, Tom and Alice seemed to be everyone's parents.

And, surprise, all the actors were uncommonly good! Not at all the overacting hams I'd been expecting. I thought, Is it possible this job might not be so bad after all?

FIRST REHEARSAL

My first script arrived the next morning, along with a four-paragraph description of my character, both written by Bill Bell.

ABOUT BRENT DOUGLAS (January 15, 1970)

> We will first meet Brent in the state penitentiary where, as the cell mate of Bill, he will be paroled about one month after Bill begins his sentence. Brent is very male, handsome, articulate and disarming—a young man of around twenty-eight who has lived by his wits. The police classified him as a confidence man when he was arrested and convicted for selling worthless securities. At the time of his arrest, however, the police were unaware of—among other things—Brent's brief venture in the "badger game," which for the uninitiated means using women to shake down men.
>
> He rarely loses command of a situation or of himself, and what he lacks in conscience he makes up for in his perseverance and sheer determination.
>
> Brent is more comfortable with women, and it follows that they are more gullible and vulnerable to him than men.
>
> But make no mistake, Brent Douglas is not merely a personality boy. He has depth and substance to his character—as well he must if he ultimately is to inspire the trust and confidence of our characters.

Having done many inane juveniles in the past, I was indeed turned on by Bill Bell's description. I was surprised, however, to read that Brent was supposed to be only twenty-eight. I was already covering gray streaks.

Wednesday, February 4, finally dawned—my first rehearsal day. I arrived at noon, just in time to watch Episode 1078 being taped. It happened very fast: cast, crew, cameras, cable pullers, microphone booms, lights, props, costumes, set painters, hairstylists, directors, producers, all working together like the proverbial well-oiled machine, an ensemble of

professionals dedicated to turning that forty-page script into a meaningful drama, completely recorded on tape—in less than fifty-five minutes.

My preconception of soaps as a lower form of art faded. At age
forty-four, I was rediscovering the adage We are never too old to learn.

The taping wrapped at about twelve forty-five. Some of the actors
wiped off their makeup and headed home, others nipped out to Ben's
Truck for a cold taco and a warm can of juice on their way up to the
DOOL office for the read-through of the following day's show. For
those working on consecutive days there was no lunch break.

Wes Kenney, coffee in hand, barreled into the office and extracted a
script from a pile on his desk. He would be directing my first episode,
which was comforting.

He introduced me to other cast members, including John Lupton (as
Tommy Horton) and Edward Mallory (as Bill Horton), to script girl Helen Hall (lovely, classy, sharp) and producer Jack Herzberg, an old-
fashioned Hollywood type, who said, "Oh, Bill, I loved your performance
in *Come Blow Your Horn* in Vegas last week." And then Macdonald Carey
came in and greeted me warmly, making me feel even more at home.

We opened our scripts and read through the scenes for timing and cuts.

Ed Mallory, who was working every day that week, appeared to be
reading his script for the first time. I watched him rip through his scenes
with pretty blonde Kay Peters, who was playing the prison psychiatrist.

Without adding any extra time to the stopwatch, Ed reacted verbally
to his own lines as well as Kay's, adding a running commentary of wit
and nonsense:

"That's narrative! What is this, a radio show?"

"That comes dangerously close to deus ex machina!"

"At Carnegie Tech that was a no-no!"

Ed's favorite word was "dork," and he could make the weirdest
sound effects: a World War I machine gun shooting down an enemy
warplane, an old vacuum cleaner. He was a bright, mercurial, excellent
actor, and I was happy my first scenes were going to be with him.

I was used to learning all my lines before coming to rehearsal. In fact,
I couldn't have gone to sleep the night before if I hadn't memorized my
words. And here Ed was etching those lines into his memory box
merely by reading them out loud. I've always had to labor long over

learning dialogue. When I finished school I had even said to myself, "Man, I am done with memorizing!" (Naturally I've spent my career—it'll soon be sixty years long—memorizing thousands of song lyrics, plays, films, commercials and TV shows!)

After initial timing cuts were announced, Wes Kenney led the pack to the other end of the hall, to that beige room filled with plastic chairs, where he energetically blocked the scenes. The mood was jovial. It all happened so fast I barely had time to write down my moves. Discussions about lines and scenes were terse. I was shocked at the level of acting know-how in that room. It was so high it crackled! Wes, the last one out of the room, pointed at me and said, "See you at seven!" I was left with the darnedest feeling of being at home.

FIRST TAPING

The next morning, since my call was seven a.m., I naturally arrived at six thirty, being used to the rule of theater that says you always check in a half hour early. The Artists' Entrance to Studio 9 was locked, so I went around back and came in through the elephant doors of the Scene Dock. There a lighting person told me, "Oh, they do their first two hours in Rehearsal Room Three, over at the main building."

I ran over to Rehearsal Room 3. Nobody was there. The lights weren't on. I was about to go look somewhere else when a prop man came chugging up with a cart of donuts and coffee, gave me a welcoming "Good morning," switched on the lights, rolled the cart in and was gone. Helping myself to a donut and coffee, I sat and read my script.

At six fifty, the other actors began to stroll in. Stage manager Britt Lomond arrived next, script in one hand, stopwatch in the other, a pencil over each ear, and making jokes in a terrible German accent. At six fifty-eight, Wes Kenney charged into the room and went to work.

He reestablished the blocking, shoving desks and tables and chairs around to suggest the sets, then did another run-through top to bottom for timing. There were a few comments on content, now and then a question about which camera was on whom. Ed Mallory still had the script in his hand, but referred to it less each time we went through. Done, off we went to Studio 9.

By nine a.m. the scene design crew had finished building and dressing the sets, lights had been aimed toward colored-tape T-marks on the floor, and the cameramen had already spent an hour meticulously aligning their cameras to the intricate test patterns.

Wes had us speak our lines and walk through our moves for the cameramen and microphone boom operators. Props were placed and tried out. Ed still carried his script, though by then he wasn't looking at it.

Recalling my initial moment on camera is easy because of my first line. I was sitting on the lower bunk polishing an old pair of shoes when a guard unlocked the prison-cell door and slid it open with a clang. Bill Horton, convicted of manslaughter in the strange death of his sister-in-law Kitty, entered apprehensively, the guard slammed the bars shut and we heard the bolt lock into place. Without looking up, I said, "Put your hand on my bunk and I'll kill you." (Oooooh.)

At ten a.m. we ran through the show again for timing. The five sets were circled like wagons around a campfire, with cameras and microphone booms in the center, cable pullers snaking the thick cables out of their way. I wanted to watch the other scenes, but was advised this was my time to get into wardrobe and makeup.

Dress rehearsal was at eleven a.m., after which we were given final cuts and changes. Ed Mallory by this time was whipping out his lines as if he'd been performing them for weeks. Me? I was sweating in the lower bunk, trying to match his lickety-split rhythm with my two-page speeches of exposition.

Notes came not only from Wes Kenney but also from Betty Corday via Jack Herzberg. Wes: "Not defensive, but no smile. Just matter-of-fact. Brent's unhappy about being in prison, but shrewd enough to keep a low profile. Know what I mean? And always remember: P and V [pace and vitality]." Betty and Jack: "Bill, button your shirt one button higher, and get makeup to powder you down. You're glistening."

We were down to precisely twenty-four minutes of story. We went on tape at the stroke of noon. Though videotape had been in use at NBC for twelve years, *DOOL* still had no editing capability (budget?), so we started at the top—as if it were a live presentation—and went straight through, leaving a sixty-second "black" between acts for the subsequent insertion of commercials. When we hit a snag, we couldn't just stop and pick it up again the way we do now; we had to go back and begin the scene over.

Ed Mallory and Wes Kenney were so much at ease that the taping seemed quick and effortless. Afterward I went into the control booth and asked Wes if he was going to look at any of the scenes. He grinned and said, "No, that's it. You were fine, Willie. See you next week." He tossed his script into the circular file and flew out the door. I scratched my rookie head, hung up my prison denims. My life as a soap actor had begun.

BILL MEETS MORE OF THE DAYS FAMILY

I enjoyed working with Macdonald Carey, who was really an old shoe. An inveterate reader, Mac always had a hardback along with him, usually from the *New York Times* bestseller list. He owned more than four thousand first editions, many of them autographed. He certainly was an experienced actor, but I felt he never was at ease learning long-paragraph soap speeches. Sometimes, when the little red light would go on, Mac would develop a tremor, and I think that was just nerves. When he wasn't nervous and just played his scenes, he was gloriously good.

On my second show I met the elegant, beautiful, superb actress Frances Reid, Alice Horton in the show, and I couldn't imagine anyone more perfect for the part. Smoking a cigarillo, she had an air of Katharine Hepburn about her. Frances had been called to testify back in the McCarthy hearings twenty-five years earlier, hadn't talked, and was still smoldering over the injustice of it all. Her personal attitude helped create the feeling of family in the company, and every year she would invite the whole cast to her Brentwood home for a Christmas feast.

The next day I experienced the Junoesque Susan Flannery, playing Laura. She, like Ed Mallory, appeared to learn her lines by osmosis. She was so real I had to follow along in my script to see if it was Laura speaking or Flannery. Like Frances, she also smoked little cigars and loved to be profane.

On my fourth show I got to meet the actor playing Mickey Horton, John Clarke. I was happy to see that John arrived at the studio already knowing his lines; he had lots of lawyer speeches to rattle off in court. So at least I was not the only one who had to work ahead of time. Also tall, with an opera singer's robust voice, John was a formidable actor who called everyone "turkey." He made his editorial comments in a Donald Duck voice.

On my eighth show I met Denise Alexander, in the role of Susan Hunter Martin. An electric actress, Denise read through her lines once out loud and then carried her script only to make changes. I couldn't believe those actors—they learned their lines so fast! I was elated that I would soon be doing scenes with Denise.

Suddenly I wanted to be in every episode. I was falling in love with the *DOOL* cast!

In addition to Wes Kenney, there were three other directors who worked the show, all first-rate.

Joe Behar, who had directed the *DOOL* pilot, was laid-back but quick. To this day, Susan and I quote Joe's directions, like, "Cross to her elbow." People don't know right from left, but they recognize an elbow.

Dick Sandwick, allegedly a toper, was comical but knowledgeable. He would give directions in the voice of W. C. Fields and then get serious: "I need a real curtain for the end of that scene. Give me something, will you?"

Frank Pacelli, a brilliant director who became a best friend to Susan's mom, was maddeningly impatient in the studio and drove the cameramen and stage managers crazy by directing the furniture and props as well as the actors.

All of them did their homework, planned the emotional "moments" before taping, but were quick to adapt and "wing" changes to catch actors bringing something unexpected to the scenes. The cameramen were given shot sheets, but always had to be ready to catch in their lenses those beautiful unforeseen tears or heightened emotions that put icing on the cake.

The directors' workday began at three a.m., when they walked the sets and placed those little T-marks that showed the lighting director where the actors were to stand. The lighting crew also started at three a.m.

It seemed there was work being done in the studio around the clock. The sets used one day needed to be taken apart, carted away and stowed before the next day's sets could be assembled. There were furniture and props and occasionally gaslit fires, lamps that could be turned on on camera, telephones that were connected to one another, water that visibly came out of faucets, and other appurtenances, such as the beautiful miniature Horton house at 280 Harris Avenue, which was frequently used to lead us into a scene in Tom and Alice's living room or kitchen. (Sound-effects specialist Bob Mott always contributed a barking dog.) Studio 9 was a busy little factory.

BILL BELL, THE INCREDIBLE

William J. Bell, head writer of *Days*, presented a large and colorful tapestry, weaving real people back and forth through theatrically tailored plots. Whether he was doing a story about a current social problem or dealing with the innermost feelings of characters involved in real-life problems, he never resorted to histrionics that were out of character.

Immediately after each day's air show, Bill called Wes Kenney to give his appraisal of the episode. He critiqued each character and scene. Then he would call Betty Corday and discuss the various actors' impact on the show.

What a tower of talent Bill Bell was! As experienced as his scriptwriters were, he always retained the right to edit their work. And the result was glorious! He oversaw the work of a strong team of writers with varied styles.

Tall and voluptuous Pat Falken Smith thought sexy and wrote sexy. Her scenes were always fun to play and were—for me—the easiest to memorize. Each line or thought led directly to the next.

Natty, slender Bill Rega, a sensitive man with emphysema, wrote himself into his work. He was the best at bringing a scene to a tearful climax, and occasionally could be very funny.

Quiet Margaret Stewart wrote parallel soliloquies, so her characters seemed to converse without listening to each other. Though dramatic, her writing was impossible to memorize.

BILL GOES ON CONTRACT

Although my seventy-year-old parents had agreed to share a home with me in Tucson, it was never my intention to saddle them with the constant care of my children. They'd already done enough of that.

But somehow that's the way it seemed to be working out. My home at the moment was Tucson, and I now was working sporadically on *Days of our Lives*, commuting back and forth to Burbank.

Since I sometimes taped on consecutive days, I rented a cheap room and kitchen on Havenhurst in West Hollywood, where the maids were light-fingered and late-night Jimi Hendrix music from a nearby pad crashed against my ears relentlessly.

In my first eight weeks on *DOOL* I did a total of ten episodes. Ten times $186 is $1,860. Gross! Take away $185 a month for my Havenhurst digs, plus the cost of airfare for the commuting, and my wallet told me it wasn't working out. I was only at home with the kids *part*-time instead of *full*-time, and I wasn't being paid enough to make ends meet.

Dr. J. Roger Miller, Dean of the School of Music at Millikin University, offered me a job to create a department of musical theater for him. And his salary offer of $16,000 for eight months' work came to more than twice what *DOOL* was paying me. He promised to make me a full professor and a department head. I told Roger I would take it.

When Betty Corday heard about my plans she immediately called Sylvia Bloom with a three-year contract offer: first year at a $26,000 guarantee (two episodes a week at $250 per episode); second year $28,000 ($275 per episode); third year $31,000 ($300 per episode). And they promised generosity in allowing me to get out from time to time to supplement my income by doing other TV shows or theater dates.

What to do? I had spent every minute of the last twenty-three years following my heart to a life of professional performing. I was an actor, not a teacher, and I knew it. I grappled, fought with myself, argued both sides, teetered on the brink, and fell.

I phoned Roger Miller, who graciously let me out of my verbal commitment, then called Sylvia and told her to go ahead and make the deal.

My accommodating folks bought my half of our Tucson house, so I had enough cash for a down payment toward a residence in Los Angeles. I made a quick search and bought a house near a junior high, a senior high and the NBC studios.

Closing my eyes and exhaling a long sigh of relief, I was now free to return to that cramped cell with Bill Horton. So, as they say, meanwhile . . .

PIGEONS AND GREENBACKS

. . . back in that cramped cell, Brent Douglas pricked up his ears when Bill Horton heard from Susan Martin that she had just inherited $250,000. In Brent's eyes that was a gold mine and he was the prospector. So when Bill was out of the cell on visiting day, Brent sneaked a peek at the letter to get all his facts straight.

Later, when Bill was attacked by that hardened lifer Ribiwitz wielding an ice pick, Brent jumped Ribiwitz, wrenched away the ice pick and held him until the prison guards took over.

Filled with gratitude, Bill invited Brent to come meet his family and friends in Salem when he got out. With visions of pigeons and greenbacks dancing in his head, Brent said, "Why, sure, Bill. I'd be glad to do that."

Having finally served his hard-time prison term, Brent bought some cool new duds, changed his name to Doug Williams, and headed for Salem.

DOUG'S DUDS

There was a small wardrobe budget for the ladies, but none for the men. When Brent Douglas finished serving his time and changed his name to Doug Williams, I had to costume Doug myself.

First I bought Doug "seventies mod": flowered shirts, striped bell-bottoms, wide belts with oversized buckles, suede half boots, a wide-lapel fitted suit, and some daring ties and colorful neckerchiefs. I decided against headbands, but every now and then would add some red, white, and blue "love beads." I wanted Doug Williams to be completely different from Salem's staid doctors and lawyers. I think even the producers and writers were jolted.

Soon Doug met Susan Martin, the intended victim. He sang "The Look of Love" while tossing a salad for the two of them, and came on to her with some forcefulness.

Susan, realizing that Doug was a scam artist on the make, figured he was heaven-sent in her rivalry with Julie. She told him, "I'm on to you, and I'm not interested. But I have a proposition for you. If you can break up my friend Julie's marriage to Scott Banning, I will give you ten thousand dollars cold cash."

He couldn't believe her audacious proposal (and neither could the audience). Doug okayed the deal, set himself up as an expert in stocks and bonds, and prepared to stalk his prey.

And that brings us right up to that fateful day when the actor playing Doug met the actress playing Julie.

SUSAN

I boomeranged onto *Days of our Lives*. Before the show debuted in 1965, I was interviewed for the role of Julie, a troubled teen and core member of the Horton family.

Days was created by Ted and Betty Corday, husband-and-wife producers unique in television. They envisioned a show where good people experience hard times but are not destroyed by them, where respect for family and hope for a better future are center stage. This philosophical tone would make *Days* a long-running gift to its viewers.

Soap operas were my strong suit. I'd played a little blond vixen named Dorothy one summer on *General Hospital*, whose overexposure at the seaside sent her into the emergency room with a severe and well-deserved sunburn. The last black-and-white TV soap, *The Young Marrieds*, occasionally featured me as Carol West, artist's model. When the show got canceled the artist went blind, and my true-blue character tried to stop him from blowing his brains out. Final scene, final episode:

Carol's at the front door screaming, "Walter! Walter! Noooooooooo!" Offstage *bang-thud*. Fade to very black.

Before I was old enough to vote I was a veteran of daytime court shows: *Youth Court, Divorce Court, Day in Court.* Those slice-of-unreality dramas were largely unscripted and tested my improvisational skills. I could make a scene out of any situation, witness or defendant. Crying and pleading were my specialties. So when executive producer Ted Corday thanked me for my reading, I decided to clinch the deal by offering him a copy of my performance highlights from *The Young Marrieds.* I'd paid over $100 to get these scenes copied and edited, and by God I was determined people in power should look at them.

The next day I got a call from my agent, Lew Deuser, normally a mild-mannered silver-haired guy in a suit. He was angry and upset. "Why did you give him that damn tape? You had the part till they saw you on camera!" The Julie character was a teen, a young, willful, immature kid. The Carol role was a fashion model, sexy and savvy. I came across as far too much for a Horton girl. My look drove the nail into the casting coffin.

In the 1960s, taped half-hour shows on the networks' daytime schedules were produced cheaply and reaped fat rewards. But actors were on the cheap side of that equation. No wardrobe was provided, though I was "modeling" a new outfit while being drawn for advertisements during each appearance. Actors received a $5 cleaning allowance, and that was all. After doing fifty or so episodes on *The Young Marrieds,* I was down to posing in my terry-cloth bathrobe. We did our own hair for that "natural look," but makeup artists were provided and I encouraged them to plaster on some glamour. Plaster plenty, actually.

God knows how strange my getups were on that tape I'd forced on Corday Productions. Deuser said something about my eyelashes getting a bad review. Anyway I blew it, and watched *DOOL* premiere and run for three years with other girls playing Julie.

SUSAN GETS THE JOB

While playing in the extreme outfield of show business, I attended Los Angeles City College night school, worked some, and considered becoming a history teacher. When *another* interview to play Julie got scheduled, I was shocked. Hadn't that ship sailed? Apparently the chemistry for Julie had never been achieved and now Bill Bell, the most creative writer in the medium, was aboard with big plans for little Julie.

By 1968, Ted Corday had died and his widow, Betty—with huge eyes and mezzo voice—was doing the casting. Betty guarded the family legacy with tireless devotion. While raising two boys she scrutinized every performance and word of dialogue daily. Like a general giving orders in a war, she gave notes with formidable thoroughness that kept the *Days* style real and warm.

All the actresses reading the audition scene would work opposite Denise Alexander, whose reputation was so excellent Ted Corday had said he wouldn't go on the air without her. The scene this time was as meaty as a slice of raw liver. Julie, older now, pregnant out of wedlock, attempts to terrorize her archenemy Susan (Alexander) into having a heart attack. In the verbal duel Susan survives and Julie brings on her own labor pains (nothing small-time about *this* show). There would be no screen test, so this time it was do-or-die in the casting office.

Denise and I tattered that scene. I remember thanking everybody in the room when it was over and staggering out the door, a broken thing. I once asked Bill Bell what he remembered about my performance that morning. "Your smile," he admitted. Ah! Go figure.

Wanting it so much, I felt an almost out-of-body experience when Deuser called, this time full of good cheer because Betty had chosen me and the job would start immediately. Would I darken my hair to match that of the girl I was replacing? You bet. I changed my hair color at home almost monthly in those days anyway. No contract was offered, since I was the fourth ingénue to attempt the role and everybody understood I was on trial, especially me.

Fortunately, Julie had grown out of the pouty kid into a passionate adult while I was waiting in the wings. That baby I'd encountered in the audition material was the center of a child-custody battle now. Julie had left town for a few months to give the viewers a chance to accept yet another new face. The reentry scene was brief, a split-screen phone call from San Francisco (foghorn sound effects) to Salem, telling Grandma Horton (Frances Reid) I was coming home.

John Clarke was playing my uncle Mickey. We had played Earp family members together on "The Gunfight at the OK Corral" segment of *Death Valley Days*. We'd gone out a few times when Lew Deuser, who represented us both, thought a match might be made. John was a lonely widower then, but we struck no sparks. Since then he had found a perfect wife in Patty and was much more at ease than I remembered.

Physically I looked average: chin-length dark brown hair, size eight, generally a little tense. Bill Hargate, the talented costumer, dressed me in lots of little navy outfits.

All the ladies' clothes came from the Broadway Hollywood, which received only screen credit. The guys got bupkes. John Clarke chose to wear the same brown suit for years. Though playing a well-to-do lawyer, he trotted it into court many times a month.

Tommy Cole, former "Mouseketeer Tommy," ran the makeup gang and kept everybody looking very natural by my standards. My standards were pretty low, but I needed to fit in. To hell with false eyelashes, lip gloss and my dreams of being a second Marlene Dietrich. *DOOL* was all about the acting, the stories and the conflicts. Glamour and "diva dish" was on nobody's mind then. We had our hands full grinding out twenty-four minutes of fresh material each day, five days a week, fifty-two weeks a year.

As a child I'd worked at the NBC lot doing *Hallmark Hall of Fame* and many productions of *Matinee Theater*, live and in color. Warner Bros. was around the corner, where I'd had the most fun of my career working on *77 Sunset Strip*, *Cheyenne*, and all the other detective and Western shows. My eyes teared up driving over the Cahuenga Pass, cruising into downtown Burbank and up to the studio with a parking pass. Johnny Carson was down the hall. This was tall cotton, all right!

Seaforth had been rejected only to return on target, a living example of the boomerang effect. Because of *Days* I would fall in love forever, my mother wouldn't be poor anymore, Hopi Indians would know my name, and I'd actually see boomerangs fly from Aussie hands. My heart would also be broken many times over, but that all lay ahead. For now, just driving through the NBC gate was my trip to Oz.

VINEGAR AND HONEY

As a little kid I'd heard lots of radio soap operas because my aunt Gertrude was deaf, and she had the voices of *The Second Mrs. Burton* and *Stella Dallas* blasting away through the whole house. Sitting beside the big brown Philco radio, I relished my favorite programs, too. *The Lone Ranger* ("Hi-yo, Silver!") and *Sergeant Preston of the Yukon* ("On, King!" "Woof!") enthralled me.

Television entered our lives in 1952, and nighttime viewing, especially old movies, was a delightful reward for a hard day's work. Davis, Dietrich, and Crawford pervaded my consciousness. My ideas of what a leading lady should be were certainly molded by their films.

Mother was an actress with many years' experience in radio drama, but by the fifties those shows were gradually disappearing, so she transitioned into film and TV acting. She often played character parts, wearing her hair in a bun and a disapproving expression on her face in hundreds of black-and-white half-hour shows. She brought brio to those bits. Elizabeth Harrower had brio in life generally, but never what you'd call steady work. No studio contract.

When and if my time came for a big job, I planned to act like Bette Davis and look like Marlene Dietrich. More practically, Mother put me in Jeff Corey's acting class to learn "The Method" when I was fifteen.

Now I had a contract, but I had to learn everything about being part of an ensemble and *staying* part of an ensemble. On *Days of our Lives* they didn't need a Dietrich or, God forbid, a Davis.

I rehearsed lines with my mom and was grateful for direction from Wes Kenney, the producer, who did everything with gusto. Wes won Emmys for every show he ever captained and made us feel a daily excitement at tape time. It's hard to have a sense of "curtain up" on a dark, cold soundstage five days a week. Wes would walk through the sets after dress-rehearsal notes, coffee in hand, shouting, "Have a good show, everybody!" Wes would tell you privately the point of a scene, then tell your cast mate something entirely different. This made for instant conflict that played wonderfully. The new Julie wanted Wes's approval more than most. Since I was raised without a dad and missed paternal pats on the head for twenty-five years, his praise was catnip to me.

Jack Herzberg, the other line producer, was a whole support system in one charming package. He watched my back and was a protective friend to me.

"Don't ever lend money to _____, if he asks you."

"Do you have a dentist in the San Fernando Valley? Here's my guy's number."

He bought my oil paintings to decorate his bachelor digs, and made sure no actors got fresh with his actresses. Because Wes was so overwhelming, nobody took Jack too seriously, but he made the set civilized, and he watched the budget, the clock and my feelings perfectly. If Wes was a father figure, Jack became my favorite uncle.

The ladies of *Days*, Frances Reid, Susan Flannery and Denise Alexander, were all extremely well read, self-assured and witty. Frances told me she'd accepted being hired to play a woman older than she was in life. This was typical of soap-opera casting, an actress of forty-odd playing mother to actors of thirty-odd. So the elegant, natural beauty was shrouded in the housedresses of a character woman. Mac Carey's Dr. Horton character played things warm, but not sexy. Frances never moped. She did complain if her character lacked brains, however. So did everybody else.

The core of drama is conflict, we know, and to achieve that somebody somewhere on some scripted page has to make a mistake. The making of a mistake is not always surrounded with Shakespearean grandeur. Many situations seemed stupid, not tragic, to the actors at first reading. And, since we were *never* given a peek at the long-range plan, there was a lot of daily grousing about, "How dumb can my character be?" Dumb enough to be interesting, of course.

Scripts had a good deal of repetition as well. "I said this ten times last week and already twice on page five," was a common complaint. Later, after many years of meeting fans face-to-face, I was surprised to discover they *loved* reciting your most repetitious lines back to you—with relish. Fans understood the story, got the main points and saw disasters coming. Repetition made things clear to a wide audience, and it was up to the actors to give it variety.

So the more the Horton family reiterated, the more the country lapped it up. Yet all those witty actors wanted to change dialogue and fought for their own opinions.

Soon Seaforth was smart-mouthing about her copious pages of dialogue, too, and feeling justified and at home. (After all, I remembered, Bette Davis went head-to-head with Jack Warner over her material.) Whipping pages back and forth, pointing my pencil, making derogatory cracks, getting muffled laughs from the cast at read-throughs, I was feeling my oats after a few months.

Then Mac Carey took me aside in the hallway one afternoon. Even under the fluorescent lights his looks and charm were arresting and my nostrils flared at the attention. "You'll get more flies with honey than with vinegar, my dear. That's no way to get what you want," he advised this little wisecracker. I was surprised. Didn't everybody do it? I guess Mac cared enough to stop me from going in this self-destructive direction. My remarks were always remembered. Saying too much to get a laugh from cast and crew was always my biggest fault. To be cautioned by the show's father figure slowed me down. Nobody loves a wiseass.

SNAPPING BEANS

Putting all backchat aside, the instinct to protect your character springs from a sound motive. Any character is invented by a writer, but is partly the thespian's creation, too; it's the actor's art. So when a show runs on for years, you've naturally grown into thinking you own the role. You and who you play are completely entwined in the audience's belief, and many a player comes to love that part dearly.

The pitfall comes from being too close to see the bigger effect a character's actions have on a show and from wanting to protect the character from taking chances, trying on new attitudes or making mistakes. It begins with a remark in rehearsal. "I would never say that." (Watch it, careful with that personal pronoun.) It continues with a trip to the producer's office "to set them straight," and ends with "I quit!"

On *General Hospital* I'd watched a pair of young actors cast as lovers fall in heat with each other, get over it and hate the situation so much they couldn't bear to come in to work anymore. They mocked the characters for being stupid and took it all so personally they finally ended their daytime careers.

All I learned from their sad example was to never fall in love with an actor you work with. The larger lesson—that living and breathing the character's world for years on end can undermine your grip on reality—escaped me.

Bill Bell said the ideal soap character is a young girl, a woman on the brink of life. Stories will rise off of her like steam off a racing horse. You could look at the history of *Days* that way. Julie had an eventful run from adolescence into edgy womanhood, usually setting free her libido in the most risky circumstances. Then her character's stepdaughter, Hope (Kristian Alfonso), had a decade of story driven by her impetuous behavior. Now the psychiatrist-twisted kid Sami muddies and manipulates the waters three shows out of five. These girls, with internal-combustion hearts, are fascinating. Adventures happen to all female soap stars all the time—kidnapping, stalking, lost desert-island episodes without end. But the acting heat sticks to actresses who play crazy, mixed-up bitches.

Well, I became Julie, and who was that? In my first shows I was a regretful sinner, a muted girl snapping beans in Grandma's kitchen. (Wes loved actresses snapping beans along with their dialogue.) Then, her role established, she girded up to fight for custody of her own little baby boy, adopted by Scott Banning (Mike Farrell) and babysat by Susan Martin (Denise Alexander).

Denise's character, Susan, loved Scott secretly, and the baby, too. She was a homebody, a maker of donuts, a real sweetheart headed for heartache. Julie hated Susan—an old boyfriend conflict started it—and was angling to get her son back more out of spite than mother love.

Uncle Mickey took Scott's case. Julie acted as her own lawyer, which meant lots of big speeches for me and showers of tears. Justice was trumped, and bitchy Julie got the baby while Susan and Scott mourned. Then, to put the elephant garlic in the stew, Julie dangled the baby boy—David—in Scott's face. He married her to reclaim the child he loved. Julie didn't give a rat's ass about Scott but had momentarily ruined Susan's life. Ha-ha, ho-ho!

Now the actor Mike Farrell was an all-around terrific guy, well informed, gifted and serious. He gradually became crushed by the spine-lessness of Scott Banning, the white-collar architect character that Bill Bell had written. Events passed over Scott, who never seemed to take action, and he was more a pawn than a person to Mike. Whatever it was that turned him off as an actor on *Days*, he left. Mike later emerged as a major talent on *M★A★S★H*, that milestone nighttime series. I regretted losing him as an acting partner and was eager to get a replacement who could have a good time doing soap.

After I'd spent about a year on *Days*, viewers loved Denise and hated me. Who could blame them? I loved Denise, too. We were both child actresses in the same era. We both had grown up in the Christian Science faith, with strong mothers. She had long, dark red hair and a no-ticeable bust. Since we had such parallel lives, I began to adopt her look. I started lowering my necklines. The hair was easy: I bought some for $35.00, a dark brown fall that attached at the crown. I named it "Cochise."

My life before *Days* had centered around Los Angeles City College, working in filmed television, and watching the news.

Newscaster Hal was the one romance to cross my path before destiny stepped in. We had met through my tiny political connection (a married man trying to get elected to congress).

As boyfriend material, Hal qualified. He wasn't married. That was a big change for me because I'd been hanging on the sleeves of married guys for years, dreaming that with enough tugging they would actually leave their wives and marry me. I mistook their weakness in dallying with me for worldly wisdom. What a waste!

Hal had a steady job commentating in TV news, for minimal money, I suspect, but he always indicated wealth was lurking on his horizon. His passion was flying the red single-engine Piper Comanche he parked at Santa Monica Airport outside Howard Hughes's old hangar. All his dates got flown to Catalina Island's "Airport in the Sky" for a thrill and a hamburger. That airstrip stuff served him well, but the girlie turnover was high because Hal demanded a loyal cheering section twenty-four hours a day. He called constantly to check your enthusiasm for his per-sonally written news stories (often cadged from the *New York Times*). I knew how to be a good audience, while his intellect and wit got me past the thick glasses and thin hairpiece. Proving myself a worthy companion, however, was taking years. I had to watch two hours of KTLA news a day, every day. After the ten p.m. broadcasts we rehashed his best on-camera bits while he downed a martini and exchanged his ideas with himself. Weekends were spent at the plane, polishing it or flying to local airports. I saw lots of California from the air and, in six years of relationship, must have spent a good two thousand hours looking over a wing for a wind sock.

His was a superior attitude, and I helped prove his superiority. All my opinions were molded on his, like gum on a shoe. Thanks to his caustic sense of humor I laughed my way through many many moons of wishing I was perfect enough, talented enough, to someday be his bride and the mother of—what else?—"Little Harold," the fantasy child who would rule the world.

A good ten years older than me, Hal had been a political science professor who became locally famous as part of George Putnam's news team. George, the anchor, was a hearty conservative given to straight-shootin' editorializing. He was more or less the model for the character of Ted Baxter, the blowhard anchorman of *Mary Tyler Moore Show* fame. In life George was a darling guy, needlessly in awe of Hal, whom he called Doctor, when actually my friend had never even written his dissertation.

George and Hal were pinfeathers on the conservative right wing, and, however distantly, they made me feel connected to big events. It took me a while to judge the meaning of little events. My little events. During my early months on *Days*, he seemed surprised that I was getting almost as much air time as the news. He preferred the master-handmaiden relationship. Hal consistently refused to spend time with my family and friends, found my career amusing and treated me like an amiable child. So I would stage fights to prove I was actually a tempestuous woman he could not take for granted. More folly. This required weeks of me repenting, crying, and gradually being allowed to sit in the plane again.

My grandmother Jessie invited the object of my affections to Thanksgiving dinner in our home one year. Between shows Hal appeared, met the guests, and endured more than enjoyed my grandmother's beautiful meal. She served raspberry sherbet between courses, "to clear the palate." Hal eyed it suspiciously and let his portion melt into a mess on the tablecloth. My mother had invited an actor I had worked with on TV Westerns to liven things up and irritate Hal. Jeffrey owned a hound dog named Louie, who accompanied his master everywhere in the form of his hair, which clung to Jeffrey's clothing. Hal loathed him on sight. That night the lights blew out during the turkey service, and helpful Jeffrey found a dead mouse behind the refrigerator while he was changing a fuse for Jessie. He also enjoyed the sparkling wine and got on a crying jag after he said "fuck" at the table in front of a family friend's ten-year-old girl. At that critical moment Hal rushed off for the ten o'clock broadcast. Mother was delighted by these entertainments. Though my grandmother was a George Putnam fan, she never beamed when Hal's toupee turned up, on-screen or off.

Of Prussian origins, Hal, a nonpracticing Jew, assured me the Prussians beat the German Jews right down to the ground in every way. Despite all the joking on the subject, I think he believed it. Opera had to be German, never French or Italian. I listened to so much Wagner during this period that I once dreamed of the *Siegfried Idyll*. All this negative nonsense didn't register with me until I wound up at a psychiatrist's office, where my doctor, also an intellectual Jew, suggested I had been dating a Nazi!

On birthdays and holidays I always received a present of jewelry. The box would be small, and I would think, "Ah, here comes the ring," but it would turn out to be a watch, a pin, or the noncommittal pendant. One Christmas I showed my mother the new trinket, a half-karat diamond set in black enamel, encased in anodized gold. "Looks like a fly's eye," she said.

1970, YEAR OF CHANGE

Oh, those sixties, America's conflicted decade. Vietnam's long-running war had become a conundrum. Drugs, sex and rock and roll were shaking the props out from under every form of accepted authority. *Days* wasn't exactly reflecting that world. The Horton family was drawn from such Midwestern God-fearing folk you could almost smell the apple pie through your TV screen. But Julie had plenty of the era's restlessness, and her dissatisfaction with the status quo reflected some genuine social change.

Slowly, I also realized this life of mine could be what I made of it. I started trying to learn lines without my mother's coaching help. I had become a functioning part of the *Days* acting ensemble with a contract. The meager salary and guarantee was proof to me at least that I belonged in show business.

The viewers hadn't singled me out for special notice though. Nobody thought of me as romantic material. Julie and I were more headstrong than loving. And we, though both set for life in relationships that looked okay from the outside, hardly qualified as passionate. But now I was flinging that long mane of false hair over my shoulder and curling my eyelashes on the sly. I hadn't left home, but I had started a savings account and occasionally toyed with a liberal thought. Interacting with so many new people and listening to their daily experiences intrigued me.

The ratings were good. The cast was good. I felt good. Soon all this personal comfort would be forgotten when my priorities changed forever. My heart was about to catch on fire.

3

Doug and Julie Kiss,
and Kiss, and Kiss

BILL

Head writer Bill Bell could create suspense. I knew that. The trouble
was he was also keeping *me* in suspense. And he knew that.

The day Susan and I met—and for the following *nine years*—he had
us working in the same episodes, but not with each other. Okay, it was
only nine days, but it *felt* like nine years. If I'd been writing the story, I
wouldn't have had the heart to torture me and the audience like that.
But that's why Bill was the head writer and I was playing scenes with
every character on the show but Julie.

I did get to meet Maree Cheatham, the gorgeous young Texan who
played Sister Marie Horton (without a hint of her natural Texas accent). One of the early plans for Doug Williams was to involve him ro-
mantically with Sister Marie and get her defrocked, but Betty Corday
and Bill Bell figured the story of breaking up Julie's marriage to Scott
was better.

At last Susan Martin introduced Julie and Scott Banning to Doug
Williams, whose expertise with stocks and bonds would surely help
them in their current precarious financial situation.

Scott Banning was a pleasant nerd. One hundred percent inept. He
knew zip about stocks and bonds, and that's why Doug took over their
portfolio. He couldn't make a martini, so Doug mixed and stirred.
When Scott and Julie went out to dine with Susan and Doug, Scott was
so befuddled by the menu that Doug ordered for everybody in French.

It was even intimated that Scott was unsuccessful in the bedroom, making an unsatisfied wife of Julie.

Naturally, Scott couldn't dance, so Julie and Doug eyed each other suggestively while "gettin' down" to some raucous dance rhythms.

Bell toyed with his audience through May and June, bringing Doug over to Julie's apartment whenever Scott was working at the plant. Doug would spread out his portfolio recommendations while Julie served coffee. Viewers bit their lips as Julie looked more and more at Doug in his mod suit and less and less at that tedious prospectus, and knew that one day Doug was going to pounce.

"IT'S YOU!"

One afternoon at the studio I had a phone call from Joan Blondell, shrieking into the phone, "It's you! You're in my story!" Joan and I had performed the eleven-month national tour of *Bye Bye Birdie* together. I played Albert Peterson, movie-star Joan my mother, at the old Philharmonic Hall on Pershing Square in Los Angeles. That's where, ushering way up in the top balcony, seventeen-year-old Susan Seaforth had caught my act.

Joan Blondell had started watching *Days of our Lives* when it premiered, and planned her life around its air time. If someone offered her work on a film or TV show, she'd accept only if they put it in writing that she could not be called to work while *Days* was on the air. (The world before VCRs, remember?)

I invited her to dinner at my house (spent two days preparing and cooking), and connivingly asked Denise Alexander and Susan Seaforth to join us. Since Joan idolized them both, and all three of us idolized her, it was a perfect evening. She drove herself over from Beverly Hills with a full-sized balloon man in the front seat next to her for protection. She called her mannequin, who came complete with mustache and a smart black fedora, "Mister Dick."

Denise, Susan and I were fast becoming friends. Early in July, NBC Publicity sent the three of us with studio photographer Gary Null out into a patch of wildflowers and shrubs in bloom. Two sexy girls and me in a purple shirt. One of the shots they wanted was of Susan and me kissing. Did they know something we didn't?

"HERE YOU HANG ONE ON HER"

Julie and Doug's first on-camera kiss took place on my forty-fifth episode, July 23, 1970, directed by Dick Sandwick. Unforgettable day.

The scene not only involved our first kiss—a deep and soulful osculation complete with bodily embrace (always genteel, Sandwick had said, "This is not just honey-foggling in the boondocks. Here you really hang one on her!")—it also included my putting a record on the stereo and starting the mechanism so we could hold each other and dance. For some reason I couldn't seem to get that starting lever to work, so we had to do the whole scene over and over, at least half a dozen times.

With no editing capability, we had to go back to the previous commercial and start the scene again: long romantic dialogue, steamy kiss, put on the record, start the stereo, 1-2-3. We worked up to that climactic kiss several times. Donnie, the prop man, looked at me sideways and showed me how simple it was to start the little turntable. I wasn't trying to goof it up; the darn thing just wouldn't engage. That's my story.

And, between you and me, Susan Seaforth was putting her soul into those kisses, and with each take she got more into it. When that sixth or eighth kiss finally took place (and the needle actually dropped onto the record), it was a magical, sexual moment! She shuddered!

Afterward, Sandwick said over the PA system, "Bill, you can pay me later." And then Wes Kenney came out of the booth, walked up to the two of us and just stood there grinning. I may have been perspiring; I know I was still breathing hard. Wes said nothing, nodded, and walked away.

SUSAN

Hayes is eating a hard-boiled egg with a four-ounce can of grapefruit juice for lunch. He opens his briefcase, draws out the egg, *tap tap tap*, peels slowly, then munches the creamy oval without salt. Now for the juice, at room temperature from a long morning waiting in the case. The acidy drink washes down any crumbs of yolk . . . ahhhhh. A Spartan repast, consumed sensuously in silence while all around him the cast chatted and carried on as usual.

How much can you learn from watching a guy eat an egg? Bill was disciplined, tidy, and possibly broke. He was also soon to be on camera with me, and I was pretending to myself, the cast, and especially my newscaster that it was all business. But it wasn't. I was smiling constantly. Denise had also brightened up a bit around "Doug." Everybody liked him, and his theatrical attack on the material had energized our little cast, energized the females most.

Sometimes you're in a plot and don't know it. The onstage pairing of Doug and Julie was orchestrated by Bill Bell from his Chicago apartment towering over Lake Michigan. Offstage, there was no pairing of Bill and Susan at all. But when Hayes had conversations with other people, I listened attentively to find out more about him. Walking into the makeup room one day, I saw Bill perched on the sink counter finishing a heart-to-heart about his divorce. His tone wasn't the usual cheerful one. "How could a woman do that?" he sighed with such pain and fresh anger.

There was a deep sadness in him, all right. Daily I reminded myself this person was weighty with the baggage of a previous life: five children, twenty-three years of marriage, a huge collection of family, and a professional biography that would make your eyes pop. He was older than me, too, and, most damning of all, an actor.

But he was finished with the marriage and trying to find his way in a new city. The teenage children would soon be arriving, his closest friends were all back East, and the cast, which had gotten to know him, wanted to help. Susan Flannery explained where he should look for a house, marking up city maps with suggestions. I'm sure Herzberg mentioned his dentist to Bill, because we both ended up going to Dr. Shulman. Then Denise sent him to the neighborhood where he actually found a house. I kept thinking this was none of my business. Besides, I was no expert on making a new life; I still lived at home with my mother.

Now the whole object of daytime drama is to capture the stay-at-home viewer in a web of romance. There are many kinds of stories, murder with mayhem, power plays among family dynasties, lost treasures and found children, amnesia victims and visitors from outer space. But the surefire story has always been two people fall in love and . . . things happen.

Recently Flannery's character, Laura, had been wooed by two Horton brothers and married the wrong one. This was classic soap plotting, with a situation that could provide scenes for years. The acting was first-rate, too, but for me it had limitations. Those characters were doctors and lawyers; how crazy could they get and keep their licenses? Fresh out of prison, Doug was a wild card, and Julie was an oozing hormone, panting for a change of partner.

MATING DANCE

Bill had seen the wife of his youth walk out the door. He was more than alone. I was exhausted from years of accommodating a mismatched relationship. There we were, living putty in the hands of dream makers.

Our mating dance began with a dance. Doug was visiting Julie's blue apartment set, delivering lines like, "You've got a lovely little place here; how about some music?" And Julie was thinking, "I've got a little something else here. Oh, could we have music? My husband never thinks of music." And Susan's thinking, "No Wagner this time!" And Bill sort of slides me into his arms for this inevitable kiss—the kiss called for from Chicago—the kiss that makes girls leave home—the kiss that's supposed to be just acting—and I feel his body and its heat matches mine.

Kiss completed, he moves to turn on the music, too. The needle swings, rises, and fails to drop. "Cut! Cut!" So, we must go way back to the beginning of the scene. In fact, the control booth must go back to the commercial that precedes the scene. It's Campbell's Cream of Shrimp Soup, with a winsome cartoon shrimp tapping around the waiting bowl. Perky pink feelers wave at us from the monitor.

"Okay, check that needle, Bill. Five, four, three, two . . ." Soup, scene, kiss, needle. "Cut!" Over and over. I lost count after six takes.

The needle wouldn't drop, Bill's temperature was rising to a fever, I had stopped touching up my lipstick, and the scene had achieved a level of steam nobody had expected. Dreamed of perhaps, but not expected. Finally the needle hit the vinyl and we danced into a slow soulful fade.

To this day I adore shrimp.

4

The Setup

BILL

For an actor, what can be better than working opposite cooperative, capable coactors? And what is more fun than being given scripts so exciting and surprising you can't wait to open them to find out who's going to be doing what to whom?

That's the enviable position I was in from the moment Doug took up residence in Salem and set his predatory sights on one victim after another. The character was so fully conceived, and so exhilarating to perform, I just sat on top of his words and hung on for a swooping, daring, diving roller-coaster ride all over the sky.

In 1970, I acted basically with three *genius* talents—Edward Mallory, Denise Alexander and Susan Seaforth.

I worked with Ed, of course, when we were playing cell mates in stir. And, after both characters were released from prison, they maintained a best-friend relationship for a long time. When Doug started singing at Sergio's, he inveigled Bill Horton into playing his piano accompaniments. There were rehearsals of new songs, Horton family members to meet, new girls to talk about.

What new girls? Well, before Doug got caught in true love's sweet snare, he bounded joyously from woman to woman in the open market. Making advances toward Susan and Julie in the daytime merely whetted his appetite for other available ladies in the evening. And, for a while,

Doug took advantage of every opportunity. After all, he had been behind bars for a long time.

He flirted with every female he met, even sang "My Best Girl" to Alice Horton, and was, for a while, an incorrigible ladies' man.

To me his most memorable conquest at Sergio's was a gorgeous nineteen-year-old with natural blond hair that cascaded over her neck and shoulders. The blonde came on to Doug, introduced herself as Diana, Goddess of the Chase, and looked at him expectantly. At the piano, Bill Horton was left with his mouth open as Diana and Doug glided out into that hot September night with only one purpose in mind. The actress was Farrah Fawcett, and in just five lines, her charisma and innocent sexuality had jingled every guy in the studio.

Was there a parallel in my life to that of Doug Williams? I had been single now for a year, and though I was not looking for a permanent relationship, in fact could not imagine ever remarrying, I did enjoy female companionship. I had not sworn off sex, and it was reassuring to discover there were in this world many women who were likewise seeking companionship without commitment.

In those days, most of our scenes on *DOOL* were fifteen to seventeen pages long. They were continuous, spread out over two acts or more, constructed with a beginning, middle and end. Today's audiences have a much shorter attention span, and soap writers have cut the length of scenes down to two pages or less.

For me, to play those longer scenes took deep concentration. Susan Seaforth and I would rehearse the lines with each other while the hairstylist was putting Susan's hair up in curlers. If we were dressed and ready, one would whip down to the other's dressing room and run them. And, finally, we began to call each other the night before to run lines on the phone.

I loved Susan's acting! She was always hauntingly real, totally incapable of dissembling. What she thought came out, and I believe that's what audiences found attractive about her.

One script called for Susan and Denise to create a flashback of a scene that had supposedly occurred long before the story was on TV. It was a confrontation that went all the way back to when Julie and Susan were fourteen-year-old chums.

I made a point of watching while they shot it, and was really impressed. Here were these two actresses in their mid- to late twenties, shrieking in adolescent voices, their gestures and body language not at all adult. They both had suddenly transformed into "little girls in grown-up bodies." I walked out shaking my head.

That day, while driving back to my room in West Hollywood, I began to think about what it meant to me to be a coworker with these talents. All my life one of my deepest ambitions had been to be a good actor, working with good actors, and here I was acting opposite three of the best in the country in this wonderful plot created just for us.

And, naturally, when you work with good people you are challenged to be better than you've been before. I was studying long and hard on my characterization and lines to try to come up to what Ed, Denise and Susan could do.

BILL GOES HOLLYWOOD

I closed on the house near NBC, the kids and I packed all our worldly goods into a moving van, and on July 16 we took up residence in our new home. What a good feeling it was to have a permanent job and be living only ten minutes from work.

Mary had married the man she'd left me for, and I felt relieved that they had legalized their relationship. But in my gut I was still churning at her, starting every day shaking my head in disbelief of her callous disregard for me and the kids. Whether she was happy or unhappy I didn't know. But, worse than that, Cathy and Tommy and Peggy didn't know either. Though I asked them never to speak ill of Mary, there remained a deep chasm of estrangement between the kids and their mother for a long time. No communication, no cards, no letters, no phone calls. Nada.

My anger at Mary ruled my waking moments. Because of breaking up with her, I didn't want to have anything to do with the past twenty-three years and all it held. For instance, I didn't want to hear the records we used to listen to together, so I gave my opera collection to Charles Nelson Reilly.

If I went out with a lady—to dinner, a show or movie—I could enjoy myself up to a point. But if my date looked at me with "commitment to the future" in her eyes, my heart just blocked up. Stop! Not me, babe. Out of here! Good-bye!

Into my new life came this booty-cutie who was deeply involved with another man. I'd even heard she was engaged, which was a big relief; it made her okay to befriend, spend time with, and not worry that she was going to ruin it by getting serious on me.

Interesting brush with irony: I was invited to audition for the newly conceived *Mary Tyler Moore Show*, so I went to MTM and read for the Ted Baxter role. Jim Brooks and Allan Burns said, "Very funny, Bill. However, we had more in mind a blustery George Putnam type." Not being from L.A., I had no idea who George Putnam was. That night I watched George (and his pal Hal) on his local Los Angeles news program.

After we unpacked stacks of boxes and settled into the job-and-family routine we'd needed for so long a time, I got Cathy started with an orthodontist, and enrolled Peggy and Tommy in school. Progress was slow, but at least I had made a beginning.

Now I could devote my attention to playing Doug Williams, rogue that he was.

SUSAN

Hal was speeding up the hill when we crested the top and crashed into the tail end of a flock of sheep. A thud, a swerve, a woolly mess. The good part was the rental car hadn't flipped over into the deep desert ditch below. The bad part was a shepherd's tragedy lay before us, with undigested grass from the creatures' last graze penetrating the engine clear through to the glove compartment. What a smell! So ended my first trip onto the Hopi Reservation of northern Arizona's Indian Country.

There was nothing to do but low-tail it back to Winslow. The great mesas would have to wait for another day. The surviving sheep milled about as sheep will. A baa here, a baa there, but nobody stepped out of the rocks to say, "White man drives like idiot." Hal assured me the thing to do was give ten dollars for the dead ewe to the first Indian we spotted. None turned up. In Winslow we used a little car wash and hosed the pesto-colored mess off the dented grill. "Third accident today," sighed the woman at the rental-office counter, eyeing our vehicle. We paid up and flew toward L.A. in Hal's airplane, through bumpy air inside and out.

"If I hadn't been rushing . . ." "We should have stayed overnight . . ." "If you didn't still live at home, Susan . . ." As always, it was my fault things weren't going more smoothly, despite his best effort. The sun sank in disgust, and my reservations about Hal's reservations were growing. Lamb was going to be off my menu from that day on, and my personal tastes were changing, too.

I believed my life was entwined with "the news" until Bill Hayes came along. His casting unraveled my old relationship like a sweater in the wash. Very occasionally Hal would watch me on *Days of our Lives* to critique my performance and explain the significance of my character on the larger canvas of, say, Western civilization. "You are . . . the bad girl." I already knew that, but he reassured me it was coming across. Also coming across was the powerful sexual chemistry between Seaforth and Hayes on-screen. "It's all acting. That bit there, that was directed," I lied, embarrassing myself when we watched scenes together on his big Magnavox TV.

FLIGHT OF FANCY

Time passed, the anchorman and the ingénue flew every weekend, and I yammered on about these trips to the cast a good deal. Bill innocently asked if he might fly with us sometime to Tucson, where his parents had retired. Were we heading to Arizona?

We were always heading to Arizona, but Hal balked. "We've already done Tucson" (Colossal Cave, chimichangas, and so forth).

"This would be a kindness, and I'd really like to visit again," I ventured. Hal must have caught on to my deeply hidden agenda, yet we made the trip. Peggy, Bill's blond youngest, sat in the back with me, and the two men sat shoulder to shoulder in front of us. Peggy sighed, gazing out the window. Hal let Bill point the plane for about two minutes, and I noticed how far it was to Tucson when you're emotionally stressed.

At the General Aviation Terminal we parted company, Hayes off to meet his mom and dad, us to some cactus patch. "Care for a munchie?" Bill artlessly asked, offering the group chocolate bars.

"No, thanks. We're going to have a fine dinner," Hal snapped. I wanted to sink into the sands. A munchie sounded so delicious.

I should have made a graceful exit from the newsman sooner, but I didn't. The next months of doggedly dating Hal and joyously working with Bill culminated in my recurring dream: An automobile is moving through deep gloom. In the front seat two men are facing forward shoulder to shoulder. I'm in the dark backseat, definitely not in control of the car. Silently I raise a twelve-inch crystal cone, pointy and cool. I slice the driver's head in two. Alarming? Well, yes. That's when I booked an appointment with a psychiatrist and began to investigate what I wanted out of life. It was Bill.

5

What It Was Was Music

BILL

Exposition! If we're going to tell our story we've got to give you some exposition! I mean, who is Bill Hayes and where did he come from? What formed him? And Susan Seaforth. What made her the woman she is? Who were her role models?

Each of us journeyed some time before our life paths crossed. Truth be told, I journeyed eighteen years and five weeks further than Susan. So, since I arrived before Susan chronologically, I'll sketch out my background first.

THE CLARION QUARTET

This is my first vivid memory.

I couldn't have been more than three when, one night, in my pajamas and supposedly already asleep, I heard my dad's quartet begin to sing. I climbed over the tall slatted side of my crib, sneaked out into the hall to the top of the stairs, lay down and went to sleep listening to the Clarion Quartet. They were nonprofessional singers who owned their own tuxedos and performed in the Chicago area, and sometimes even got paid (but more often not).

We lived in Harvey, a factory town on the south side of Chicago. Many of its sixteen thousand inhabitants were impoverished immigrants from Poland, Germany and Russia, and about 15 percent of our population was African-American. Lush green elm trees softened the factory starkness, though by 1950 they were all gone, victims of Dutch elm blight.

Dad had been the school principal in nearby Dolton, but when he began selling the World Book Encyclopedia door-to-door, he and Mother moved to Harvey. Moved there, in fact, just in time for me to be born on June 5, 1925, a 105-degree cooker of a day, at Ingalls Memorial Hospital. Mother's one request was an electric fan.

Except for the constant rattle of freight and commuter trains, it was a quiet neighborhood we grew up in, with little green grass snakes in the fields, meadowlarks warbling their distinctive song, robins vying for the fat worms.

Dad had a deep, lusty baritone voice and sang every day of his life. He woke me and my brothers George and Phil every morning singing "Oh, How I Hate to Get Up in the Morning"; he sang "You Belong to Me" in the shower, "The World Is Waiting for the Sunrise" to Mother, and "The Wedding of the Sunshine and the Rose" while doing the dishes, a chore he never grumbled about.

He bought music for him and us boys to sing together, and long before our voices changed we were singing "Home on the Range" in four-part harmony. Those harmonies became so much a part of us that George, Phil and I all sang in quartets for years.

As a little tyke, I used to make up songs and sing them for my parents. "Do you wike that song, Daddy?" "Do you wike that song, Muvver?" They always did.

Dad knew hundreds of songs from the 1890s and early decades of the 1900s. When he sang those songs, I could hear the chords in my head and sing harmony with him. At an early age I discovered that I could pick out the chords on the piano, so I could accompany us by ear in any key.

Mother, sensing that I had some talent, started me on piano. Though my teacher, Miss Irene Olson, was a statuesque young lady with a Marilyn Monroe figure, she was absolutely unbending in her pianistic pedagogy. She gave me a book of simple pieces to practice, and I found I was able to play them in any key. I was proud of that, but she always disapproved. "That's wrong, Billy. The piece is written in C, but you played it in F [or G or E-flat]." Sounded fine to me, but she definitely did not want me to play by ear. Finally I told Mother I didn't want to take any more lessons with Miss Olson.

Mother said, "It's all right for you to stop taking piano lessons, but you and I both know you want to play some instrument, so think of all the instruments in the band and orchestra and pick out one you want to learn to play." I chose the violin.

I started taking lessons from Mr. William Montelius. Finnish and with a chiseled, character man's face, Mr. Monte conducted the orchestra at Thornton Township High School. He'd traveled Europe as a concert violinist and also as a professional magician. He taught me how to make playing cards disappear, and I can still do it.

Mr. Monte taught me to read music, think notes in my head, play in tune, conduct, and play with authority. One day he asked me, "Billy, do you have lead in your pencil?"

I smiled. "Of course. What do you think?"

He said, "*Play* like it. Leave it to the old ladies to play like old ladies. Loud or soft, fast or slow, when you play you let everyone know you've got lead in your pencil."

GOING PUBLIC

My folks belonged to the Federated Church of Harvey, a federation of Congregationalists and Presbyterians. Dad was the leading singer of the bass section, and I dreamed of the time when I could sing in the choir with him.

Meanwhile, I made my public singing debut when I was in third grade, performing "I'm a Robin Red-Breast" for the P.T.A. That's when I first noticed that little girls in spangley leotards could tap-dance. I knew right away that I wanted to tap-dance, too. Winnie Seidel taught tap, but all her students were girls, and at that age to go into a class of all girls was just too embarrassing for me to consider.

What we did in our neighborhood was play baseball. We roller-skated around the block, I broke my shoulder playing sandlot football, we swam in the summer and ice-skated in the winter, but more than anything else we played baseball, every single day.

Lou Boudreau lived across the street from us. Louie was three years older than my big brother, George, and as kids we used to watch him play on the school baseball and basketball teams. Though only five feet seven, Lou Boudreau was a genius at both sports. At age twenty-four, he became the playing manager of the Cleveland Indians. He was one of my boyhood idols.

GRANDPARENTS

For years we climbed into our old brown Auburn with the chromed spare tires alongside the hood—and superchargers!—and drove out west to farm country, to Oswego, where we'd have Sunday dinner with Grandma Mitchell, Aunt Nellie and Aunt Vera. The routine was the same every time. Mother would join her two sisters and their mother in the kitchen with the big wood-burner stove, preparing food and laughing at Aunt Nellie's jokes. Dad would turn on the Cubs game, lie down on the davenport and go to sleep with the funnies over his face. George, Phil and I would fend for ourselves, playing Pick-Up Sticks on the floor, creating endless oval patterns on a little gadget called the Hootenanny, or stacking buttons from Grandma's button can.

Grandma Mitchell raised all her own food, so dinner was chicken, diced potatoes, corn on the cob, green beans, rolls with "apple jell," and always freshly made piping-hot pies. After the dishwater was sluiced out onto the back lawn, the ladies would join us in the parlor, Aunt Nellie would sit at the piano, and we'd sing from the sing-along songbook. I'm sure, when we hit the chorus of "Little Liza Jane," the neighbors a block away could hear us very well.

My dad's father, Grandaddy Hayes, was a lawyer who'd been a singer and choral director before he lost his hearing. He'd had a fever as a boy that caused the nerves in his ears to atrophy, and after age forty he never heard another sound. We used to talk to him with our hands, utilizing a two-handed alphabet.

Distinguished-looking Grandaddy, with his soft voice, was not a complainer. He wrote briefs for other lawyers until age eighty-eight, taught himself to read foreign languages, rode his bicycle to work (all dressed up in a coat, vest, tie and hat), and lived to be ninety-six. He had a fine memory for the old hymns he used to sing, and would often pick out the melodies with one finger on the piano and ask me if we were still using that hymn tune today. He taught an adult Bible-study class until he was ninety-two, made his pupils study other religions and think for themselves. He wrote and published poetry and lyrics to hymns, a history of Owensboro, Kentucky, and a detailed genealogical history of his family. Grandaddy Hayes was one of the inspirations of my life.

SCHOOL DAYS

My brother George was a hard act to follow. He did his homework, made it to first chair in the high school band, got good grades, and never seemed to get in trouble with his teachers. But it was my lot to follow him—same teachers, same classes, lower grades. They'd even say to me, "Billy, why can't you act like your brother George?" I got in trouble with every teacher I had. Once Mr. Zevenhouse, my sixth-grade teacher, kept me after school for talking out loud and paddled me with a board that had half-inch holes in it. My behind had blisters for three weeks.

When I got to high school I immediately joined the glee club, the chorus and the orchestra. The music we played in orchestra was classical and challenging, from Franck's Symphony in D Minor to Beethoven's Fifth.

Our collective forms of entertainment in those high school years were (1) the athletic games, and (2) dancing. We held at least one school dance every weekend, with music supplied by a full dance band: piano, bass, drums, four saxes, three trumpets, two trombones. And name big bands were playing all over the Chicago area. I first heard—in person!—Benny Goodman, Glenn Miller and Tommy Dorsey.

At fourteen, my voice changed, and I was finally able to join the tenor section of our church choir. One of the thrills of my life was processing shoulder to shoulder with my dad. I liked that we sang different composers, different styles, different periods. We'd go from "Dry Bones" to a Bach cantata. I loved the choir—especially singing with

Dad—and have continued to sing in my church choir wherever I've lived ever since.

SINGING TELEGRAMS

Between my junior and senior years in high school, I worked all summer for Western Union, delivering telegrams on my bicycle. They gave me a snappy blue uniform, and when I questioned wearing the thick leather puttees in the heat, my hungover boss with the greasy black mustache gruffly told me, "You'll want them on!"

He was right. I found I was easy prey for yippee little dogs, who snapped at my ankles and shins.

I learned a few other things. Telegrams decorated with two red stars had to be delivered in person to the addressee, because they carried news of a death. Those with one star were almost as important—they gave arrival information. And people only tip telegram deliverers in the movies.

What made the job fun for me was the then-current custom of sending singing telegrams. My boss knew I liked to sing, so he gave me all those to deliver. It was the summer of '41, and there was an ASCAP-BMI war (strike) going on, meaning I could only sing a melody that was in the public domain. Western Union decreed that every telegram had to be sung to the tune of "Yankee Doodle."

Sometimes it was a snap:

> *Happy Birthday, Miss Berovik,*
> *Happy, Happy Birthday!*
> *Bill and Susan Hayes wish you a*
> *Happy, Happy Birthday!*

But not all the messages were that accommodating:

> *Congratulations, Mr. Swyrszynski,*
> *You've caused us great elation!*
> *You've sold more bras and girdles now*
> *Than anyone else in the nation!*

The pay was 25¢ an hour, ten hours a day—$12.50 a week. At the end of the summer I bought a '36 Ford sedan for $100, so you could say that was my first professional singing job.

Senior year, George invited me to come visit him at DePauw University, a small Methodist college in Greencastle, Indiana, surrounded by waving cornfields. Although I agreed to go look over the school, I was only mildly interested. But when I arrived, I was swept into the excitement of college. Hitting a ten on the excitement scale was the music! I couldn't believe what I was hearing.

Though the men did not have "hours," the women did. They had to be in their dorms or sorority houses by ten p.m. Sunday through Thursday, eleven p.m. Friday, and midnight Saturday. The result Sunday through Thursday was that more studying got done. And on Friday and Saturday nights, serenades! The men's groups—dorm or fraternity—would go stand outside the women's houses—dorm or sorority—and sing an opening number. Then the women (all in bathrobes) would crowd out onto their porch and sing a reply. For the next half hour the two groups sang love songs and novelty songs to each other, back and forth, all in four-part harmony. I've never heard any more beautiful, romantic, heart-stirring music in my life. After hearing one serenade, there was no question as to whether I would go to DePauw. I immediately applied for admission. Oh, the sweet power of that music!

PEARL HARBOR

Singing second soprano in the high school chorus and playing piano in the orchestra was an adorable redhead named Mary Hobbs. Since I was a senior and she was a sophomore, we knew each other but were not really close. We never had a date, and certainly had no idea that one day we would marry and produce five children. We were both sitting in the orchestra that day in December 1941 when President Roosevelt gave his "Day of Infamy" speech (a radio broadcast piped into all the classrooms) and declared war on Japan and Germany, changing our world forever.

Many of our seventeen- and eighteen-year-old high school buddies left school following that broadcast and enlisted in the service. It was as if the entire country jolted awake. Our factories immediately retooled to start producing war matériel. A strange mood swept over the nation's draft-age men and women, a feeling of, "Well, I'm going to be killed anyway, so I might as well enjoy myself." Couples got married quickly, before the men shipped out. Wives followed the men as long as they could, then came home pregnant. Women began to take over men's jobs. Empty seats appeared in all our classrooms. George enlisted in the Army Air Corps. I was still sixteen, so I decided to work through the summer, then go ahead and do my freshman year at DePauw.

INDIANA HARBOR BELT

A dilemma caught me the weekend before graduation from high school. The prom came on the same night as commencement of Thornton Junior College. I made the mistake of taking Barbara Snyder to the big dance when I should have been playing "Pomp and Circumstance" in the orchestra. It probably wouldn't have made any difference in my relationship with Barbara, but it did make a devastating difference in my relationship with my violin teacher, Mr. Montelius, who expected to see me there in his orchestra.

Up until that weekend I still had a chance of getting some scholarship help at DePauw. But Mr. Monte gave me an E, settling that question. F was failure; E was just one tick above it. I graduated, however, on June 4, 1942, the night before my seventeenth birthday.

Two days later I applied for a job as a crew dispatcher on the Indiana Harbor Belt Rail Road. The man looked at me and said, "You have to be eighteen to work on the railroad."

I said, "I'm going on eighteen."

He asked, "When did you turn seventeen?"

I said, "Day before yesterday."

He grinned and hired me anyway.

The job paid $50 a week. Room and board still being free at home, I put my money away. I was hitting the high life, right? Well, sort of. Those railroaders were as low-life as any I've encountered anywhere.

My task was to make sure there were three switchmen on every train. Their bump-board system worked by seniority, the switchman with the

greatest seniority being number 1 and the most recently hired appren-
tice being number 161. It was simple: The men with the lowest numbers could pick the best jobs. If number 4 picked a train, that bumped
the highest number off that train. I had to call that man and say, "You're
bumped," and then he'd pick another train and bump somebody else. If
number 4 called in sick, then I called number 5 and asked if he wanted
to move up, and so on.

I wasn't there very long before I found out that when number 33 was
working the hump on the West Yard, number 39 was over at number
33's house humping his wife. They'd even call in and ask what jobs the
others were working so they could plan their days. I was supposed to
keep two sets of notes: If "Jones" asks what job "Smith" is on, tell him
the eleven fifty a.m. East Yard, and so forth.

In addition, the drunk rate was very high, and I'll never forget the
salesman who came by every Monday with his large suitcase of dildos,
extensions, vaccu-jacks and eight-pagers (little X-rated cartoon books).
He did a landslide business.

Well, it was a job. I went off to college with a thousand dollars in the
bank.

COLLEGE

My freshman year at DePauw was all flux and transition. As time wore
on all the men either enlisted or got drafted into the service. The music
of the serenades changed drastically as families and couples were being
torn apart by the war. Tall, handsome Bob Daugherty sang the solo on
our sentimental rendition of "Home":

> *When shadows fall and trees whisper day is ending,*
> *My thoughts are ever wending home . . .*

Then Bob went off to England with the Army Air Corps, crashed, and
never got to go home.

My Lambda Chi Alpha freshman pledge class was outstanding. Out
of a dozen, three became doctors, one an attorney, two became nationally syndicated cartoonists, and one a very successful political writer in

Washington. They were high-quality people who taught me courtesy, generosity, how to study, how to be responsible, and the meaning of true brotherhood.

I grew closest to Jack Lewis, from Princeton, Indiana. A pink-skinned Welshman whose father was a coal miner, Jack and I immediately became singing buddies. We argued endlessly about how to end the war and treat the enemy, but we were always totally in sync when it came to harmonizing. We'd start the same song in the same key at the same time and then leap to the same harmony note at the same time. It was uncanny. That's never happened to me with any other singer. He and I sang together every day. Jack became a doctor, practiced in Dayton, and is now retired, but we've never lost touch, never stopped harmonizing. I've never met anyone I feel greater kinship to, probably because of that mysterious musical tie.

My brother George had earned a four-year scholarship to DePauw, and half my Lambda Chi brothers had done the same thing. I had gotten myself a lousy E in orchestra, eliminating my scholarship chances. If I could finish my first DePauw semester with a half-A, half-B average, I could earn a scholarship for the next three and a half years. I set out to do that, applied myself, worked hard, probably averaging three hours of sleep a night that first semester, and then got a C in Spanish. I had an A going into the final and blew it. I was devastated! Downhearted. *Low.*

I walked around Greencastle and had a talk with myself. I said, "You're throwing away your life. You have the potential, but you're not taking the challenge. What are you going to do about it?"

And I answered myself, "I will enlist in the most difficult branch of the service I can find, and if I can succeed in that, then at last I will feel I am worth something."

ANCHORS AWEIGH, MY BOYS

I found out that Marine pilots were being taken from the top 5 percent of Navy pilots, and that's what I set my heart on. In March 1943 I hitchhiked down to St. Louis and enlisted in the Navy Air Corps. They signed me up and said I'd hear from them soon.

All alone in St. Louis, I had some sort of epiphany. "Hey, if I'm old enough to get shot at, I'm old enough to have a peek at the seamy adult world." So I bought a pack of cigarettes and lit up, went into a dank, smelly bar and chugalugged a shot of whiskey (I can still smell it), then went to a burlesque show (I can still smell it, too). I slept on a wicker train seat all the way back to Greencastle, then called my folks and told them I'd enlisted in the Navy Air Corps.

I got my letter of "Greetings" from the Navy on my eighteenth birthday and was in uniform by July 1, 1943.

While I was stationed at the Naval Flight Preparatory School in Wooster, Ohio, our platoon was out on the dusty field drilling one day when a lieutenant stopped us and said, "At ease." Then he told us the base was going to put on a show Saturday night, and they were looking for cadets who could entertain, any volunteers?

Five of us stepped forward. One cadet could imitate Donald Duck. The other four of us said we could sing. The lieutenant said, "Okay, fine. You four are now a quartet." Talk about luck. There's no way he could have picked four better voices to go together. Kenny Pope sang lead, I sang baritone. Bull Durham was a perfect top tenor, and Monk Eakins was a low-low bass. We instantly became a barbershop quartet.

Meanwhile, George had been called to the Pacific Theater, bombed Tokyo, was shot down, and made it to Iwo Jima. My quiet brother, who never talks about it, was a hero of World War II. Phil, fortunately, was too young.

My personal goal was set: to become a Marine pilot. The syllabus of ground school and flight training required only nine months. But victory at the Battle of Midway had changed the war so much that, by summertime, fewer fighter pilots were needed. So they began to stretch out our training schedule.

We were sent (in uniform) back to college for two semesters. Then to Naval Flight Preparatory School in Wooster, Ohio, for four months of ground school: engines, navigation, Naval history, code. Then to Pre-Flight School at Iowa City, Iowa, for five months of physical training. Our entire day was physical: an hour of football, an hour of track (including a killer obstacle course), an hour of swimming (jump off a fifty-four-foot catwalk, swim five miles clothed), an hour of wrestling, an hour of boxing, an hour of basketball, an hour of jujitsu, an hour of skeet shooting. We were taught combat skills, how to kill in hand-to-hand fighting, and how to shoot somebody with either a rifle or a pistol. Five solid months of it. We were fighting machines.

Then (at last!) we went to Ottumwa, Iowa, to learn to fly. N2S Stearmans, the old yellow-peril biplanes from "The War to End All Wars," were our first planes—open cockpits, no radios, stationary landing gear, built-in ground loops. All our training, first day to last, was aerobatics—Immelmanns, split-Ss, slow rolls, snap rolls, loops, stalls, spins—plus how to land, tail-first, in a fifty-foot circle. Four months of flying, then they lopped off the bottom 60 percent of all classes. Ooh, the tension! Cadets began to put their own bunk mates on report, break each other's bones in the contact sports, anything to stay ahead of the swirling scythe.

In April 1945, the war ended in Europe. VE day. Mop-up began in the Pacific. We were sent to our final destination—Pensacola, Florida. We flew SNJ Texans—closed cockpits, radios, retractable landing gear. Then it was May 1945, and my time was running out. Night flying, instrument training, tight-formation flying, and always dogfight-style aerobatics. Instrument landings, carrier landings, bombing and strafing runs. I was in line to be a Marine pilot, green uniform in my closet, and . . .

Hiroshima! Nagasaki! And VJ day! The Japanese called it quits. Unconditional surrender. The captain of the base got on the horn and said, "Now hear this! Now hear this! The war is over! Everyone who is not on watch is now on twenty-four-hour liberty! Go!"

Buses were crammed going into Pensacola, the Waves singing at the tops of their lungs, "Roll Me Over in the Clover!" All of Pensacola was in the middle of town, elbow to elbow, laughing, crying, kissing, hugging, jumping up and down, singing, yelling. Someone gave Bull Durham and me a bottle of Southern Comfort. We walked around town and mingled with the sweaty, exhaustedly excited townspeople. We got pretty jazzed drinking the Southern Comfort and chasing it with cigarette smoke. We weren't used to it either. We picked up a Wave named Mary. Bull passed out on the porch swing of a bed-and-breakfast. Mary and I went for a wander and finished off the bottle. We were kissing in somebody's backyard, and she asked me, "How high can you piss with a hard-on?"

I said, "Over that fence and hedge."

She said, "Prove it."

And I did. Way over! Into the next yard.

I took her back to the bed-and-breakfast, spent my last $4.50 on a room for her, and then went to the Knights of Columbus, lay down on a pool table and went to sleep.

The next morning it was a bedraggled gang who returned to the base. There's a scene in the movie *Mister Roberts* that comes close.

All training stopped. The Navy offered us two options: (1) accept your wings and commission immediately, stay on active duty two years, then inactive duty for twenty more years, or (2) be mustered out. I figured I had earned my commission and my wings, whether I actually got them or not. So, having achieved my personal goal, I ran to sign option 2 as fast as I could.

Two days later, Bull Durham and I got on a train to Great Lakes, Illinois, the huge naval base north of Chicago, to be mustered out of the Navy. We passed through Princeton, Indiana, in the middle of the night, stopped right at the crossing, two blocks from Jack Lewis's home. There I was on the train, between cars, hollering to my singing buddy, out into the night, "Hey, Lew-ass! Lew-ass! I'm here! Are you here?"

BACK IN CIVILIAN CLOTHES

I returned to DePauw to pick up the pieces of my life. Bull Durham joined me. And Monk Eakins, our bass. And with Jack Lewis back out of the Army (yes, he had been at home that night, on furlough!), we quartetted through the rest of school. Monk Eakins died some years ago, but Jack, Bull and I still manage to sing together every year. Fortunately, Jack's son Bill is a bass and knows all the songs, so we press him into service often.

Also at DePauw at that time was the cute coed I'd known in high school named Mary Hobbs. Mary and I studied together, sang together, fell in love, dreamed youthful dreams, believed in the future and the luck of the young and courageous. I cashed in my $225 worth of war bonds and bought Mary a ring. With no job, not even any prospects, not a cent in the bank, we married the weekend before our final semester, and got our bachelor degrees in June 1947.

Graduating from DePauw at roughly the same time, seven couples—including Jack Lewis and Bull Durham and their wives—got together to vacation for a week in Old Mission, Michigan, on the peninsula above Traverse City. The same group still meets at the same place every summer, and we still sing the same songs, from "My Evaline" to "Coney Island Baby." Only now we're just the first generation. Our children, now mostly in their fifties, comprise the second generation. And their children, in their twenties and thirties, make up the third generation. All are my family.

I double majored in English and music. Mary had ended up a zoology major, and where the two of us thought we were going is anybody's guess. I vaguely thought I might get into choral conducting and arranging. Mary knew shorthand and figured she could get a secretarial job anywhere. But before I even opened the want-ad section to see what was available, fate—in the person of my younger brother, Phil—surprised me with a look into the world of professional entertainment.

ENTERING THE CIRCUS

Phil, having learned that the Rodgers and Hammerstein smash-hit musical *Carousel* had closed its Broadway run and was beginning its national tour in Chicago, wrote to the stage manager, saying, "If you need a tenor replacement for your singing chorus, I would like to audition."

The stage manager sent Phil a penny postcard that read, "Please come to the Shubert Theater on Tuesday, at two p.m., and present this card. Be prepared to sing a song."

I arrived at our home in Harvey to find Phil in bed with strep throat and no voice. There was no way he'd be able to sing the audition, so I took the card, grabbed Dad's copy of "I Love Life" off the piano, surreptitiously changed the name on the card to read Bill instead of Phil, and took the Illinois Central train into the city. I located the stage door of the Shubert Theater and introduced myself to the stage manager.

He pointed me out into the light. I handed my music to the accompanist and sang. A voice from the darkness asked me if I knew "Make

Believe." I sang half a chorus of "Make Believe," and the same voice asked me how tall I was.

I said, "Five feet nine," and that did it. I fit the costume and was offered a job singing in the chorus of *Carousel*, opening one week later, at $70 a week. Phil shook his head philosophically at the odd turn of events, but never gave it a begrudging second thought. After all, it stayed in the family.

Fate had smiled on me and I didn't have to go through the disconcerting process of looking for a job at all. I was immediately employed. My rehearsal consisted of watching the man I was replacing, to see what his staging was, and memorizing my two lines and the tenor parts to "June Is Bustin' Out All Over," "Blow High, Blow Low," "This Was a Real Nice Clam Bake" and "You'll Never Walk Alone."

Up until that moment, I'd had no idea a person could actually make a living by performing. I'd just never thought about it. Teaching, yes. Conducting, yes. Arranging, yes. But singing and acting? What a propitious discovery!

I found out, however, that all my previous singing had not prepared me for the rigors of singing in theater. Blending in a quartet or choir was one thing, but being heard in the back row was a whole new ball game. My new singer friends in the show urged me to take some voice lessons and learn to *project*.

The GI Bill had paid for the completion of my undergraduate work, and I still was eligible to get some more. So I promptly went up to the Music School at Northwestern University in Evanston and enrolled in a program for a Master of Music degree. My reasoning was: If I don't enjoy the performing and prefer to teach, having a master's degree would be a good thing.

But I did enjoy it. Being in *Carousel* was a thrill, every performance. The story moved the audience to tears, and I stood at the side of the stage and lived through Billy Bigelow's "Soliloquy" as if I were singing it myself.

Well, why not? Mary and I had conceived our first child, and like Bigelow I was dying to know what it was: "My little girl, pink and white . . ." or "My boy Bill, he'll be tall and as tough as a tree. . . ."

When the show completed its Chicago run and packed up for its next venue, I turned in my notice, preferring to continue my studies at Northwestern. I was learning a lot from John Toms, my voice teacher, and realized a legitimate foundation in vocal technique is a valuable asset.

But now I didn't have that weekly paycheck coming in, so I needed to look for ways to make rent-and-food money. But I didn't want just any job. I wanted employment related to my new line of work, *showbiz!*

First, I became the choir director at my home church in Harvey. They had a big library of music (and no music budget). I just poked through their stacks, made my choices and started. Rehearsal Wednesday night, service Sunday morning.

Next, Temple Beth Am hired me to lead the tenor section in the choir and sing all the tenor solos. My Hebrew wasn't bad, but the joke was that I sang the "Avinu Malkeinu" with an Irish accent. The vocal demands were nearly operatic. Rehearsal and service—Friday night.

I succeeded in talking my way onto a live musical show on WJJD-radio: "Songs You Remember." Every Tuesday and Thursday morning I sang two songs. Rehearsal nine a.m., show ten a.m.

And I did my first television, singing second tenor in a jazz quintet as background for the WGN musical series called *The Adventures of Homer Herk*. I ate up all those jazz licks. No vibrato, *very* close harmony, altered chords: for me a totally different type of singing from what I'd done before.

I bought monthly commuter tickets, took my briefcase of school-work wherever I went, and settled into a routine of studying on the trains. I took a voice lesson every day for the next eighteen months, and was home for dinner every night except Friday. (Fortunately, the temple offered crullers and coffee.)

I was working very hard, flying from one job to another, doing my theory, composition and orchestration while jiggling and bumping on the trains. But it never was like work to me. It was all musical, and everything I did was either performing or related to it. If you really enjoy what you're doing, you've got the world by the tail.

I added singing, on average once a week, at the Cordt Funeral Home in Homewood. Most requested funeral favorite: "Danny Boy." And I began to get hired to sing tenor solos in oratorios and cantatas all over northern Illinois.

On March 21, 1948, I was singing Dubois's *Seven Last Words of Christ* with a chorus of 600 and an orchestra of 150, when my first child was born. There is no greater moment in life than having a baby! What a treasure! It was "My little girl," and we named her Carrie.

One month later I gave my graduate recital of art songs and opera, picked up my master's degree, auditioned for Olsen and Johnson of *Hell-zapoppin'* fame, and was invited to join them as their vocalist. That meant pulling up stakes, quitting all my jobs, going on the road for a while and eventually moving to New York. When they offered me $250 a week, Mary and I agreed we could live on that. Still not a penny in the bank, but what could be more secure than show business, right? Off we went to the Big Apple.

Ole Olsen and Chic Johnson, purveyors of low-vaudeville comedy, were spectacularly successful with their circus-sized extravaganzas. Becoming their featured singer, I was taking my first harrowing steps out of the chorus and into the solo limelight. Being innately shy and used to being in the background, it was nervous-time for me as we played the 16,000-seat Chicago Stadium, the Canadian National Exhibition (26,000 seats in the open air—June Johnson and I made our entrance in a helicopter), and Madison Square Garden in New York, with close to 20,000 seats.

Television had remained experimental until September 1948, when the *Texaco Star Theater* premiered, starring Milton Berle. Overnight, television burst into its first full glory. By summer 1949, Berle was "Mr. Television," the darling of the country, and Olsen and Johnson had just the right bag of sight gags and silliness to stand in for him when he took his first hiatus. And I was their singer! I did a few of the stooge crossover gags on the show, but mainly I was used as a musical contrast to their outrageous puns and tomfoolery.

On our October 28 show, Chic Johnson—knowing that Mary and I had a bag packed at the theater and were on our way to the hospital right afterward—gave me a big grin and said, "Hope it's a boy!" Our second child was born that night. He's "My boy Bill," the second treasure of my life.

Olsen and Johnson's baby gift to Mary and me was a *huge* white wicker crib that they'd used as a prop in their shows, so that Billy would have a bed to sleep in. They knew we were living more on dreams than money.

Now a family of four, Mary and I borrowed down-payment money from her dad and mine and bought a little attached house in Jackson Heights, Queens, for $9,600. Our furniture consisted of Billy's whopper crib, one bed, one chest of drawers, and a dozen orange crates. Carrie slept in a dresser drawer, on the floor. Sometimes you just have to believe in the future.

The future jingled when I received word that producer Max Liebman had seen me on the Olsen and Johnson show. He was casting a new series for NBC, to be called *Your Show of Shows*, and wanted me to come sing for him.

A producer asking me to come sing for him? That was a stunner. I was in the circus, balancing precariously on the big red-and-white balls with the other clowns, and the ringmaster had just catapulted me up onto the high wire. I could hear the drum roll.

When I look back at that moment, still fresh after fifty-five years, my heart quickens. And when I think of all the thousands of songs I've sung since then, I know I've been blessed. Music, the one true divine language, has enriched my life beyond all my dreams. And it all started by listening to my father's quartet singing as I slid into dreamland so long ago.

6

1353

SUSAN

Alvarado Terrace is a block-long street in central Los Angeles that runs between Pico Boulevard—named for the last Spanish governor of California—and Hoover Street—named for the vacuum cleaner. The First Church of Christ, Scientist is on the Hoover corner, a Romanesque brick gem copied from a famous church in Ravenna, Italy. Across from the terrace is a narrow park that once was filled with camphor trees, benches and dusty bushes. Five great houses, built in 1905, face the park. Behind them an alley accesses their big detached garages.

The Raphael House, our house, was one of the five. Mr. Raphael's business was fine wood and art-glass manufacture, so the mansion was a showplace. In style an accommodating bastard-Tudor within, Craftsman without, stuccoed and half timbered, it had twenty-seven rooms stacked over three stories and basement under a red-tiled roof. The windows of the deep front porch were beveled glass. The paneling of the foyer and living room was tiger oak to match the carved staircase. In the dining room, flame-mahogany walls surrounded an art nouveau table and chairs of the same rare color that could seat twelve.

My mother, Elizabeth, put her parlor grand piano in the alcove off the living room. I could stand on a step leading into the book-filled den to sing across the Oriental rugs while she played for me. I was learning to project. Beside the staircase to the second floor were two sets of

stained-glass windows, golden ones with emerald leaves and scarlet pop-
pies, and aquamarine ones like papyrus plants. The bedrooms all opened
into each other and onto the landing of the stairs, with bathrooms at
each end. You could reach the third story from the back stairs too, solid
red oak but less grand. Up there the redwood walls were painted cream,
a fireplace cheered up the five large rooms with peaked ceilings and
dormer windows. There was electricity on the "third floor," but no
plumbing. When my grandmother Jessie purchased the house in 1945, it
contained a pool table and a painting of a blacksmith shoeing a horse.

The washing machine was in the basement. There was no dryer. My
grandmother carried baskets of wet washing up the basement stairs to
the grassy backyard to pin endless sheets on the four clotheslines. Heat
came from radiators or, on festive occasions, from the five wood-
burning fireplaces.

Off the dining room, with its built-in buffet, clock, columns and fireplace, was a little bonus room next to the butler's pantry. You could
open the pocket doors automatically by stepping really hard on a
wooden button in the floor. The only telephone was there, so we called
it the telephone room. The Chippendale secretary sat by the windows,
where Elizabeth would go over her ledgers for hours, smoking and trying to make the money match the bills.

All activities commenced in the kitchen. An eight-burner Chambers
stove, with two ovens, two broilers and something called a deep well,
dominated the room. It had been custom-built for the old DeMille star
Warner Baxter. Jessie had never met him but was very proud of his
stove. As a toddler I would polish its chrome flanks with Kleenex tissues
and spit. The doorless breakfast room faced the plumbago hedge Jessie
had cultivated ("Isn't it a beautiful blue?"). The radio was in there, a
Mission-style table for six, and a built-in marble counter for rolling pas-
try. Big flour bins were filled with linen tablecloths and napkins. Under
the cuckoo clock I ate my hot lunches, a lamb chop fried in garlic butter, sweet-and-sour beets and a big glass of milk with chocolaty Bosco
stirred in.

There was furniture enough from our old home in San Francisco to
fill the bedrooms and the halls. The paying guests, the "roomers," slept
on the second floor. Mother and Jessie and I slept "topside." We peed in

an enamel bucket at night, then carried it discreetly downstairs to the second floor toilet to flush and rinse with Lysol in the morning.

The big incinerator that immolated our trash sat in the back alley just under a monstrous date palm. The palm was full of rats, and its roots penetrated the plumbing twice a year. The Roto-Rooter man would snake the drains while Jessie, in tall rubber boots, shoveled water off the basement floor into buckets.

The garden belonged to Maggie Wylie, the Scottish terrier Mother had named after the heroine in the James Barrie play *What Every Woman Knows*. Calla lilies bloomed every spring by the clothesline. The neighbor's fence was wooden lattice, and I could peek through at their mysterious Finnish-speaking life. I played alone with Figaro, the cat, or mused on the meaning of things as I perched in the mock-orange trees.

The ROOM FOR RENT sign at 1353 Alvarado Terrace was tacked up under the mailbox on the front porch. People who rent rooms need more than a place to sleep, a lot more. We rented by the week, but most of the guests stayed on for years. Sometimes the rest of their lives.

This was the nest I was so reluctant to leave. The neighborhood was run-down and hardly safe. I attended Sunday School on the corner, as my grandmother wished, and tried to sell Avon to all the Latino families around us when I graduated from high school in 1960. Across Terrace Park stood the California Lutheran Bible School. That institution eventually supplied us with renters after the dear old salesmen I'd grown up with passed away.

Jessie Harrower, "Grammie," had adopted my mother, Elizabeth, out of an orphanage in 1918, when she was nine months old. The flu pandemic was raging, and babies were thought to draw the disease. Mother dead, father shiftless, Mother had been dropped off by her surviving relatives. A German surname was a strike against her as America entered the Great War. But Jessie wanted a baby, so. . . . She herself had survived being an orphan, raped, seduced, abandoned, prostitution, VD, alcohol and widowhood. Her cultural advantages had been few, beginning with birth in a log cabin in southern Ohio. As for education, the Fourth McGuffey Reader was her last textbook, but she made the most of it. Jessie made the most of everything. Nature gave her gorgeous legs and hazel eyes. She was loving and wise, with sparkling eyes no man I ever knew could resist. All the hard times she'd seen never clouded them.

When my grandfather, Bill Harrower, made an honest woman of her, their first wish was to have a family. Conception was impossible, even with love, because her first husband had made the doctor tie Jessie's tubes while she was in surgery for a ruptured appendix. Nobody asked the woman if she wanted such a procedure, of course: it was 1903.

Harrower was from a large Scottish immigrant family living in Oakland. He loved the sea and, in 1901, earned his certificate of First Class Engineering Compentency in Hong Kong. Perhaps he caught his wanderlust from his schoolmate Jack London. After a colorful youth in the Pacific, under steam and the last days of sail, he married the sassy Jessie and worked as chief estimator at Moore Dry Dock Co. on San Francisco Bay.

My grandmother wanted her darling baby girl to have all the lessons and chances money could buy. The mother had great expectations, the father doted on his girls. Luckily Elizabeth turned out to have talent.

If history and World War I brought Jessie and Elizabeth together, the famous stock market crash of '29 propelled them to Hollywood. When Harrower's salary was halved due to production cutbacks, Jessie took her teenager out of the fine girls' school they could no longer afford and set up housekeeping off Hollywood Boulevard at the Padre Hotel. Elizabeth would "break into pictures."

Success did not descend like a snow-white dove. The era of British casts in studio costume flicks was in full swing. Mother mastered accents and tried out Englishy names like Eve St. John and Beth Alden. As a bottle blonde at fifteen, she was cast in *Becky Sharp*, the first full-length feature film in color. With her salary she bought a riding habit, and carried a crop to parties. By her twenty-first birthday she had developed style and beauty, but Jessie stood guard over her virtue. That invitation to San Simeon, William Randolph Hearst's fabled ranch for the raunchy and famous, was refused! She got engaged to silly actors lightheartedly and frequently, but remained intact.

Radio was a perfect medium for the beautiful voice she had cultivated. All those amazing accents were castable, and Elizabeth worked on all the big shows of the late thirties and early forties: *Lux Radio Theatre, The Edgar Bergen Show, The Bob Hope Show.*

Pearl Harbor changed things. My grandfather's company was taken over by the U.S. Navy, and boyish officers with ninety days of training were giving orders. The pressure of seeing his experienced advice ignored, and ships going to sea improperly prepared, was wearing down Mr. Harrower's heart and mind.

Elizabeth got an outfit that looked very military and began to search for a man to go with it.

My father, Harry Seabold, grew up in hardworking circumstances in Hillsboro, Oregon. One year he spent a semester in Berkeley, and that's where he met Mother, in the fifth grade. The handsome blond kid returned to the tall timber, but Mother drew hearts with his initials in them and never forgot Harry. He was a cadet in the Army Air Corps when he looked her up again. She was a glamorous woman, wearing her hair in a soft pageboy style, dressed in formfitting jackets with a silver Prince of Wales pin on the lapel. He was smart as a new nickel in that uniform. All the good guys were shipping out, and Harry was plainly more of a man than those Hollywood boys with their pencil-thin mustaches.

So quickly they married, strangers to each other at the altar one hot sunny morning in Bakersfield. They kept house while he was in basic training in Oklahoma City for ninety days. I was conceived, Harry flew off to his war in North Africa and Europe. Mother went home to San Francisco and did radio shows. Jessie rejoiced at my birth, while Mother sent letters twice a day to her husband and food packages to our Scottish cousins under the guns in Europe. Dad became the youngest major in the Air Corps, and had an adventurous war in Egypt and Italy.

My grandfather's health failed and he suffered a nervous breakdown. The doctors urged Jessie's consent to give shock treatments to him. Since she was a devout Christian Scientist, I doubt she understood the gravity of the procedure. The gentle husband and father was handed over to the white coats and machines. Twenty-two times! He came back an invalid, unable to work. The devastated women were told to take him to new surroundings away from the sea and every single place he loved. So they sold the family home and headed south to Hollywood for good.

The first thing I remember is that long drive to Los Angeles. Jessie was at the wheel, and a canary in a cage swung over the backseat beside me. Friends who ran a rest home put us up while Jessie drove around for nine months on rationed gasoline looking for a house to buy.

"I've come home," my grandmother announced the first time she set eyes on 1353. The mansion cost $19,000, and we had zip. "We'll rent rooms to officers' wives." Mom was an officer's wife, and we had lots of furniture. My grandfather padded about, I learned to talk, and Jessie kept house for over twenty people while Mother worked in radio and dreamed of Harry's return. The house filled up with those pompadoured ladies of "the Greatest Generation," hoping, smoking and laughing. When the war ended they moved on into the future and peace.

Dad was gone for thirty-three months without taking a U.S. leave. Then finally, quite finally, he showed up, to tell us he was not going to stay. The divorce was as quick as the wedding. My grandfather died in his daughter's arms that same year.

Mother never quite believed Harry wasn't coming back someday to love her, that I was going to grow up without a father. Jessie had lost the best man she'd ever known, and had a heartbroken daughter and a baby on her hands. The rooms were emptying fast and we had no savings. My support check from Dad was $42 a month.

The matriarch principle kicked in. Jessie was the sun we revolved around, radiating energy and love. She worked sixteen hours a day, every day. She laughed and prayed and cooked and cleaned up. Like a general in her Eisenhower jackets, slacks and aprons, she would repeat each morning to me, "To those leaning on the sustaining Infinite, today is big with blessings." That darling woman never doubted for a moment her girls were meant for greatness.

The guests became more varied. Growing up, I inhaled the rich fragrance of Maxwell House coffee along with a hundred life stories.

The master bedroom rented for $10 a week, the smaller bedrooms went as cheaply as $6. Jessie and Mom provided "hotel service," making beds, dusting, dumping wastebaskets, tidying rooms and swabbing the bathrooms daily. Visitors were welcome downstairs. Officially, meals were not served, but people would drop into the kitchen and linger. Long. There was no outside help and no time to look for better-paying work.

THE ROOMERS

Nathan Lakowski moved in. A gnomelike Jewish bachelor from New Orleans, he worked on Los Angeles Street next to the Midnight Mission at a toy-and-novelty wholesaler's. Nathan grasped our rather desperate situation and began to do what he could. Each day, after selling in the toy store, the talkative man with the crooked leg went to the garment district to work some more, not for salary but for beautiful little dresses for me.

On Saturdays he limped onto the streetcar and rode to the flower market, bartering his labor for flowers to send home. Bundles would arrive by messenger about eleven a.m., gladiolas, daisies, sweet-smelling stock, and boxes and boxes of vandal orchids from Hawaii. Jessie filled the steep vases to overflowing. Light from the gold stained glass poured over the wing-backed chairs and the Italian tables.

Nathan loved the grandeur. He was well past sixty, and had never had a family. His first job was delivering buckets of beer in Storyville; then he sold scanties to the whores of that fabled red-light district. I can't imagine our lives without him. Toys? I had everything he could loot from the store inventory. When I was five the Easter Bunny showed up at my egg hunt in the backyard, dressed in cuddly fur and silently delivering baskets. When I became five and twenty I realized that bunny had been Nathan. He paid for dinners out at Rand's Round Up, where I first tasted prime rib, then fancy meals once a week on Restaurant Row. What did he ask in return? Just his room, a little attention. Never a date, never a hug. Such unqualified love was my first lesson that great souls can come in unexpected packages. Whatever brought him to California, it was Divine Providence. Nathan was our blessing.

This childhood had no children in it. I played alone by the stairs, while adults and adult dramas kept coming up the terrace.

For about ten years Pat Wallace lived with us. Once upon a time she'd been Miss Illinois, but now she modeled for sportswear firms in the fashion district. Spare, tall, square-jawed, absolutely stunning on the runway, she was heavy-footed and raucous in the kitchen. Tramping in after work, she would throw down her huge purse and pull up a chair in the breakfast room to tell us about her day. We listened, finishing up Jessie's glorious tomato soup, rich with beef bones, or a plate of stewed chicken over bread slices. Pat's irregular love life and glamour was fascinating to us. Mother devoted megawatts of energy to counseling the needy and nervous girl. Packs of Pall Malls went up in smoke in that little red, white and blue room (Jessie was a patriot). Finally, I'd throw open the window and breathe in the snap of clean air from outside. "Time for the grooming bit," Pat would say on a dateless Friday night, and drag her perfect size-ten body upstairs to wax, shave, curl and cream it. The vocation of beauty took hours.

There was Guido, the mysterious Bolivian he-man. After a bar fight one night, he was dropped off at the plate-glass front door, a bloody, unconscious mess. He surprised us by marrying the lady with a small mustache from the back bedroom. Yan and Gregor, two Russian guys who flirted with Mother in shifts while she did the ironing, littered their room with orange peels and thought American canned food was poisoned. Lynnette was a plump Southern lady who read stacks of paperback bodice rippers. Once a week she dusted her mirror with face powder to cheat time. Val lived in the $6 room for fifteen years, speaking Hungarian to his brother on visits, blasting the radiator on high and reading Louis L'Amour. Jessie thought they were engaged in "secret work." These were the Cold War days.

Mercedes, the Mexican Madonna type, got pregnant and hysterical until Jessie pressured her soldier boy into marrying her. Their baby spent his first year in the master bedroom, being danced around by all of us until Pop came home from duty overseas. Aunt Gertrude, the demon relative, came and went, with her teeth in a glass and mutiny in her heart. Mother told me that all three of her husbands had died insane. There was Clyde, the truck driver with wavy hair, who had an affair with Pat and deeply regretted it. The man who showered for forty minutes at a time and tried to take a strange woman upstairs (Jessie shook him down for his room key and showed him the door pronto). Chester, the retired vacuum salesman from Toledo, who saw his old dog in a dream. "Hello, Chet," it woofed. Jerry, the Australian boxer, whose mother sat on our sofa singing "My Yiddishe Momme." The Polish couple who made love so intensely Mother had to change the sheets every day. Well, it was never boring.

WE THREE

At night we'd creep up to our big room, where three single beds sat in a row. I would dance to Yma Sumac on the record player in my red nightie, leaping by the mirror, or, in quieter moments, do embroidery cuddled up to the radio. Nathan gave us a television set in 1952, so there was wrestling and *Spade Cooley's Western Jamboree* to watch, and, of course, *Your Show of Shows*. Maggie, the dog, slept in the rocker. On the Fourth of July, we could see the Coliseum fireworks from the dormer windows.

Mother never learned to drive. When she landed a theater job, my grandmother drove her to work. There was no thought of a babysitter. We sat in the car together for hours, reciting Bible verses and passages from *Science and Health* while Mother rehearsed or performed. Jessie would tell me selected stories from her life. Finally they realized if I was there I might as well be in the show, too, so when Mom played the Woman of Samaria at the Pilgrimage Bowl by the Hollywood Freeway, I was The Littlest Child in the temple scene. At the Pasadena Playhouse I moved up to productions with just me in the cast, and Elizabeth coached me, trying not to be a stage mother. I loved the responsibility, the excitement, and making my grandmother say, "I was tempted to be proud."

Television turned out to be where we worked most—live shows like *General Electric Theatre*, where Mother noticed the host, Ronald Reagan, so meticulously combing his hair. Church shows for the Missouri Synod Baptists were low budget, but you got lots of dialogue (I died of pellagra on the episode about Vitamin G), and Mother played Susan B. Anthony in biographical shorts for Encyclopaedia Britannica Films. The Westerns were great sport; we'd spend a day and a half shooting a script on the dry hills of the western San Fernando Valley. Our mother-daughter team appeared together only once in film, as low-life hillbillies on a segment of *Wyatt Earp*.

Elizabeth did small parts in big features, too, getting to play a scene with Clark Gable himself. He was no disappointment; he rehearsed with

her carefully, and charmingly admitted he couldn't be photographed after four o'clock, due to age more than inclination. She had a long run at
MGM in *Plymouth Adventure* with Spencer Tracy, who was happy on the
days Hepburn visited the set and a little drunk on the days she didn't.

Our own cast on the second floor kept changing. When I was sixteen
and graduating, valedictorian of my class (no big thing, with only
twenty-three students in the school), Dad paid us a visit at last. Harry
was ill at ease and seemed to sense he may have missed something. Still
living in Hillsboro, Oregon, he had remarried. Of course, Mother
hadn't even considered it.

Jessie was over eighty, but she climbed three flights of stairs dozens of
times a day. While Mother and I went to the movies one night, Jessie
decided to press some sheets on the big industrial-sized mangle Nathan
had given us years before. She caught her hand in the machine, a terrible accident. Two young girls who were living on the second floor
found her in a pool of blood. Skin grafts and bone surgery were performed on her hand and arm that night. In a few days the doctors also
found cancer in her intestines. I felt the world changing like an eclipse
of the sun. After the next surgery, a colostomy, Jessie never came home.
We found a decent rest home nearby on Hoover Street, where she
faded . . . faded . . . almost away.

THE ROAD TO ROMANCE

1967 at 1353. All girls, all the time. They were students from California
Lutheran Bible School, in their late teens, living away from home for
the first time. That home was usually somewhere in Minnesota or the
Dakotas. Every other lass was named Linda, and not one of them had
ever eaten that elliptical mystery, an avocado. This was the reign of
Elizabeth, and she poured herself over the white-bread babes with
gusto, to make and mold them into the types of people she enjoyed,
reverent yet high-spirited. In short, fun. With Jessie no longer there to
say her nay, Elizabeth became the final authority on all subjects, and
loved the part.

When I wasn't juggling my love life, or *Days*, I played the older, sophisticated sister. A photo layout in *Daytime TV Magazine* came out on

me titled "The Girl in the Stained Glass Window." There was a picture of two girls in pirate outfits, fencing on the front steps. That was Kathleen, my new foster sister, and me (Mother had plunged into caregiving). The old house turned into a background for our socializing attempts, and a den of delight to all those Lutherans.

Denise Alexander and Susan Flannery were the guests at my first dinner party. "Where's Bill Hayes?" Flannery asked as we passed the hummus dip. So astute, she knew it was only a dress rehearsal for the big push. "The entrapment of Billy" was accomplished with many a meal. We started with a small lunch of chopped-olive sandwiches in the breakfast room. He loved 'em. Unlike Hal, he enjoyed my mother, the girls and the big house. Investing in some cookbooks seemed wise. I picked up the Time-Life International series one at a time.

Spain, Germany, Morocco, I planned each dinner to have a theme and never repeated myself. The girls all helped, so the guest list became as ambitious as the menus. Dinner for ten, twelve, even fourteen. We used the Spode Pink Tower dishes, and the good crystal was polished to a diamond shine. Mood music and candles were set out; we laughed hysterically cleaning house, then clearing up. We invited the world we knew: our Lutherans, of course, sometimes dressed in my extra polyester gowns, friends, cast, crew and producers from NBC, beloved teachers, other girlfriends, and "extra men," usually gay guys. The one person invited first, each and every time, was Mr. Hayes.

Bill was a wonderful man, stepping carefully through a crossroads in his life. To me he was like a noble prince who has lost his country and must search for another. I wanted to be part of his adventures and be there when his new kingdom would come.

Jessie got to meet Bill just once. We slipped into her rest home together and hung over the bed. Grammie looked so little. What did she think when she took his hand? Her eyes sparkled as she glanced between me and the handsome stranger. My heart was shouting, "This is him! This will be my own true love!" I didn't say it out loud. She knew. It means everything to me that they met and that she saw us together. A short time later, death came to visit. I had no more chances to share my happiness with the woman who never doubted I would find it.

Bill Bell had written Doug to be a sleazy predatory type in his twenties. Bill was an ageless, irresistible charmer, then in his forties. The Corday casting huddle had changed the character concept and snapped him up. Then Bell remembered that the man with the bedroom eyes was an accomplished vocalist, and Doug was put in a nightclub setting, warbling weekly to Julie. Hayes was the first actor on daytime TV to burst into song.

He sang at our parties, too, playing chords and leading the group in ditties of the "When You Wore a Tulip" vintage. Tommy, his teenage son, made the guest list, and charmed the girls even more than his father did. Lorna, our Lutheran accordionist, was quite smitten. On Mexican night we made margaritas from scratch, with plenty of Triple Sec. The ladies passed out before the enchiladas were served. Bill and Tommy carried those who could be roused up to their beds, turned off our oven and went home to Studio City.

My house was full of curious young folk, and so was Bill's. We drove around Burbank after rehearsals to be alone, perhaps enjoying a tall glass of iced tea at the Pickwick Bowling Alley or, more likely, stopping at a scenic parking location, overlooking the smog, where restraint was sorely tested.

On a hillside in the Westlake District, a girlfriend from college kept a little flat. Connie was studying to be a CPA and a belly dancer, both of which she accomplished. Thanks to her humor and generosity we had a trysting place. Bill's favorite color is red, the only color I now wore. Amazingly, Connie let me paint her bedroom walls crimson, and I brushed over the windows, too, to make them look like stained glass. "It's a firecracker!" she laughed and let me keep a key. The stage was set. Bill and I rendezvoused on a blistering summer afternoon. The moment was passionate and perfect. I felt like the Queen of Love.

The grandest party had just two guests: Bill Hayes and Bill Bell. I was deeply excited to welcome the man who had done so much to change my life. I never forgot for a moment that all the acting opportunities, wonderful stories, the casting of Hayes, and the popularity of the show came from this one man's wise and handsome head. Bell was in town from Chicago for network meetings, and Bill had shanghaied him to Alvarado Terrace. We had two hours' notice. Lorna, Kathleen, Mother and

I flew around the homestead, but our catering skills were smooth now. We all put on red dresses, placed red posies on the table and poured burgundy wine.

Looking beautiful, Mother turned to daytime's reigning lord and asked, "Mr. Bell, will you say grace?" The girlie heads bowed. Bill Bell hadn't said a grace in decades. He was thrown and, I believe, charmed. Because he was a writer, a smooth devotional dropped like pearls from his lips. Things went well. He recalled that night for years—"All you ladies in red, and Elizabeth made me say grace. Remember?"

MY FAVORITE ACTOR

My leading man and I couldn't always book Connie's hideaway. Of course, lust burned regardless. A quickie in the car was often our only option. When interviewers ask, "And what was your most embarrassing moment?" we never tell. But this was it:

The scene: Through the manicured streets of neighborly Toluca Lake a green station wagon is slowly cruising, easing past the lovely homes and rosebushes. Behind the wheel is Bill, a pixie smile and dreamy look in his eyes. Across his lap an ardent female expresses her oral devotion. That's Susan. As the pinnacle of feeling approaches, Bill pulls to the curb. But look, over there, crossing the street is a man walking his dog. The man sprints toward the station wagon. "I can't believe it, I can't believe it!" he cries. In an uncoordinated manner Bill grabs a wrinkled road map and tries to cover Susan up. The man thrusts his head through the open car window. "You're my favorite actor!" The road map heaves. The man looks down. Bill gives an autograph and hits the gas.

7

"Forsaking All Others"

BILL

On April 14, 1970, the day Susan and I met, the injured heart inside my breast blared, "I will not ever get married again!" And I meant it.

Yet, on October 12, 1974, I openly declared to Susan, before God and some pretty meaningful witnesses, "I will" and "I do." And I meant it.

Never say never, right?

When I had married Mary on February 1, 1947, during a two-day blizzard between our final two semesters at DePauw University, our wedding included the traditional vows: ". . . forsaking all others . . . to love and to cherish, till death us do part."

Well, death didn't part us. But something did. It may have been our immaturity—Mary was twenty, I was twenty-one. It may have been sex—whatever I did was not satisfying to Mary, and she first said "no" in bed just four months after our blissful nuptial day. It may have been our lack of communication—in my family we never discussed problems until we were cornered; in Mary's family the favorite expression was "Don't tell Dad." And it may have been the work I gravitated to, the mistress of all who are addicted to being onstage, that splitter of unstable couples—*show business!*

I was passionately in love with performing; Mary was not. She wanted me to be happy and abided it for a while, but as years passed her opinion of my lifework tarnished from bright to dull, like a brass knocker. She was jealous of my playing opposite beautiful, sexy young ladies, rehearsing endless hours with them, singing love songs to them.

Travel is an integral part of the entertainment business and, since hormones never sleep, being apart is devastating to the relationships of the young.

As long as I worked in New York we did pretty well. I did my studying of lines and songs on the trains as I commuted to and from work. Most rehearsal schedules were ten a.m. to six p.m., so I could race to the subway and make it home for dinner at seven p.m., and still have time to sing lullabies at put-to-bed time.

But by the 1960s, the jobs increasingly took me away from home. I played more clubs, toured more shows—eleven months on the national tour of *Bye Bye Birdie*, eleven-week tours of *Foxy*, *The Student Prince* and *Camelot*—and that's when the strain of being apart pulled at us without mercy.

Mary, needing my time and attention, would ask, "Could we join a bowling league together?"

And I would answer, "There's no way I can say I'll be there every Monday night."

And again she would say, "Can we play bridge every Friday night or a round of golf every Saturday?"

And my reply was the same. Trying to do the best job at every booking I got, I devoted myself to preparing and improving my abilities, constantly honing my skills. Show business is a relentlessly jealous type of work, and if you don't work at it, there are others who will beat you out. The same, of course, is true of marriage.

Alcohol played a major role in separating us. When we married it wasn't a part of our lives, but over time it sweet-talked its way between us. In the early fifties, Mary discovered that whiskey sours were tasty, and after two she was no longer shy-and-retiring Mary, she was life-of-the-party Mary. So for a while it was a sweet relaxer, and for a while I welcomed the addition of alcohol to Mary's life. It not only seemed to make her happier, it acted as an aphrodisiac. Denial in any form, of course, is a bitter pill, but the denial of sex in the marital bed is impossible to swallow. So, if alcohol raised Mary's level of carnal pleasure, I was happy to spend the money and the time.

But alcohol has an escalation clause in its contract. I'm sure Mephistopheles softened up Faust with a little convivial libation before offering him Marguerite on a platter. I discovered that aphrodisiacs have no conscience, and, once inhibitions are circumvented, the party goes on with whomever.

Mary and I never agreed to have an open marriage. We just tacitly decided that our marriage would be successful in all but sex. Somewhere along the way that one traditional vow about forsaking all others lost its sacredness.

I'm sure we loved each other. We certainly both loved our children. But during the social upheaval of the sixties we began to break apart. Even the difficulties we had faced together were not strong enough bonds. And, being married over twenty years, we did encounter some very serious times. The worst was probably in 1951, when at the age of twenty-four Mary was stricken with polio.

Off she flew to the hospital in a siren-screaming ambulance, pronounced highly contagious. Nobody knew how to arrest polio. When she was taken away in that shrieking ambulance, I stumbled into our tiny clothes closet, shut the sliding door, started crying for the first time in years, and began an earnest conversation with the Almighty. Asking forgiveness for whatever Mary and I might have done wrong in the past, I prayed that good health would return to her soon. I promised to increase my search for God and to devote myself to his church for the rest of my life. It was a real foxhole prayer.

The polio fever remained damaging for only three weeks; then her temperature dipped and mercifully dropped back to normal. Her doctors confirmed that the ravaging part was over and she could go home. For the next six weeks I carried her back and forth to the bathroom, and then her recuperation started. Did I feel childish as I expressed my gratitude to God for the way things turned out? I did not. Did I go to the Garden City Community Church that Sunday? I did, taking my three-year-old daughter Carrie with me. Have I continued to be involved in the ministry of caring in local churches ever since? I have.

But even that intensely bonding experience and all the others we shared lost their holding capacity. We began to face things separately. The combination of opposing factors wore us down—the lack of communication and the vagaries of show business, all exacerbated by a liberal use of alcohol—took their toll, and new social patterns emerged. Time with drinking buddies was time well spent, all other time was a drag. I tried to keep up, but alcohol has always been destructive to my voice. Sometimes at three a.m., when I needed to go home, I would pull Mary bodily to the car while she was beating me with her purse. After the second drink, she became a master of the cutting remark.

Our marriage was probably already over, but I refused to acknowledge it. I doggedly believed I would be able to find the answer to Mary's needs, even saying to her, "If you want me to quit show business, I will. I'll find something else to do."

Her response was, "No, you love what you're doing too much to give it up."

I still believed Mary and I loved each other, and when she moved out in 1969 and went to live with another man, who had left his wife and children, it killed me. I was so shocked and angry at her for breaking up our family unit, I could barely think.

My frayed heart was saying, "I never want to go through this again. I can't." And that's pretty much the way I felt through the first four years of the life of Doug and Julie and Bill and Susan.

But, at the same time, I was coming to know Susan as a truthful person, a family-oriented person, a caring and loyal person, in addition to being an extremely talented person. I enjoyed her priceless wit. I could see that she was vulnerable and had been hurt. She could be combative with others, but never with me. Over the four years, I stifled my feelings of affection for her. We sort of courted. After she said good-bye to Hal, we spent more and more time with each other, going to see operas and plays. I found myself really enjoying our times together, our conversations, our critiques of the shows we'd seen and books we'd read. I could see that she enjoyed me. Her kisses were soft and warm and I reacted. Yet still I could not picture myself marrying a second time. The anger and the hurt were too fresh in my heart. Until 1974, my year of change.

On February 11, my parents celebrated their fiftieth anniversary. And what a party! Friends and family by the hundreds gathered in Tucson to applaud and congratulate them. It was a clear affirmation that a sustained, happy marriage was possible. I had just spent five years saying,

"No! No! It's not for me." But the love that filled the air that weekend shone on my heart as from a great distance.

Then Peggy, my youngest, graduated from high school, relieving me of certain parental responsibilities. I could relax a little, and the distant light grew stronger.

On June 1, my son Billy got married, and what a happy gathering that was! Family and friends singing and laughing, time moving forward, new dreams, vows of ideal love pledged, thoughts of the future. Mary had planned not to be there, but I called her and said, "You have to go."

She said, "It will make people uncomfortable."

I said, "No matter. It's Billy's wedding, the most important day of his life. You must be there." She came. It was the first time I'd been with her since she began her new life, and seeing her wrenched my heart. But Susan was also there, looking like a Botticelli painting, and I discovered my hand wanted to hold hers, and when photos were taken, I felt like standing next to her, not Mary. The light at the end of my tunnel glimmered like a Christmas star.

I had wanted to take all five of my children around the world, to open their eyes to the beauty, art, history and tradition of other cultures. I had always hoped this event would take place right after my youngest graduated from high school, when all the kids would be old enough to appreciate what they were seeing and experiencing. Now was that time.

My having no money put a temporary crimp in the plan. I couldn't pay for a trip around the world for all of us. I lowered my sights just a little and settled on London, with side trips out into the British countryside and to Scotland. I projected a budget for a month that came to a little over $20,000. So I borrowed from the Toluca Lake Bank, my AFTRA/SAG Federal Credit Union, and my lover-friend Susan. She didn't hesitate; she just wrote out a check.

My budget paid for round-trip transportation for eight: Carrie and her husband, Dean; Billy and his bride, Bonnie; Cathy, Tommy, Peggy and me. It paid for four rooms at the Harley House Hotel, a bed-and-breakfast in Russell Square. It paid for BritRail passes, meals, tours to all the great attractions (Stonehenge, Stratford, Westminster Abbey, Windsor Castle). It paid for a day at Wimbledon, and thirteen West End shows.

The eight of us exhausted ourselves running through the crowded railway stations, from one Underground line to another. Susan and her mother, Elizabeth, joined us for our third and fourth weeks, and the two ladies and I made the rattly rail trip (on "The Flying Scotsman") to Edinburgh together. We visited their cousins Evelyn and Euphan, and the 800-year-old Norman Chapel of St. Margaret, where Euphan had wed. That little side trip was another affirmation of the meaning, the closeness, the value of family.

The whole London experience bound me and the five kids together in an even newer way. Shared experiences like that can never be taken from us. I'm sorry for those who have never blown all their money on an experience like that. Susan and her mother probably felt like outsiders, overwhelmed by being entangled with a man who had all those children attached to him, but it gave them a perfect opportunity to see who I was.

And you know what? A curious contentment spread itself over me. I felt like huge boulders had been lifted off my neck and shoulders. And, most important, I suddenly felt no longer mired in the slough of despond. The acid of anger and revenge vacated my gut. I woke up one morning saying, "Mary, I forgive you. I hope you can forgive me. And I wish you a happy life." I meant it. She is still married to Ed, and I'm happy for them.

On Sunday, September 29, 1974, I realized several things at once: (1) I was finally free of my past, free to once again enjoy life, to have a future; (2) somewhere along the parade route I had fallen seriously in love with Susan Seaforth; (3) she was in love with me, too; and (4) she and I might make each other happy if we married. Sound simple to you? It wasn't. It had taken me years to precipitate those few earthshaking ideas in my head so that I could feel them in my heart.

That very day I said to Susan, "How about a week from Saturday?" She knew exactly what I had in mind, and when we kissed on it I knew from that moment everything would be all right.

8

Three Weddings and a Magazine

SUSAN

We married on an Indian-summer evening in Bill's living room. By 1974, a great many people knew we were in love. The immediate family of twenty-two Hayeses knew, the cast knew, and most daytime viewers were pretty sure. To love is much. To marry is more.

Somehow, after twenty-eight years of cold feet, I had left home. My grandmother was gone and work was steady enough for me to pay for a nice place to live. I searched for one within trapping distance of Bill. Four blocks away on Acama Street I found a two-bedroom apartment to put my records and red dresses in. At Christmas I baked sixty macadamia nut pies for my new family, the cast and crew of *Days*. All the quiet, and being alone so much, was a shock. Of course my darling made romantic visits, all the more so when he made a surprise entrance climbing over the patio fence. It was a relief as well as a victory when he offered his own guest-house as my next address. "It needs some fixing up. You can decorate it and stay for free." I moved in immediately, before Bill's mind cleared.

Bill had joined the choir of the First Christian Church, one of the San Fernando Valley's oldest congregations. I began warming a pew in the colonial sanctuary. We both loved the preaching and the music. Meanwhile, back on Alvarado Terrace, the Community Redevelopment Agency had declared the street a heritage site, but they had not a penny to preserve or protect the terrace. It took Mother almost two years to sell 1353, and it went for peanuts. She found a little one-story in the

Valley. "Off Riverside," she said vaguely, when I asked the location. It was also four blocks from Bill's.

Having been born a Caucasian woman in mid-twentieth-century America gave me more privilege, freedom and fair treatment than all my sisters could have imagined generations back. Mother put me in show business, where I was never exploited or cheated as a child performer. Some honest aptitude for the acting craft took hold, and without seeking it I was given a profession before the age of twelve. So getting to be onstage was never my first goal. My first goal was marriage. My mother was an unwilling divorcée. That used to be called a "grass widow," and I often thought she might tempt some new bulls into her pasture, but she locked the gate and took no new lovers or chances. This example of a lifetime wasted in longing was forever before me.

My grandmother had been unmoved by the wet dreams of love. She despaired over the eternal torch my mother carried for my father. Together Grammie and I would dry the dishes and discuss the crucial mysteries of life and love. The creation of a home that sustained the body and the spirit was her notion of what a good wife did, and as for love, it didn't last long without mutual respect. Her ideas came straight out of a nineteenth-century sampler, but then so did she.

I had dreamed of a strong marriage, the sampler I would stitch my life into. There would be the space for my creativity to color, framed by the oak of sanctity and decorated with the golden molding of love. Yet I hadn't seen a long happy marriage in my life until I met Bill's parents. Those "roomers" of my childhood and the self-absorbed actors of my girlhood hadn't given me a clue of how beautiful a lifetime of loving can make you. The senior Hayeses were platinum-haired lovers, proud of each other and courteous to one another from the first morning kiss to the last good night embrace.

In my heart commitment to Bill was complete, and Bill was dating only me.

Unquestionably Bill's attention to his children and his track record as a responsible dad were virtues in my eyes, not a matter to be jealous over. The man had embraced being a parent. I longed for a home with a dad in it as well as a friend and a lover. Bill was all three. He was unaware of his power over women and treated them like delightful equals.

Most important, his style of problem solving and cheerful courtesy to all was what I wanted to emulate.

Basically, I just wanted to eat Bill up like the delicious cookie he was. Emotionally I wanted to copy his recipe for living. Secrets, lies and cheating—I'd been there and done that. Life would be so much easier and sweeter if founded on honesty. I didn't think about changing the man I loved. It was time to change me.

Bill always plots his movements on paper, drawing up calendars on yellow pads with boxes for special events, like vacations or visits. That year there had been a great Hayes gathering to celebrate his parents' fiftieth wedding anniversary, and all his children and their spouses had spent a month with him in London. How magic it was when he stood in the guesthouse door with a yellow homemade calendar that said *Wedding*. This was our time. "How about a week from Saturday?" How about it!

For fifty dollars I found a long ivory dress, then asked NBC wardrobe to shorten it. "Is this for something special?" asked Jody, my dresser, giving me a wise look. "Uh, no . . . just liked the color," I stammered, stuffing it into a plastic bag.

Opting for secrecy, we got the blood tests and license in downtown Burbank, a place dull enough to keep a secret. I asked Wes Kenney's wife, Heather, my longtime friend, to be matron of honor. She also sang the solo and baked the wedding cake. Carrot.

William Foster Hayes II, Bill's father, was best man. Kathleen, with ribbons in her hair, was the rest of the wedding party. Wes wrote a funny description of our courtship to read before the ceremony. Our loving minister, Bob Bock, presided. William Lockwood, who had been Bill's pal since DePauw days and was my voice coach, played a Puccini prelude and the "Wedding March" on the baby grand.

We invited sixteen souls. The princely Jimmy Starbuck, the man closest to Bill through all his New York days and dreams. The Hayes daughters, Peggy and Carrie, would come, and David, the first of the grandchildren. The two-year-old locked himself in the bathroom I'd painted fire engine red. Getting him out was a real icebreaker.

After much soul-searching we called Hillsboro, Oregon. My dad, Harry, got on a plane. So Mom could be assured of being teary-eyed? No, to heal an old, old wound.

Our beautiful mothers wore long dresses and sighed over the Puccini melodies while Kathleen lit the candles. Wes made everybody laugh. Heather sang like an angel. It was time to step into our new roles. A husband. A wife. Bill had on an ivory suit. We walked into the living room arm in arm.

This was real life. I knew in marrying such a good and honest man that this commitment was forever. Reading from the Song of Songs and the Book of Ruth, my voice failed, and not because of the tears or the emotion. Marriage is a sacrament to both of us, and we were standing with the generations of our families beside us. "Thy people shall be my people and thy God, my God." In that private place where man faces the infinite we stood together and pledged to be together always.

Then joy. Kisses and singing. A happy, happy wedding supper. We called Betty Corday, who wasn't surprised at all. Everyone danced. Gifts were opened. I watched Harry fall for that famously happy couple, Bill's parents. My good years with my father began that night. Saying good night, Jimmy Starbuck blessed my husband. "So many memories, Bill," he sighed. Our two mothers glowed with love for us and each other. Our two fathers were both great guys. And my darling Bill would be mine all the days of our lives.

BILL

Of course it was an exciting day! We were getting married!

But what made it really special was that Susan's father, Harry Seabold, was there. After he had dissolved his marriage to Elizabeth, Harry remarried and fathered three more children in Oregon. They had had no communication for years, though Harry did keep some tabs on Susan. He went to her high school graduation. But that's sparse.

I'd had my dad as a part of my life for nearly fifty years. We'd played catch, camped out on the beach, taken trips. He taught me how to drive, instructed me in the ways of the world, set me straight when I needed it, and had given me his unconditional love and support every second along the way. And Susan had had her dad . . . one . . . night?

Well, Harry's presence turned that ordinary exciting day into a fantastic exciting day. And the best part was it didn't stop there. Our wedding day was just the beginning of a whole new relationship for the two of them. An executive of a large construction firm, Harry began to make frequent runs to meet with clients in the L.A. area, and he always made sure that he and Susan spent some quality time together. For birthdays and special occasions he found sentimental cards for Susan and wrote loving notes on them. He arranged for us to go salmon fishing with him and his Oregon children and ferryboat riding up to Vancouver. Obviously, Harry was trying to make up for lost time.

In the four years I'd known Susan I hadn't heard her say a good word about her father. For a while, though she was happy to have him in her life, she was still vulnerable and was wary of this show of affection. Once, when we were in the Portland airport coffee shop, she vented all her pent-up anger, asking how he could keep her out of his life all those years. Harry sighed a yes, since his second marriage he'd let too much time pass and he was sorry. He wanted them to be close, and that he indeed did love her dearly. Tears. Relief. New life.

Susan stayed close to her dad until the day he died. When he passed, their years of estrangement faded into the forgiving past. All four of our parents are gone now, but our fond memory of their smiles on our wedding day will always be with us.

I count that day as the beginning of the second half of my life, and a satisfying, joyful thirty years it has been. Every day I register my gratitude to God for the gift of Susan, and I silently thank the three who created her: her grandmother, Jessie, her mother, Elizabeth, her father, Harry.

SUSAN

ART MIRRORS LIFE

Back in Salem our characters smoldered with love, but again and again circumstances kept them apart. The prowling tomcat Doug married Julie's mother, Addie, for her bundle of cash, but the marriage turned into a love match while Julie ate her heart out (and her husband, Scott, was fatally hit in the head by a passing beam). In the spirit of cynical revenge, Julie trapped the richest man in Salem, Bob Anderson, and enticed him to the altar. And so it went. Head writer Bill Bell had sworn he would never let Doug and Julie marry. But Bill was gone. CBS had offered him carte blanche to do whatever he wanted, and he went on to create and produce *The Young and the Restless* and then *The Bold and the Beautiful*, two great soaps that will remain on the air as long as daytime serials last. Bell continued to influence our lives as my mother's writing mentor, but he was no longer writing *Days*. So, in 1976, Corday gave Doug and Julie up to marriage, that state of romantic fulfillment the fans were begging to see.

Days had swollen to an hour-length show after Bell departed. Profits were large for soaps, and compared to nighttime budgets, ours was cheap as dirt. With this new sixty-minute format all contracts were out the window and the Hayeses, like the entire team, had to renegotiate. We expected a raise. Double the salary sounded nice, but Columbia Pictures Television executive John Mitchell pooh-poohed that. "We're going to add new characters. You won't be working more. Actually you'll be working less." Well, how encouraging. In the end we both got very small raises, no perks, and a pat on the head from Mitchell. Of course, the hours in the studio turned out to be twice as long, as we had feared, and we were both stretched to the max, but the show was a smash as an hour.

Time magazine chose to write a feature on soaps in 1975. Writer Leo Janos interviewed Betty Corday, Pat Falken Smith (our new, libidinous head writer) and ultimately Bill and myself. Betty didn't seem to enjoy *Time*'s style of scrutiny, a serious study of us and every other soap on the air. Would the piece be a colossal put-down? Janos found the executive branch very closemouthed and Miss Smith colorful and blabby. We were told to cooperate and, since Janos was charming and candid, we did. In New York and Hollywood *Time* did layouts of all the shows' current hot story lines. Planning for our Kodak moment, I found a red negligee to match *Time*'s red cover format. I asked makeup to put oceans of glycerin tears under my eyes as well. Then the wonderful photographer got in the groove and began to give directions as we posed against a maroon wall from the Doug's Place set. "You're pleading with her, Bill. . . . Reach your hand out. . . . You're saying no, Susan . . . yeah, good!" I tugged at my neckline, tossed Cochise the hairpiece and moistened my lips. Bill looked as desperate as you can in a coat and tie. The whole thing happened while the crew took five. It was brief. It was posed and way over the top.

Then weeks went by. Big news stories ran in *Time*. Heads of state died or, worse, didn't. Had the whole rushed intrusion been a fantasy? Then 1976 rolled around, and one day we were dragging through the NBC cafeteria line at lunch. Publicist Norm Frisch, a warm and experienced staffer, came over and opened his preview copy of the January 12 issue. "Sex and Suffering in the Afternoon" read the title. It was us. Susan was inclined downstage weeping like a willow; Bill was upstage in soft focus, pleading. We made the cover. See the sex? Neckline, lips. See the suffering? All that glycerin. It was my big "aha" moment. Granted, our names were not on the cover, but a long and semi-accurate column about us was inside. The salary figure cited in that story was oodles more than we were making. I assumed Pat Smith had sexed up our money in her mind to give the show prestige. No matter. All the casts of all the other shows hated us that week. In faraway Oregon, my father's second wife hid the magazine from him. The idea that he had ever loved my mother, even for ninety days, was too much for her, and my existence was a sore point in their marriage. Somebody saved him a copy though.

"The first daytime actors to appear on the cover of *Time*," our bios have trumpeted ever since. It is prideful to add, but I must, the *only* daytime actors to land there. The editors never plowed that field again. It was a pop-culture moment, glory to serial drama for a week, then on to the next big thing. Still, it's wonderful to be collectable. Bill's taste for my red dresses had a big payoff.

Steven Spielberg's *Close Encounters* had a clip of Doug and Julie on Richard Dreyfuss's character's television screen. Bill and Susan were jammed into one box together on *Hollywood Squares* as semiregulars. Fan magazines were bestowing awards on us for most popular male and female on soaps. We each received multiple Emmy nominations for Best

Actor and Best Actress in Daytime. The show was center stage in televi-sion, and we happened to be onstage at the time.

The viewers wanted a happy ending. "We know they're married in real life, so why not on the show?" the producers' mail kept whining. A soap commandment is never give the audience what they ask for. But ultimately the producers caved in and made the most of the obvious.

THE GRAND AFFAIR

Entwining Susan and Bill's love with Doug and Julie's turned out pretty well. After we were asked for suggestions by the writers, the Scripture we had recited in our living room made it into the shooting script. First Corinthians 13 took a big cut, but Ruth and the Song of Solomon got to tape. Wes Kenney let us fill the church set on Stage 9 with some fam-ily, so Kathleen was there again.

Days costumer Joe Markham made a big satin bridal gown of palest pink (Julie had been down the aisle a few times before). This was no off-the-rack fifty-dollar job like my real wedding dress. "And of course . . . a Watteau back," Joe said and grinned. He well knew I'm in love with the eighteenth century, so he okayed a waterfall of fabric to the floor, plus a cathedral train, all in the manner of the French artist's paintings. Yes, I was "Watteau" all the way, with five talented bridesmaids to flip this creation around. The characters' honeymoon took them to Italy. We shot those scenes before the big wedding day. Dick Contino serenaded us in a fake gondola. The prop men lay on the floor moving pie pans full of broken mirror to duplicate moonlight on the Grand Canal. We dressed as Antony and Cleopatra for a masquerade scene in our Burbank Naples. A picnic with wine and soulful kisses supposedly took place in the ancient Roman Forum, à la *Love Among the Ruins*.

NBC set up a satellite feed to Australia on the wedding day to say hello to *Days*' enthusiastic fans Down Under. There was a special green-room for press and fans to watch the event while we taped it. Elizabeth was with the press, being "the mother of the bride," getting to enjoy a bigger affair than even she could have planned. A spike in the ratings was expected, so Pat Falken Smith chose to write daytime's first inte-grated kiss into this episode.

Shooting took hours and cost a fortune. Betty Corday gave us a gorgeous ceremony that was deeply personal to us. People across the country threw parties and dressed formally to watch that day.

BILL

THE SAME VOWS, BUT PUBLIC!

Elizabeth had wanted us to have a big wedding and this was it. Instead of sixteen people crammed into one small room, Doug and Julie were wed before 16 million guests in rooms all across the country. I think we heard from every one of them. Several thousand crowded onto the NBC lot to eat a piece of wedding cake on the evening of our taping. They had to step around the klieg lights and remote trucks set up to beam a satellite-remote of the ceremony to Australia. And on the day our wedding aired, viewers in thousands of American towns and cities made a special effort to join us. Some cut classes, others called in sick or took extended lunch breaks, and several—so caught up in the story—dressed up and gathered to be participants in the festivities. At some of those gatherings, ladies served cake and champagne to toast our future. We know this because of the many snapshots we received, along with over a hundred wedding gifts and thousands of wedding cards. For those 16 million viewers, the 1976 Doug and Julie wedding was a fitting climax.

Of the many *Days* episodes in the past thirty-five years in which there were parallels between what Doug and Julie were feeling and what Bill and Susan were feeling, that one episode surpasses all. The Hessian Inn, the Variety Show, the 1981 wedding, and all the other heart-jangling memories included, nothing will ever top the high of highs of that day.

SUSAN

TUBEROSES

A TV wedding between beloved characters is always outstanding and warmly remembered. We had something extra to give, though. My character, like me, had been selfish and flawed, then changed by love. Bill's love was changing me, too. Every day I felt empowered to do my work well and acknowledge that this was our special golden time. We felt the moments flying by but lived in them and shared everything one hundred percent.

That dear daytime audience had watched us fall in love. When Bill read from the Song of Songs, "Arise my love, my fair one, and come away," they understood what it meant. This happy ending was just the prelude to life's next opera. Those women out there on the other side of the TV screens knew real love takes a long, long time.

After the fourteen-hour shoot, we flew off to our much-delayed real-life honeymoon in Italy. In Venice, a magical bouquet appeared in our room at the Hotel Fenice. It was from Betty, Wes, John Mitchell and Pat: "Happy Honeymoon!" We breathed in the fragrance of tuberose together. All the excitement and joy of our union seemed to rise in that flower's perfume.

BILL

WHITE WATER

Years roll by, NBC executives change, producers come and go, writers replace writers, fresh ideas point the characters down different white-water rivers. That is the precarious constant of the forty-year novel called *Days of our Lives*. We actors cling desperately to our characters as we bob down the rapids, paddling furiously around treacherous rocks, hanging on for dear life as we plunge over fearsome falls. Some are dislodged, never to be seen again, while a few masterfully hurtle down the rushing course, defying death at every turn. What I mean is, the actors, who are most visible to the audience, are never masters of their own fate.

Doug and Julie, finally together and happy in their marriage, became too content for their own good, and every writer since Aristotle knows that conflict is the basis of drama. What to do? In this case the viewers all know Bill and Susan are happily in love and Doug and Julie are actually the same couple, so we can't break them up. Can we?

Along comes a new head writer, who says, "You want conflict for Doug and Julie, I'll give you *CONFLICT*." The new head writer with endless ideas and courage beyond belief, stepping up like Gary Cooper in *High Noon* unholstering a six-gun, was little Elizabeth Harrower, mother of Susan Seaforth Hayes.

Elizabeth determined our fate for less than a year, but during that time she sent us through numbing white water. She had Julie open the oven door on Maggie's farm, catch fire, and burn until Maggie could put her out with a big hooked rug. The burn, a third-degree alarmer, left a scar that started just under Julie's left eye and stretched all the way down onto her left breast. The scarring caused Julie to become reclusive, and it unhinged her mind into believing Doug could only stay with her out of pity, so she flew to Mexico and obtained a quickie divorce.

Doug's long-lost brother, Byron, appeared (doing the telephone calls between Doug and Byron, and playing both parts, was fun!), but soon Byron expired. His widow, Lee, showed up, zeroed in on newly divorced Doug and somehow got him to marry her. The wedding took place on the same day Julie took off her bandages to see that her cosmetic surgery had been successful. Julie arrived at Doug's Place just in time to see her true love introduce his new wife and serenade her by singing "The Second Time Around."

Shortly after this, the powers that be took away Elizabeth's six-shooter, thanked her for doing what she said she would do, and turned the show over to another storyteller.

More rapids to run, more madness. Julie and Doug return to their senses. And plans are made to remarry the star-crossed supercouple.

SUSAN

WOULD THE THIRD TIME HAVE CHARM?

A remarriage: the occasion for a modest trip to a judge's chambers, and perhaps one hopeful private toast? You would think. As we know, however, in television if it's worth doing once it's worth doing over and over.

Al Rabin produced Doug and Julie's 1981 reunification. The network was paying for another blowout. The location was to be Descanso Gardens, an old romantic spot, full of camellias and azaleas in spring. Again we were asked for input and again we made suggestions. Bill unearthed a poem written by his granddad to his grandmother in the nineteenth century that sounded like a valentine to us. Lee Smith created a dress in peach parfait for the one and only time I weighed 116 pounds. Best of all, my own darling was to sing "Till There Was You."

For this wedding the characters had found their way back to each other after stormy times. Bill and I hadn't been apart for a moment since '74 and loved and respected each other much more than when our romance began. "Praise to the Lord the Almighty, the King of Creation," everybody chorused as we practically pranced across the green lawn. We were blessed, the cast got suntans and everyone made lots of overtime.

BILL

ROSES

Swish pan to Descanso Gardens on a bright, hot, sunburny day in 1981. Once again the writers asked us what we would like to have as a ceremony. You understand, this never happens, so, both surprised and pleased, we wrote out our next wedding, choosing the rose as our theme. Roses symbolize love (every day of our life Susan cuts roses from our own garden and places them in our home). Trish (Patty

Weaver) sang "The Rose," and Susan and I recited Robert Burns's "O My Love Is Like a Red, Red Rose" to each other. And, following our reception in the sun, we trotted off to our future in a romantic white carriage drawn by romantic white steeds.

THERE COMES A TIME MAGAZINE

It always amazes me when Susan and I go to a fan gathering and someone pulls out a treasured, faded copy of that magazine cover for our autographs. I should be used to the fact that soap fans, and *Days* fans especially, are unlike any others, but they always surprise me. Many have watched from the show's inception and retain vivid recollections of everything our characters have gone through—Addie and the birth of Hope, singing duets with Robert LeClere, our wonderful Variety Show—and they proudly say, "I've watched every day since the story went on the air." What loyalty!

Without those fans there would have been no Doug and Julie wedding. Without their reaction to our looking goo-goo eyes at each other on camera, maybe Susan and I would have rafted down a different river. I can't imagine it. I can't imagine not having that exciting day back in 1974. It was the best day of my life.

SUSAN

SANDS OF TIME

Our romance began with an hourglass, an ancient measuring of sands and time. *Kismet*, by Forrest and Wright, contains this song:

> *Princes come, princes go.*
> *An hour of pomp and show they know.*
> *Then over the sands, the silent sands of time, they go.*
>
> *Wise men come, ever promising the riddle of life to know.*
> *Wise men come, and over the sands, the silent sands of time, they go.*

Lovers come, lovers go,
And all that there is to know, lovers know.
Only lovers know.

And we do.

Part Two

9

Your Show of Shows

BILL

AUDITIONS

I rode up the creaking elevator and entered a grimy rehearsal hall, complete with chicken-wire-in-glass transom windows (unopened), choked with stale cigar smoke, butts and ashes galore, a cigarette-burned upright piano topped with coffee cups, and a loud piano pounding in the next room accompanied by staccato bursts of tap riffs and locker-room laughter.

A distinguished middle-aged man, five feet seven, in a rumpled suit and frizzled toupee, greeted me. "Hello, Bill. I'm Max Liebman. Thank you for coming." He sat down on a bentwood chair and waved at me to stand near the piano. "Buck will play." I had just worked with handsome Buck Warnick, who lived in New Jersey and had six kids, on the Olsen and Johnson shows.

Buck smiled at me. "Hi, Bill. What'll it be?" I felt like we were in a movie with Dan Dailey and should be wearing polka-dot bow ties and yellow straw hats.

"Morning, Buck. G chord, please." Most vocal auditions at that time required that you be able to sing (1) a ballad, (2) a rhythm song, and (3) something that showed your range. I first sang "East of the Sun," slowly, as a love song.

Max smiled and said, "A rhythm song?"

I snapped my fingers to give Buck the tempo and sang "East of the Sun" as a rhythm number. We had sung the song on serenades at De-Pauw both ways, so I was on familiar ground.

"Something with a little more voice?"

I said to Buck, "B-flat seventh," and sang the old chestnut "Without a Song," showing that I had some high notes and could project.

"That was nice. Do you read music?"

"Very well."

"Can you come sing for me again at ten o'clock Thursday morning? I want the rest of my production staff to hear you."

"I'll be here." He rose, we shook hands, and I eased out of the room.

On the subway home I drew a picture in my calendar book of my left hand, with the first two fingers crossed. I sketched over it and over it until the drawing was very black. I'd enjoyed my time with Olsen and Johnson, but their plans were to continue playing vaudeville and night-clubs and *maybe* bring a show to Broadway. I recognized that television was the medium of our future, and I didn't want to drag Mary, Carrie and Billy around the country in a theatrical trunk. We'd bought the home in Jackson Heights, and I desperately wanted to stay in New York and do Max Liebman's new show.

On Thursday, at ten a.m., I reentered that same dreary rehearsal room, which was now even thicker with cigar smoke. Max introduced me to his two writers, Mel Tolkin and Lucille Kallen. Born in czarist Russia, Mel Tolkin had emigrated to Montreal as a boy of twelve, was tall, deadpan and dry, an accomplished pianist and composer. Lucille Kallen's impish look betrayed her ability to turn every situation into satire. Max said, "I believe you worked with everybody else here on the Olsen and Johnson show."

He sat on the same bentwood chair, waved at me to sing, and said, "Irv will play." Former big-band pianist Irwin Kostal, with horn-rims and the longest, slenderest fingers I ever saw, was hunched over the up-right. Irv had been our orchestrator on the last five O&J shows.

Max said, "Sing what you sang for me the other day." So I sang the same three songs and stood there, heart pounding. The clock ticked. Max slowly struck a kitchen match from his coat pocket, relit his dead cigar, took a few puffs to get it going, blew out the match, and finally said, "Rehearsal here Monday morning, first show Saturday night, it pays a hundred and fifty dollars a week, thirteen weeks." Then he smiled. "There, are you happy?"

I nodded, gulped, grinned, sighed and chortled, tried to put my hands in my pockets, pick up my music and shake his hand all at the same time, saying something about as cool as "Yea-bo!"

Max said, "Well, welcome to *Your Show of Shows*." I nodded and grinned my way out the door and leaned against the wall.

Then the gang from Olsen and Johnson came out into the hall, thumping me and saying, "Congratulations! Knew you could do it. See you Monday." It was a group I'd come to know as close as brothers: costume designer Paul du Pont, set designer Freddy Fox, vocal arranger Buck Warnick, orchestrator Irv Kostal, and musical conductor Charley Sanford.

I floated down in the ancient elevator, bounced to the subway, danced home and nearly cried with happiness when I told Mary I was going to be on *Your Show of Shows*. I'd been in the right place at the right time, and I knew it.

FROM THE MOUNTAINS

From the thirties to the sixties there was a phenomenon most New Yorkers knew as the "mountains hotels." Some were small and "cost-effective," others were grand in size, amenities and price. Each establishment developed its special ambience, and getaway New Yorkers would try several until they found one to fit their particular needs. Some places were dressy, others casual; some welcomed families, others provided games for singles. Within two hours' driving distance of New York City, all afforded a pastoral change of scenery and a respite from the noise and grind. Most were in the Catskills, some in the Poconos, others up along the Connecticut coast. Nearly all were operated by and for the Jewish community, and borscht was on the menu daily. Hence the nickname "borscht belt."

At the hotels that catered strictly to Jews, Yiddish was spoken almost as much as English. They offered tennis, golf, swimming and sunbathing, rowboats and canoes, card games, tango lessons, inordinate amounts of food (you could easily put on a pound a day), social dancing and . . . shows! When they were jammed they presented shows every night; when they were less occupied, shows were still offered on Friday and Saturday nights. Comedy was king and, on nine out of ten show nights, the fare was the same: singer, dance team, comic.

Max Liebman, an immigrant from Vienna, became a writer and producer for vaudeville acts, then gravitated to the mountains hotels.

In 1934, when taking a job as social director at Tamiment, a large, not strictly Jewish hotel in the Poconos, Max decided his Saturday-night shows were going to be different. Other entertainment throughout the week could be the usual—movies, vaudeville acts, concerts, formula shows (I appeared in that beautiful rustic theater once, opening for Jackie Mason)—but Saturday night would be special. He would write and produce a completely different show every week.

For years Liebman wrote and directed sketches and songs, creating weekly revues. He developed a scenic department, costume shop, music library and Saturday-night shows that became so successful he finally was able to hire a cowriter, Sylvia Fine. Sylvia's husband was the handsome singing comic Danny Kaye. For years Max utilized Danny's performing abilities, then added Broadway star Imogene Coca.

By 1949, when television was finally coming of age, Max and his assembled staff came of age, too, producing a sophisticated revue every week. Sixteen years of preparation had made him the one person capable of creating such a show for TV. Adding the heroic talent of Sid Caesar was a no-brainer.

THE COMPANY

On our first day of rehearsal, up in those grungy Malin Studio rooms, I met Sid Caesar and Imogene Coca, Robert Merrill and Marguerite Piazza, and our guests for the week: British theater star Gertrude Lawrence, and Burgess Meredith, now probably best known for his role as Rocky Balboa's trainer in *Rocky*.

I met choreographer Jimmy Starbuck and was amazed at how quickly he could stage songs and dances. Jimmy had toured with the Ballet Russe and had sung and danced on Broadway, and not only was he one of the main reasons for the success of our show, he was a beautiful man.

He adopted me and my family, invited us to the ballet, and lavished Christmas gifts on my children. He taught me a lot as a performer.

I also met the brash kid Sid had brought in to help write the show— Mel Brooks. The conversation between Sid and Max had gone something like this:

Sid: "Max, I want Mel Brooks to be a writer on our show."
Max: "He has no taste. Everything he does is in bad taste."
Sid: "But, Max, he's funny!"
Max: "I have no budget to pay him."
Sid: "I'll pay him and you'll give him a writing credit."
Max: "Deal."

And that's how Mel Brooks became one of our writers. Max rarely liked what he wrote, but Mel was incorrigibly creative, bubbling with energy, always funny, and especially adept at creating monologues for Sid. Mel would frequently drop in to our music rehearsals, suggest a song or two, do a quick imitation of Al Jolson or Bing Crosby, and then bow out to imaginary applause.

He always called me by my whole name. "Hello, Bill Hayes! You hate me because I'm Jewish, right? If only you had chutzpah, Bill Hayes, you could be a big star! You know what you should sing, Bill Hayes? 'I Was Lucky to Be Born at the Same Time as You.' I'd mention it to Max, but I don't think he likes me today. But keep it in mind. Or"—and then he'd sing "A Million Dollar Baby (in a Five and Ten Cent Store)" à la Jolson. "Ah, Bill Hayes, if you were only Jewish, you could go a long way."

Howard Morris was used sparingly during our first thirteen weeks. He was a fine actor and could do whatever they asked him to do, but it took a while for the writers to figure out how to use him. Sid, who was very strong, had no problem picking up—by the arms or the coat lapels—all 140 pounds of Howie. They used this disparity of size often in sketches, with Sid tossing Howie around like a sack of Ping-Pong balls. And, of course, Howie's funniest bit was playing Uncle Goopy in the "This Is Your Story" sketch, hanging on to Sid's leg while Sid stumped around the stage.

Max knew right from the start how he wanted to utilize Robert

Merrill and Marguerite Piazza. He wanted first-class opera to be a part of every show. Jimmy Starbuck would stage a scene with the ensemble or Jack Russell (resident baritone) and me (resident tenor), and then Bob or Marguerite would sing an aria. The two of them sang so effortlessly, so beautifully! Bob was a slack-jawed singer, and if his aria had a lot of p's and f's and s's in it, whoever was sitting in the chair in front of him was in for a lot of spit. But it was worth it. Bob not only was a major talent, he could sing those incredibly difficult arias the first thing in the morning! And Marguerite, the Southern belle from Memphis, was an Italian beauty who had a voice that was soft and round (Southern), but had guts to it (Italian). When neither one was available, Max would bring in another star from the Metropolitan Opera Company: Jan Peerce or Patrice Munsel.

Max believed that since most television owners at that time were affluent, they would enjoy sophisticated music as well as comedy. He was proud of the mail that came in thanking him for including opera and ballet.

Though *Your Show of Shows* presented music on every episode, we—along with the vaudeville acts and concert artists—were really just the frame around the main part of the show, the comedy. And the kingpin in our array of talent was Sid Caesar. Sid, the larger-than-life hunk from Yonkers, created a new dimension in comedy. He was a very physical performer, which set him apart from the radio comedians who were moving into television. And Sid had that rare musician's ear for the lilt of languages other than American English, plus the ability to replicate them in total gibberish. His imagination was so strong and his body control so complete he only had to think a pantomimic situation and his hands and physique would perform it. Max Liebman used to say of Sid that if he pantomimed picking up an object, you automatically knew what it was and how much it weighed.

The same was true of his characterizations. The writers would tell him who he was, in what situation, and Sid would flip the switch and out would come reality and truth, heightened just enough to be funny. To me, Sid's work on *Your Show of Shows* was the peak of his powers. There wasn't a thing he couldn't do—except maybe tell a joke. I never heard him tell a joke onstage or off. His comedy was a vein of gold that came out of the ore of life.

Sid needed powerful performers to balance him, and nobody did it better than Imogene Coca. After playing leads in a score of Broadway musicals, mostly revues, Imogene had an endless bag of her own tricks. Sid was giant, Imogene petite, yet he could never blow her away. She could wither him with a look, make fun of him with one eye closed, cut him with a harridan's voice, lure him with huskiness. Imogene's comedy, like Sid's, came out of life situations and the vulnerability of everyday people living through them, and, being a singing dancer, Imogene performed something musical on every episode.

HOW DID WE DO IT?

Every Sunday afternoon, Max would gather his production staff and announce what the ingredients were going to be for the next Saturday's show. When released they all sprang into action. Freddy Fox (in his classic business suit) would start sketching sets, Paul du Pont would create costume charts, Aaron Levine located sheet music and cleared numbers with NBC and music publishers, writers would run to their typewriters and begin whacking away, Jimmy Starbuck would begin planning his staging for the singers and dancers, and Buck Warnick would rush back to his piano in New Jersey.

Buck, an experienced pianist-conductor, was our vocal and choral arranger. His product needed to be finished first. He would stay up all night Sunday writing charts for the numbers—usually six a show. Buck had eight ensemble singers who could read anything and sing anything, so he wrote accordingly—difficult eight-part harmonies, from pianissimo oohs and humming backgrounds to big legitimate sounds. When the music was to be off camera, the singers could hold their music and purr their blending sounds into a microphone at the side of the stage. When they were on camera, they had to project to a boom microphone eight or ten feet above them. The same went for all solos: theatrical-style projection was an absolute necessity. No lip-syncing!

Buck would arrive Monday morning with a fresh load of music, and copies would be made and handed out (smelling like fresh cat pee). He would take the singers to a rehearsal piano and indicate the style of the various numbers. Then we'd have an hour to woodshed it on our own before we were sent to Jimmy Starbuck for staging. We'd be holding the music while Jimmy gave us entrances, movements and exits. It was always a challenge trying to memorize vocal parts and the staging at the same time. When I had a free minute I'd jot down notes on the music: "step R, crossover step L, X Maggie, circle behind her, 2-step 4 times DL, waltz-clog, stop, clap, pose."

I memorized on the subway on my way home, as that was the only time I could really concentrate. I'd get home at seven p.m., and from that point on I needed to be husband and father, not performer. Dinner-bath-bedtimes—eventful and crucial times with endless dishes, diapers, crises and lullabies. The next morning I would solidify my memorization on the way back in—closing my eyes and singing to myself, making little representative movements, jostling the poor commuter sitting next to me as he read his newspaper. And still, when I arrived, donut eaten, coffee in hand, I frequently had to ask the others, "What did we do here?"

Was it always a scramble? Of course! But definitely worth the trouble! It was an exciting, creative, challenging time! Sometimes Max made it more difficult by giving us a new number on Tuesday or Wednesday, causing the whole process to be ratcheted up to a faster pace.

Jimmy Starbuck staged a *thousand* different musical numbers over the course of 160 episodes. I never saw him hesitate and scratch his head. He was instantly creative. Max would indicate the basic style—classical, lyrical, funny, sexy, folk—or give him a nationality—French, Italian, Mexican, Balinese, Russian, Scottish—and Jimmy would just start.

Though it was coming off the top of his head, he somehow kept it all organized. He may have been given the dancers and dance sections of four different numbers from ten to eleven thirty a.m. His rehearsal pianists would sketch out dance music as he staged it. At the same time we singers would be reading down our notes for the first time. If Jimmy suddenly got the singers for an hour, he would stage their parts. If he got me for an hour, he might leave the dancers with a rehearsal pianist to lock in what had already been set, and take me and the girl of the week to a smaller rehearsal room and stage us.

He needed to finish all the staging by Tuesday or Wednesday, so that the next step could begin—the orchestrations. A run-through would be held for Irwin Kostal, principal arranger, who could then begin writing orchestral charts.

Irv did most of the arrangements himself. He'd work throughout the week on any part of any number that had been staged, tying the pieces together whenever he got to see the rest of the numbers. And he had backup arrangers standing by to do pieces that were completed too late.

The music copyists started slowly on Tuesday, and then—like a snow-ball racing downhill—would copy all day and all night Wednesday and Thursday. Every piece of music had to be orchestrated and copied by Friday in time for our four p.m. orchestra run-through. Many times copyist Harry Battista would run in with the last-copied music—still wet on the page—for the orchestra to play.

Our camera director was ever challenged by the rehearsal schedule. He'd start the week with an empty notebook, charging around to catch whatever sketch, dance or number was being rehearsed. As the week progressed and lyrics or sketch scripts became available, he'd start to fill in his notebooks and plan shots. Stage managers timed numbers and sketches whenever they could.

THE INTERNATIONAL THEATRE

Our opening theme song was "Stars over Broadway," and we actually broadcast from a theater, rather than a television studio. The International Theatre, built in the 1890s, originally had a seating capacity of over fifteen hundred. But in 1949 it had been cut up to accommodate TV production. Seats had been removed at the rear of the center section to make way for a control booth. Twenty rows on the right had been removed to create space for our orchestra. Much of the center-front section had been torn out to allow for a camera runway, leaving about four hundred seats for live audience.

Performers always played front, to the audience and the cameras in front of Freddy Fox's theatrical drops and flats. The sound of the orchestra lagged a split second coming to the stage, so we had to take our beat from conductor Charley Sanford's arm.

We utilized four cameras: one in the middle of the balcony front row (stationary), one on the floor at stage right (stationary), one on a tripod downstage left (it moved a little), and one on a runway directly in front of center stage (it could dolly in and truck sideways). Though later in the run we were given a Houston crane camera to ply the runway, we really had very little camera mobility. And this was long before zoom lenses. Each camera was fronted by a turret of four single-power lenses—from close-up to long shot—manipulated manually. The bulky cameras required an hour of test-pattern adjusting before they could focus on anything—before every use! Though they were the best television cameras in the world, they were barely out of the experimental stage. And they could only transmit images in black and white. (Our 140th episode, on December 5, 1953, was presented in color, as was our final show—June 5, 1954—a glimpse into the future.)

THE LOOK

Your Show of Shows was a costume show from top to bottom, and every performer had several changes. Since it was *live*, with no time between numbers and sketches, most costume changes had to be made at the side of the stage. I'd be singing a number, keeping an eye on Charley Sanford's conducting arm to catch the beat (he always wore a white shirt— he was so far away!), and in my peripheral vision I could see Sid, Carl and Howie in their undershorts, changing in the wings on stage right, while over at the downstage-left microphone the singers would be oohing and aahing and tying ties and buttoning buttons, and in the downstage-right corner the guest hostess and her dresser would be shielded behind a screen making her change.

Sometimes you inadvertently got into the wrong costume and you made your next appearance dressed unlike everyone else, causing strange takes and questioning looks: "Am I wrong? Are you right?" One time, in the "From Here to Obscurity" sketch, a hilarious satire of *From Here to Eternity*, (Sgt.) Carl Reiner pinned a medal on (Pvt.) Sid Caesar, but in the quick-change Sid's dresser had neglected to put the protective pad under his shirt, so Carl pinned the medal right to the skin of Sid's chest. Ooh, the pain!

Costumer Paul du Pont, I was told, bore some unique tattoos on his body. Those claiming to know said that three little mice were depicted running up the hole in his bum, and that he sported a vine of roses spiraling up from the pubic area to the crown of his manhood. Once I asked him if this was true, and he just smiled.

What a new world I was in! I, who had grown up in the Wonder Bread, straight-arrow Midwest, with cornfields, Uncle Ezra and the Hoosier Hot-Shots, was now deep in the land of The Other. I'd tasted some of the differences along the way, of course. As a boy, many of my close friends had had skin several shades darker than mine, so that wasn't new. I'd bunked with shipmates who couldn't ask for the salt without using some form of the f-word. Working for Olsen and Johnson, I'd shared a dressing room with Maurice Millard, a white South African drag queen. So I was not totally innocent.

But working on *Your Show of Shows* with those personable, shining talents all those years did give me more maturity and understanding.

Most of the male dancers were gay, and they had the most raucously bent senses of humor. They taught me that every lyric I sang could be taken two ways. They were masters at double entendre and mercilessly funny. I came to see that, under the skin, we were all the same, and yet society had caged, persecuted and isolated them. How fair was that?

Though most of the singers and dancers were not Jewish, many of our comedy writers and performers were. Here again, those survivors of heavy persecution had developed the ability to show the world how silly it was.

Great stars like Pearl Bailey, Lena Horne and Nat "King" Cole appeared on our show. They were presented with respect, but—it's hard to believe now—they had to be introduced from a different part of the stage, and nobody from our cast was permitted to work with them on camera. Even our own regulars the Billy Williams Quartet never performed with any of the rest of us. All because they weren't Caucasian.

Amid all those vastly different non-white-bread performers, I came to a great appreciation of diversity. I do not enjoy or respect religious groups who foment exclusiveness and divisiveness, claiming omniscience. If someone has a concept of God that differs from mine, he loses no points. The person, however, who professes to have the inside track and thus the only key to the unknown is an ass. We all teach, consciously or not, by our word, our action, and our example. Too many of our fellow travelers down the journey of life have taught the negatives of hate, fear, disdain, and psychological violence. Oscar Hammerstein put it so aptly in *South Pacific* when he had Lieutenant Cable sing "You've Got to Be Carefully Taught."

MAX

Max Liebman was to me the one who made *Your Show of Shows* the success it was. All those years as writer-director-producer at Tamiment paid off, as he could make instant decisions on all aspects of the show. He always gave notes after our dress rehearsal on Saturday evening:

"Don't walk behind the cyclorama during the opening number—we could see you."

"Sid, the battered top hat is funnier than the derby."

"Freddy Fox, spread the wings on the sketch set or get us a smaller sofa."

"Carl and Howie, you'll have to underdress if you can't make the change."

"Jimmy and Buck, figure out a forty-five-second cut in the finale, or better yet, a minute."

On one memorable night we were over on our timing, so big cuts had to be made. Ventriloquist Paul Winchell, with his alter-ego Jerry Mahoney, was guest star of the week and had been integrated into the show quite a bit. Winchell's series, *The Paul Winchell Show*, was hot at the time. When Max finished announcing the cuts from the sketches, Chubby Goldfarb, Winchell's rotund, curly headed manager, spoke up. "I'm sorry, Mr. Winchell will do the sketches the way they were rehearsed."

This was followed by a stunned silence—nobody ever questioned Max's dress-rehearsal notes and decisions—because there wasn't time to quibble. The company, seated in the front ten rows of the theater, still in costume, Imogene's head in a towel (she always washed her hair after the dress rehearsal and dried it during notes), looked at Goldfarb sideways.

Max looked up from his pad of notes, smiled and said, "I'm sorry, this is my show and I'll decide what's cut." He looked back down, preparing to go on.

Chubby, believing he had Max by the short hairs, came back with, "Mr. Winchell will do everything exactly as rehearsed, or he doesn't do the show."

Without hesitation, Max went on in the same tone of voice, "Winchell is out. Marguerite, you'll do the opening welcome and introduce the Billy Williams Quartet. Judy, you'll intro the first sketch. Sid, you'll do the 'Gum-Machine' monologue in place of the second sketch. Bill, you'll sing 'Wand'rin'' in place of Winchell's single spot." Then he went on with the rest of his notes. Goldfarb and Winchell slowly got up and drifted to Paul's dressing room. Winchell changed his clothes, packed Jerry Mahoney in his traveling case and departed the theater. Neither the NBC executives nor the viewers at home ever knew such a crisis had occurred ninety minutes before we went on the air. We on the show didn't have time to hash it over. We just went to work on our changes.

THE FIRST THIRTEEN

I think Max was testing me those first thirteen weeks. He used me a lot, in a kind of background way. On our opening show I stood upstage in overalls and sang "Sweet Betsy from Pike" while Fisher and Ross danced the story in front of me. For the next several weeks it seemed like all I did was sing in lederhosen and flirt with the girl of the week.

On our fifth episode our guest host was movie-star Macdonald Carey. Not only was Mac a gracious host, he was also properly silly in the old burlesque classic "Take It from the Slap." And then, for our finale, Jimmy had staged a comic ballet for Imogene, in Indian costume and perky feather—"Pocahontas"—and Mac drolly narrated the action. Neither of us, of course, had any idea we would meet again twenty years later, on the set of *Days of our Lives*.

One of my first big numbers was memorably unnerving, "Way Back

Home," a lovely, nostalgic song with confusing lyrics. I had a horrible time memorizing the lines, which rhymed dustiest, gustiest, rustiest, crustiest, lustiest and trustiest in the first six bars. Though happy to get the solo, I was a bit wired.

Max had slotted my song, which included the dancers doing a skipping, carefree number all over the stage, to follow the "Henry the VIII" sketch. Sid and Imogene ate all through the sketch and threw chicken, bones and red wine in every direction. So much greasy debris was flung around that, before we could start "Way Back Home," the stagehands had to wet-mop and then dry-mop the stage, or the dancers would be slipping dangerously in the garbage.

Our guest host, Basil Rathbone, given the signal to stretch his announcement, tried valiantly, but there were only so many words, and finally he said, ". . . and here's Bill Hayes." Backstage, I heard my musical introduction being played, but the curtains didn't part. I could hear the stagehands flailing at the stage with their wet mops. Charley Sanford, seeing that the curtain didn't open, started the orchestra a second time. Still the curtains didn't part. Stagehands then began dry-mopping and Charley played the intro a *third* time. I, in my little set-piece cocoon, wondered why they kept playing that stupid intro over and over without opening the curtain. I got off my bench and started to leave the set to find out what was going on when—at last!—the stagehands ran offstage and the curtains flew apart.

A few weeks later I sang "I Miss My Swiss" in long stockings and—what else?—lederhosen. The number included a Swiss folk circle dance, and everybody but me had had the sense to roll garters into the tops of their stockings. As we circled, my stockings drooped, then slowly slid to my ankles. And, as my arms were around other dancers, I couldn't stop the downward flight of the stockings or the rising redness on my face. I got mail for years asking me to repeat "that song where your sox fell down."

On Monday of our thirteenth week, I cornered Max on the stairway and asked if he was unhappy with my work. He looked surprised and said, "No. Why?"

I told him I felt there were lots of strong songs around, with lyrics that could touch people instead of just suggesting a visual scene like bicycles or Switzerland or Sweden, and I wondered if he thought I couldn't handle them. He said, "Not at all!" He thought a moment. "Well, I may have one for you."

That afternoon he called me into his office and played Sammy Kaye's record of "Wand'rin'" for me. "Is that what you mean? Do you like that song?"

"Yes. And yes."

That Saturday night I sang "Wand'rin'" in a tiny two-fold flat, carrying a coat over my shoulder. The choir sang lonely oohs and aahs and the orchestra played lovely haunting fills between the phrases. That performance was one of the peak points of my career as an entertainer. People wrote to me about it for the next ten years.

The melody of "Wand'rin'" was folklike, the chords were old-timey in their simplicity, and the lyrics expressed lonesomeness so universally they touched everybody. It built to a vocal climax, with a high G-sharp, and a terrific applause ending. The response, immediate and gratifying, sent me off into our first hiatus on winged feet.

During our summer off I played four shows at the Chicago Rail Road Fair—*The Merry Widow, Of Thee I Sing, The Mikado* and *On the Town*—two weeks of rehearsal, nine weeks of performing. We did four fifty-nine-minute shows a day, seven days a week, a brutal schedule vocally. Playing in the round with no sound system, a train puffing and clanging a hundred feet to the west of our tent and planes landing at Meigs Field a quarter mile east of us demanded continuous loud projection. It was so exhausting that toward the end of the run actors began losing their voices and dropping out. At one performance of *The Mikado*, so many were incapacitated that instead of eight men singing "We Are Gentlemen of Japan," dancer Phlip Nasta was the only one left to do the song. He sang with gusto but had a difficult time keeping a straight face. We finished at the end of August, and I had a welcome week off to rest my battered vocal cords.

SECOND SEASON—THIRTY-NINE WEEKS

During the summer Max Liebman had rented two floors of the City Center Building, a happy improvement over the Malin Studios drear.

An ancient, palsied man called Pop took us up to the sixth floor and—very slowly—opened the elevator gate and door to our new home. Max now had a spacious office for himself and room for a secretary-receptionist, the writers had a room with ashtrays, the singers had a room with piano, and there was one large room with bleacher seats for rehearsing the dancers and putting musical numbers together.

As we sailed into our new season, we were joined by two new permanent members of our company: Carl Reiner and Judy Johnson. Robert Cummings was our guest star that first week, and when Carl joined him and Sid in the "Producer with a Problem" sketch, we all could tell Carl was going to kick us up a notch.

Pretty brunette Judy and I were immediately put together, doing "You're a Star," and I was thrilled she was going to be a regular. That number was the first of about a hundred we did together. Judy, who had toured with Les Brown (Band of Renown) and Sammy Kaye (Swing and Sway), and had had a hit record with "Joltin' Joe DiMaggio," added a more pop-singing style than we'd had before.

She and I, playing the young lovers on the show for the next three years, were given the best of Rodgers and Hart, Schwartz and Dietz, the Gershwins, and Cole Porter. Those duets with Judy are some of the sweetest memories of my life.

She always rehearsed with a smile and learned her part—music, lyrics and staging—quickly, delivering her lyrics right into my eyes. Since she didn't read music, whenever we were given our music for the week she and I would find a piano and I'd play the chords and sing her part for her. She learned by hearing it. And, since our numbers were beamed out *live* all over the country and we never really had sufficient memorizing time, before each show we'd make a pact, "If we have a good time the audience will have a good time, so let's have a good time no matter what happens, right?"

"Right."

"And then maybe they won't notice the goofs, right?"

"Right."

Well, of course they noticed the goofs. But egg on your face was part of the excitement of live TV.

Working under such time constraints, Judy and I depended on each other and bonded like Marines under fire. Silly jokes and caustic wise-cracks kept us on our toes, and when Judy got the giggles she would hold herself where the seams of her leotard came together and plead, "Stop! I'll wet my pants!"

MAIL

Another nice surprise I got that first day back was two large boxes of fan mail that had accumulated during our break. Preadolescents and teenagers, the fans who write more than anyone else, had picked me out of the group to write to. I personally answered the best-written letters and tried to autograph and send out eight-by-ten glossies to those who requested them, but there were just too many. For the next three years I received about a thousand letters a week, so I hired a secretary to help me read and sort and send. For a few years I had over five thousand fan clubs around the country.

The mail was a kick to read. The letter writers commented on my songs, dancing, costumes, partners, hair and height. They wanted to know the intimate details of my life, including if I was married, my phone number, my favorite foods, and so on. Many purported to be reporters for their school newspapers and asked me to fill out ("please answer in full") ten pages of questions. I was thrilled to receive them, but there was no way I could even read them all, let alone answer them. The fans didn't appreciate having their letters answered by a secretary. One mother of a sixteen-year-old wrote to me, "How dare you not respond to my daughter's invitation for you to attend her sweet-sixteen birthday party?! She was in tears the whole weekend! Shame! Shame on you!" Ah, me.

ON BEING IN A HIT SHOW

Our run of thirty-nine episodes from September 1950 to June 1951 was a smashing success. Our guest stars knew what they were getting into and they looked forward to joining the fun. Sketches were tailored for them, and the stars enjoyed them a lot more than the ten or twelve introductions they had to make, each announcement liberally sprinkled with names.

We regular cast members also made announcements, and, even though I was given the words to say and was familiar with all the names, my shyness was a monumental block to announcing with ease. The fact that Sid Caesar was not much better at it was some consolation. Sid was a tower of talent but a very shy man. Perfectly at home in any character, glib and at ease, he was never at a loss for words—until he became himself. At those times when he was just Sid he found it difficult to come up with "Thank you and good evening, ladies and gentlemen." And I loved him for it.

Imogene was, if possible, even more shy than Sid. On Saturdays, we always had fans crowding around the stage door of the International Theatre. Imogene would arrive in the morning and never leave the theater. After the show, she'd wait until all the fans had left the stage door, bundle up in a high-collared coat and dart out into a waiting cab.

Sid was always impeccably dressed, in a well-cut sport coat, slacks and tie. That didn't stop him from downing a bottle of Dr. Celray's Tonic in one long swig, putting his hand to his chest and producing a windy belch.

He and I got along just fine. Like Mel Brooks, Sid always called me by my whole name. "So, Bill Hayes, how do you explain you getting more fan mail than Immy and me? What are you doin' to those girls?" "So, Bill Hayes, your socks fell down, eh? You trying to steal the show?"

Your Show of Shows was *the* thing on TV in those years, and everybody in the country watched it. There was no place we regulars could go without being mobbed.

It was no longer easy to sit alone on the subway and memorize lyrics because everyone who recognized me wanted to talk about Sid and Imogene and the long-haired girls in the Hamilton Trio. I couldn't take my family out to dinner because everybody in the place wanted me to come over to their table and meet Aunt Myrtle, pose for pictures and sign a dozen autographs. Even in a theater, while a play or movie was going on, people would sidle through the row and stage-whisper, "My wife will kill me if I don't get your signature."

Though most fans were courteous, I discovered that—on evenings out—I was spending more time with them than with my family. It was exciting, but somehow not right. I began to not make eye contact, to shy away from people, and I discovered that if you walk fast and look in store windows or subway gratings you can get to your destination on time.

The worst part of the celebrity was the articles in those early fifties fan magazines. One had a big triangle slashed across a double-page spread, with my photo at the apex, "The husband," a snapshot of Mary at one corner, "The wife," and Judy Johnson's face at the opposite corner, "The other woman." The kids' pictures gazed angelically from the middle. I couldn't believe it!

There wasn't a hint of hanky-panky going on: Judy was not making a play for me, and she and I were not two-timing Mary. I don't know if Mary believed the innuendo, but the story certainly bothered her and embarrassed Judy, too. Dave Tebet, doing publicity for *Your Show of Shows*, told me to forget about it. "That's part of our business, Billy-boy. It's what we call 'fan candy,' and it won't do your career any harm. Just sit back and enjoy it." Well, what if it did my marriage some harm? Was I supposed to "sit back and enjoy" that?

Of course, eventually I accepted that it comes with the territory. In our business we spend exciting times with coworkers, often diving deep into emotions, portraying love scenes as realistically as we can, laughing and crying with one another, peeling back inhibitions. So show folk will always be targets for suggestive gossip. I mean, fan candy.

COMING INTO FOCUS

Carl Reiner was the best straight man of all time. His grasp of the German professor interviews was money in the bank, and the writers began a series: "Prof. Wolfgang von Lionklopper," "Dr. Sigmund Shock," "Dr. Heinrich von Heartsick," "Dr. Sigmund von Sedative," "Dr. Rudolph von Rudder," "Prof. von Lieberstraum." It was setup, boff—setup, boff—setup, belly. Every time, couldn't miss. Carl's eyes, though, used to give him away. He'd be playing his square interviewer to the hilt—but, inside, Carl was terribly amused by the nonsense of the moment, and his eyes were always laughing.

He was a great improviser. But even better at off-the-top-of-his-head improvisation was Mel Brooks. Sometimes Mel would stand out in front of the company, and they would throw him characters and situations, and he would just take off. Mel's creation of the two-thousand-year-old-man probably came out of one of those impromptu sessions.

His comedy genius was like a fire hydrant: turn it on and the gush would knock you off your feet.

One time Carl asked Mel to be a Yiddish pirate, and Mel went on and on, topping himself and creating a whole ridiculous picture of this wild-eyed Jewish-dialect Bluebeard ("Mit mein cutlet at mein belt")—twenty minutes of virtuoso display. I've not been surprised at all to see Mel's success at writing funny films and then topping them with the Broadway musical *The Producers*. His mercurial talent was always visual. Because I knew and felt close to Mel long before he became the king of Broadway, I am proud of what he's accomplished and very happy for him.

By Christmas 1950 our cast was not only working well together as a unit, we were a happy family backstage. Two weeks before Christmas, I bought a two-foot evergreen, set it on a card table in the big rehearsal room, and hung a couple of fake icicles on it. People began to bring in real ornaments and tinsel, until it was nicely decorated. Then everybody started putting brightly wrapped packages around the tree, until the twenty-fourth, when Max ordered in champagne and we all had a celebratory nip together. The Christmas/Chanukah presents mostly turned out to be gags (Sid, Carl, Howie, Mel and Mel gave the unmarried Lucille Kallen three huge squash gourds in the shape of Herculean male genitalia). It was a laughing, happy time. Our ratings soared, Max, Sid and Imogene reaped all kinds of awards, and Marguerite, Jack, Judy and I graced the cover of *TV Guide*.

When Sid, Imogene, Carl and Howie played together it was magic—old sketches dragged out of Tamiment files, traditional burlesque turns, pantomimes, spoofs of silent movies, foreign movies, classic films, and modern-day marital-problem sketches. Liebman would get the four of them together in the writers' room at ten o'clock Monday morning, the writers would throw ideas at them, and they would all edit and change, replace and revise, and laugh and shout, with the men all smoking huge cigars, until they emerged at six o'clock Thursday night with sensational results. There was never a rude put-down, a hint of profanity, a double entendre, a mention of breast or penis size, any form of bathroom humor, or even a laugh track. So different from the TV of today. It was just nonstop hilarity.

When asked today what compares with the sketch comedy of *Your Show of Shows*, I emphatically answer: "Nothing!"

"But what about *Saturday Night Live?*" they ask. It probably comes closer than any other show, but even *SNL* is caught up in the washroom humor that made us snicker and guffaw when we were sophomores in high school. The comedy on *Your Show of Shows* was sophisticated, witty, and so eloquently satirical it hasn't been duplicated for decades. *Caesar's Hour* maintained the standard throughout the fifties, spawning spectacular careers for that galaxy of writers. But despite the brilliance and huge success of *Caesar's Hour* writers Larry Gelbart, Neil Simon, Michael Stewart and others, the growing audience's inability to under-stand truly sophisticated comedy continually demanded that the prod-uct be watered down. As for the cynical sitcoms of today, there is absolutely nothing that compares.

SPRINGTIME '51

The happiest moment of spring '51 for me was the arrival of my third treasure: my redhead, Cathy. She was due in May, but during the preg-nancy Mary had developed such toxemia that her ob-gyn warned us not to go past seven months or the baby might be adversely affected.

The night before Cathy was born I sang "Eileen," an old-fashioned-sounding Irish ballad written by Max Liebman. We finished the last half hour with a twenty-minute version of *Die Fledermaus* and, though my music was first-rate, I found it difficult to concentrate. Mary was in the theater, and right after the show she and I went directly to Doctors' Hospital. She forced down her glass of cod-liver oil, which induced la-bor, and a few hours later Cathy arrived—a tiny four-pounder. The hospital kept her incubated for five weeks, until she filled out to a plump five and a half pounds and they allowed us to take her home. Then we were five.

During that season Judy Johnson and I were given six Rodgers and Hart songs to do. That's when I discovered what a special lyricist Lorenz Hart was. His songs were sensual and passionate. His witty words were always the easiest to memorize. One thought led to another: "I took one look at you, that's all I meant to do, and yet . . ." "We'll have a blue room, a new room for two room . . ." Can't get better than that.

Judy and I had a genuine live-TV experience on our final show of that season. We were doing Cole Porter's "You're the Top" and had each sung a verse and chorus. As we were about to go into a bebop chorus of angular movement our lead trumpet player turned two pages of music at once. Result: orchestral chaos! When Charley Sanford figured out what had happened, he sped up the rest of the number; dancers were crashing to the stage, and we didn't get to finish before we were cut off the air. Hey, live TV, right?

We were at the pinnacle of TV success. Awards, notoriety, ratings, adulation. We were *hot*! During the thirteen-week hiatus, I headed for Chicago, where I had my first experience with screaming girls in the audience. At the Chicago Theatre, I found if I moved or jumped or tapped or snapped to the rhythm of the music, or if I sang directly to the girls in the front rows, they all screamed. That shook me up so much I stopped moving completely.

Your Show of Shows reconvened in September 1951, with the same cast, picking up right where we left off. For me it was a whole year of screaming teenage girls. On the show, when my name was announced, the girls would scream; after my song, the girls would scream; when I walked out the stage door, the girls would scream. It bemused and embarrassed me, sometimes even frightened me. And I didn't have to sing bubblegum songs to elicit the reaction. That season I sang several songs in Neapolitan, but the darlings screamed anyway.

Their ebullience was an indication that I had a potential for something, but neither my agents nor I could figure out how to turn it into profits. Don't think I haven't fantasized about what might have happened if we had.

COAST TO COAST

TV cables were connected between Chicago and the West Coast in September 1951, so Los Angeles and San Francisco, Portland and Seattle received our show *live*—for the first time—on September 29. Prior to that they had only been shown kinescopes, which were of poor quality at best. Kinescopes were films of live-TV pictures taken off a studio monitor. They are our only record today of TV before tape, which didn't come into use until 1957.

We ended our third season on May 31, 1952, and dispersed to do our own thing. For me it was first to play *A Tree Grows in Brooklyn* in Dallas with the Broadway icon Shirley Booth (who later starred in *Hazel* on TV). What a joy!

The rest of that summer I worked at Warner Bros. in my first feature film, *Stop! You're Killing Me*, starring Broderick Crawford and Claire Trevor. Claire was a gorgeous, classy lady. Brod, one of Hollywood's old guard, talked every bit as fast as the characters he portrayed. Every afternoon (before the last setup of the day) he took me across the street to the Smoke House bar, where I would nurse one shot of booze while Brod would slosh down several. Margaret Dumont, the grande dame who had worked opposite Groucho in all the Marx Brothers films, played my mother.

My first time in Hollywood was great fun—except when the San Andreas Fault made itself known. One night I was awakened by the house bucking like a bronco and screeching like a speeding train: we were having an earthquake! Talk about a rude awakening! The following day at the studio there was a huge fire that burned up warehouses of costumes and several soundstages. We actors were hustled off our stage and told to leave the lot immediately. Hook and ladder trucks were clanging in the gate as we were driving out.

I had to wonder why they thought Hollywood was such a perfect place to make movies.

FOURTH SEASON

I flew back to New York, charged up and ready for our fourth season (1952–53), but I seemed to sense strange vibes. We began to repeat sketches and numbers. A lot. By popular demand? I didn't think so. Why? What was going on?

"Why the sameness?" I questioned head writer Mel Tolkin.

"When you've got a winning formula going you don't mess with it. Look at Jack Benny—same format for twenty years."

Well . . . maybe. I tried to analyze what I was feeling. Was Sid's cough the result of too heavy a load of responsibility? Did I hear him begin to argue with Max's decisions and taste? Were the production people getting a little testy when final decisions were held off longer than before? Was Max slowing with weariness?

I believe sometime late in 1952 the gears began to slip. Vocal arranger Buck Warnick would grimace and mutter, "It can't be done. There's not enough time." Jimmy Starbuck would lose his sense of humor and become irritable with the singers and dancers, his closest friends. Even the irrepressible Mel Brooks quit dropping by our music rehearsals. Our show was still at the top of the ratings heap, but I felt the honeymoon was in jeopardy of being over. Apathy leads to atrophy, tension to distraction.

In December 1952, as usual, I bought our annual Christmas/ Chanukah tree and set it up in the big rehearsal room. Soon the tree was covered with spangly ornaments and surrounded with gifts wrapped in red and green. The party on Thursday, the twenty-fifth, was boisterous. Sid and Imogene handed out ceramic plates to the company (with everybody's signature fired in), champagne corks popped. But to me the hilarity was tinged with sadness, as if it was a closing-night bash. The following Monday I called my agent, Charlie Baker, and asked, "Charlie, what's doing on Broadway?"

Charlie replied, "Dick and Oscar are casting their new show right now, and they haven't found their leading man yet. If you say so, I'll arrange an audition."

ANOTHER AUDITION

I had no time to think. On a lunch break from my *Your Show of Shows* rehearsals, I took some music and ran over to the Alvin Theater, slipped in the stage door and was immediately taken out onstage. The house lights were up, so I could actually see the awesome trio I was introduced to: composer Richard Rodgers, author-lyricist Oscar Hammerstein II and director George Abbott. Relieved that I didn't have to wait (while tension built to "What am I doing here?"), I sang Irving Berlin's "Just One Way to Say I Love You," starting on a high G so they'd know I had money-notes and could project. They conferred a moment and then Mr. Rodgers asked me to sing another song. I did "Wand'rin'," they conferred again, and then Mr. Hammerstein came to the lip of the stage and asked me to come back in two days to read a scene from the script. My heart was thumpin' and jumpin'.

Leaning back in his theater seat, George Abbott asked me, "Didn't you just play *A Tree Grows in Brooklyn* in Dallas with Shirley Booth?"

"Yes."

"She told me you played the part better than anyone else."

"Thank you, I'm glad." The stage manager gave me the scene, which I took home and quickly memorized.

Two days later I did my scene, with an assistant stage manager reading the other lines. The trio of theatrical titans conferred, and then Rodgers said, "Bill, that was very nice. We'd like you to do our show."

I went back to our rehearsal studios and told Max of their offer. He said, "Is that something you'd like to do, Bill?"

"Yes, it is, Max. It's Rodgers and Hammerstein and Abbott, and, Max, it's a chance to do a featured role on Broadway."

He looked at me, slowly lit his cigar, and said, "All right, we'll call it a leave of absence. When do they want you to go into rehearsal?"

"March twentieth."

"Then let's say you'll work on our show through March fourteenth. That would give you one week between. Sound all right to you?"

"Yes, Max. And thank you." I thought, What a classy guy.

A few days later Max told me he'd had a personal call from Richard Rodgers, thanking him for allowing me out of my contract to do their show.

My last two months as a regular on *Your Show of Shows* taught me how a person can be happy and sad at the same time. I was excited about going off to play an R&H show on the Great White Way, but I was plagued with second thoughts about leaving TV's number-one show while it was still leading the pack.

One episode holds a special memory for me, because I nearly got smithereened by some falling scenery. The number was "Any Place I Hang My Hat Is Home." I was standing upstage left listening to Marguerite Piazza introduce my number when two stagehands shifted some forty-foot flats and pushed them too close to the back wall. The flats bel-lied out and fell—hundreds of pounds of wood and canvas and nails and paint—and, missing me by half an inch, landed backstage with a mon-strous *ka-wham!!!* If they had landed on me I'd've been a pancake. My whole insides wrenched just as Marguerite was saying, ". . . and here is Bill Hayes." The intro started and I sauntered out onstage. Though my heart was pounding like John Henry's hammer, I tried to look relaxed and cool as I sang the opening line, "I'm free and easy, that's my style. . . ."

Most memorably, on February 28, I sang Nanki-Poo in a twenty-five-minute, modernized Gilbert and Sullivan *The Jazz Mikado*. Buck Warnick and I had been having fun at the piano one day, reading through the original Gilbert and Sullivan score, wondering if we could do a cut version of the show, when straight old Buck began to put some jazz accompaniments to the songs. We looked at each other and agreed that could do it. He worked on it a few weeks, sold Max on the idea, wrote a part for Carl Reiner (Pooh-Bah) and another for Howie Mor-ris (the Mikado), and it was just spectacular!

At the company curtain call of my last show, Max came out and pre-sented me with a gold watch inscribed, "Good luck, Bill! Sid, Imogene, Max." And, after 119 straight episodes of that thrilling show, I departed to play *Me and Juliet* on Broadway.

ME AND JULIET

To a twenty-seven-year-old singing actor in 1953, Broadway was nir-vana, heaven and paradise rolled into one. A leading role in a Broadway musical was the Golden Fleece toward which all quests were directed. The fabled Lorelei had no sweeter siren song. New York's theater dis-trict was the temple whose gods were named Berlin, Gershwin, Porter and—Rodgers and Hammerstein.

To be chosen to play a lead in a new show by Richard Rodgers and Oscar Hammerstein II—who in a dozen years had turned out *Okla-homa!, Carousel, South Pacific, Allegro* and *The King and I*—was to be knighted, blessed, beatified. The one time I sent a telegram to every member of my family, announcing a career achievement, was to trumpet this casting.

Perhaps you can imagine the helium cushion I was on when I received a call one day: "Hello, Bill, this is Dick Rodgers. Dorothy and I are having the cast of *Me and Juliet* up to our apartment Sunday afternoon. We'd like to meet everybody personally before we go into rehearsal and hope you can join us."

"I'd love to."

"Good. Oscar and Dorothy will be there, too, and we'll play through the songs so everybody gets to hear them the first time together."

Have you ever had a phone call from a deity? Have you been invited into an inner sanctum? I'm not trying to be blasphemous here, just trying to convey the awesomeness of that moment.

Dorothy Rodgers welcomed us at the door, Rodgers put on his Benjamin Franklin spectacles and played the songs for us, and Hammerstein read the lyrics, snorting at his own jokes. We stopped at one point to watch an episode of *Victory at Sea*, for which Rodgers had written the music. The score was stirring and cinematic, and Dick beamed and nodded listening to it.

At our first rehearsal, Hammerstein introduced the production personnel: scenic designer Jo Mielziner, costume designer Irene Sharaff, choreographer Robert Alton, and director George Abbott. While the stage manager was passing out our scripts, Hammerstein said a pretty amazing thing: "This is the script as I have written it. However, from this moment forward, whatever Mr. Abbott says about it, whatever changes he wishes to make, what he says goes."

I thought, How many writers would have the self-confidence and class to make such a public concession?

Then he introduced the entire cast. Isabel Bigley, Joan McCracken, Ray Walston, Mark Dawson and I were the main principals, the supertalented jazz pianist Barbara Carroll would be playing onstage (Barbara still plays soooooo beautifully!), and in the dancing ensemble was a vivacious redhead with legs up to here named Shirley MacLaine.

George Abbott was prepared, organized and a stickler for starting at the stroke of the hour, plus taking five-minute breaks timed to the second. If you were late, he let you know it: "That's unprofessional and inconsiderate. Don't do it again." He worked fast and was his best at the fast-paced comedy.

Hammerstein watched the scene rehearsals intensely, sometimes giving quiet acting notes during a five: "Think of it this way. He's trying to be all business, but can't be because he's fallen in love with her."

Rodgers, like an eagle wheeling overhead, was everywhere at once, listening to music rehearsals, checking dance staging. He gave copious notes, quick and to the point, and wanted the music sung precisely as he had written it: "No phrasing, no liberties, please. Sing it eighth-quarter-eighth-quarter-eighth, with the whole note preceded by an eighth-note syncopation."

Rodgers and Hammerstein created so many blockbuster shows that, in comparison, their lesser shows are considered failures. *Me and Juliet* was one of their lesser shows. We played nearly five hundred performances, however, all to full houses. Production costs were paid off and substantial profits went into the R&H till. So, though not in the same category as the storied five that were made into films—*Oklahoma!*, *Carousel, South Pacific, The King and I* and *The Sound of Music*—our show must be considered a success. You may quote me.

Three months after we opened I was invited to sing "The Big Black Giant" on *The Ed Sullivan Show*. My big solo from *Me and Juliet*, it's a profoundly moving Hammerstein text that speaks for all performers who are subject to the call of theater. That "big black mass of love and pity and troubles and hopes and fears" is the audience, the monarch of our lives. If the giant likes us, the show goes on. If it doesn't, we pack up and go. The big black giant of Broadway liked us for eleven months. Then we packed up and went to Chicago.

While we were playing our eight-week run there, Mary—back home—had to ask a friend to run her to Doctors' Hospital for the birth of Tommy, our fourth treasure. Tommy was already twenty days old when I got to hold him for the first time.

I did leave *Me and Juliet* one day during our run to appear on a special broadcast (in color) of *Your Show of Shows*. Max Liebman had called Richard Rodgers and asked him to "return the favor." He said, "We're going to repeat *The Jazz Mikado* and would love to have Bill play Nanki-Poo."

Rodgers didn't hesitate. "Of course, Max."

Me and Juliet was a beautiful experience, a dream come true and, as the song says, "They can't take that away from me."

AND BACK HOME

I was to do one more show with Sid, Imogene and all the gang. Max kindly invited me to sing on the final episode of *Your Show of Shows*, June 5, 1954. I sang "Rock the Joint" while the Hamilton Trio danced; I sang "Anema e core" and "Chi se nne scorda cchiu" (in Neapolitan) to Pauline Goddard; I watched Imogene sob all the way through her final number, and I took my 121st bow with the cast that was so dear to me.

For our closing-night party, NBC had taken over the Rainbow Room on the sixty-fifth floor of the RCA Building. A Dixieland band from our own orchestra lightened the mood, a feast of kings was laid out for us, and everybody cried in disbelief that the thrill ride was over.

After hugging and kissing everyone else, I sought out Max Liebman and tried to tell him thank you, but I just couldn't get it out. He understood what was in my heart, smiled and said, "Thanks, Bill." That was my twenty-ninth birthday.

IO

Great Ladies

SUSAN

Most history buffs remember that the English prime minister during World War II was Sir Winston Churchill. That twentieth-century icon of leadership, literature and cigars also had a lovely daughter named Sarah, who was a leading lady and hostess on NBC's *Hallmark Hall of Fame* in the 1950s. She was red-haired and chiseled of feature, with a fine chin and clear eyes that resembled her mother's, Clementine, who said the secret of a happy marriage was never seeing your husband before lunch. What the Churchill home life may have been like I can scarcely imagine, but it had produced a good actress with a pedigree that captured the high-class image Hallmark Cards demanded for its television productions. "When you care enough to send the very best" was quite a slogan, and nothing lived up to it like a Churchill.

The opening shot of the original series was a slow pan through a vast colonnade filled with statues of the dead and the famous. An echo-chambered voice would announce the great personage of the week. This set was actually a twelve-inch-tall miniature and the statues were teeny-weeny figurines. I was cast in the story of Catherine Paar, Henry the VIII's last wife (or main squeeze, depending on how you read history). The regal Sarah was to be Paar and I a nine-year-old Princess Elizabeth, Henry's daughter before her great days as England's queen. This was the job that made my family nearly delirious with joy, for we were Scottish by adoption, great Anglophiles, and we truly loved the overseas cousins who had just suffered through a terrible war. I had literally grown up with the Karsh photo of Sir Winston that was in our den (just below the stained-glass window with the stag's head in the middle of it). My phony British accent, which I tried to stifle around my peers in the fifth grade at Magnolia Avenue School, came out in full force.

In the teleplay Paar was under suspicion for her liberal spiritual views and risked running afoul of great Henry's murderous wrath. In one scene the princess and the queen watched from a palace window as an off-camera heretic was marched to the stake. My line was, "They are going to burn her. Oh, Kate!" Sarah shuddered, we all shuddered. It was campy and swell. The Churchill family all had great acting chops.

At dress rehearsal Ms. Churchill sat before the camera, trying on dozens of sixteenth-century bonnets, looking for the most flattering one. Whenever I see pictures of the unlucky wives of Henry VIII, I think of Sarah. What hats those queens might have chosen, given an NBC costumer.

During rehearsal week a birthday milestone passed for Sarah, and producer Albert McCleary poured champagne in her honor for all the cast, even little me. Mother slipped the wine cork into her purse and we kept it for years. Protocol was loosened, as they say, and several people asked Sarah about her father. "What was his real impression of FDR?" "Actually, he never could stand him," she volunteered, and poured another glass all round. The laughs just kept on coming after that, and I think her evening ended with a public disturbance somewhere off the premises. Such was my first brush with a name from history, and I ate it up like Yorkshire pudding. The British have an ancient aristocracy, yes, but they've cultivated an aristocracy of talent, too. Sarah Churchill was "top drawer" on both counts.

The musical *Peter Pan*, directed by Jerome Robbins, came through L.A. on its way to Broadway in 1952. The show starred Mary Martin as the ageless boy. An epilogue was being put into the show where Peter returns from Neverland to find his Wendy too grown up for more adventures, and takes her little daughter Jane off to his world instead. Miss Martin attended the Jane audition and chose me to read the scene with her. "Speak as loudly as you can," she suggested, "as loud as me." We were in the Musicians' Union Building on Vine Street, standing in a cavernous space, but when Mary gave it her all, glass could shatter. This was before the days of microphones under every wig onstage. You were expected to project the voice with breath and power enough to fill a theater. I piped up to my maximum volume, "Oh, Peter, take me with you!" and got the part. Jane would go into the show at the director's discretion. Mr. Robbins, whippet thin and eagle-eyed, was occupied with drilling the dancing pirates, lost boys and little Indians in his exciting choreography until their boots and moccasins were soaked with blood. The preparation required to make a musical seem effortless was amazing to me. I watched a tireless Mary chase Captain Hook through "Oh, My Mysterious Lady," a comic number, ten times one afternoon at rehearsal. It looked perfect when they started, but Robbins was relentless.

I felt lucky to be aboard such a sparkling enterprise and very sorry for my singing, dancing kiddie cast mates, who I attended school with five hours a day in an upstairs room of the theater complex. They were pretty much bushed. The teacher hired to tutor all us moppets, as the State of California requires, was urged by the creative team not to tire us out with book work when energy was needed for rehearsal and performance. I laid low for a week, admiring Tiger Lily's dance moves, and figured the epilogue was forgotten. Then one morning about eleven thirty, when the stage scenery was drying from a repaint in the scene dock, I was called out to the bare theater for a flying rehearsal all alone. Remember the drill? Pan throws fairy dust in someone's eyes and they can fly. Well, that was my bit. The harness you fly in fits like a parachute, with straps between your legs and a hole in the back of your costume where the wire connects to lift you twenty feet above the stage, "flying" in a pendulum action, swinging from point-start to point-stop under the control of a man on the other end of your rope. You might miss your mark and fail to arrive where expected, but, other than wrenching your spine or rotating like a sack of spinning potatoes, it was pretty safe. Now grace or dancing ability would have helped a lot, but I was hired for my loud voice. "I like the way she lands," Robbins muttered, "but takeoffs need work," and he hurried away. Five more minutes of ups and downs and I was considered rehearsed for the two o'clock matinee. Thrown into a pink-nightie costume and fitted for the harness by Mr. Foy, "the flying guru," I was called to Miss Martin's dressing room to run through our scene and have my makeup put on by the lady herself. "You probably don't have any makeup in the theater on such short notice." True enough. Now who should I call up for some courage? Miss Martin was warm and encouraging in her green and gold elfin outfit, patting my face with color from the English greasepaint tubes she favored and telling me things were going to be fine.

The curtain rose on the Darlings, Tinker Bell, the dancing pirates, and Hook, who schemed but was swallowed by the crocodile. Wendy grew up and finally, hours later when the audience was *way* ready to go home, it was time for Jane.

The violins were playing agitato as I lay in the nursery-set bed for the very first time, golden sequins (theatrical fairy dust) clutched in my sweaty fist. Peter flew through the nursery windows on a crescendo of music. The scene went well enough, my voice was loud as a piercing shriek, "Oh, Peter, take me with you!" I pitched about a pound of sequins in my face, stepped forward and flew straight into a wall. I missed the starting mark and consequently missed the mantel, with its helpful handle for flying children; I was in free flight over the stage, improvising some moves and sticking with the dialogue, which seemed to go on for pages. At last Peter caught a passing ankle, hauled me to earth, and we made our getaway out the windows to Neverland onto a big dusty mattress. In all the rushing to clear the stage for the company curtain call, I hoped nobody was thinking about my pathetic debut. How magically transformed I felt when Miss Martin called me from the dark wings to stand beside her spotlight: "Here's our little . . . Jane!" After three weeks of bliss the part was written out. Among all my tears, Mary Martin remained a green and golden memory.

BILL

JUDY, JUDY, JUDY

In 1957, during my rehearsal week of *Fanny* at the Dallas State Fair Musicals, I'd been working late at the theater and decided to go stand at the side of the stage to watch the show that was currently playing. It was a variety show, and the first half of the show was acrobats, a dance team and comic Alan King. As I stood in the wings, I was joined by this beautiful, talented legend with the tousled, boyish haircut, who was going to perform in the second half. It was *Judy Garland*! She wore a faded dressing gown and was surrounded by her three children, little miniature replicas of her. They had the same eyes, lips and gestures, and were hanging on to her legs and peeping out from behind her gown. We introduced ourselves.

"Hi, I'm Judy. And this is Liza, this is Lorna, and this is Joey."

"Hi, I'm Bill Hayes. I'm here rehearsing *Fanny*."

"I know. Bill, the boys and I are having a poker party up in the room tonight, after the show. Come have a drink if you're still up."

"Thank you. I'd love to."

Her two youngest, playing down around her ankles, started to giggle, so she shooed them all quietly back to her dressing room. That was Judy #1: Gentle, loving mother.

I remained in the wings to watch the legend work up close. She did it all, and the audience went out of their minds. One showstopper after another: "Get Happy," "The Man Who Got Away," "Rockabye Your Baby" and "Somewhere Over the Rainbow" (sitting on the lip of the stage). That was Judy #2: Onstage dynamite.

The poker party was on the top floor of the Stoneleigh Hotel, where we were all staying. Judy's dancing boys were seated around the dining table, playing five-card stud at the top of their lungs. Judy, dressed smartly in a form-fitting man's suit, topped off by a black snap-brim fedora cocked way down on one side of that devil-may-care, happy-go-lucky face, greeted me at the door, welcomed me, stopped the poker hand in progress to introduce me to the guys and told me she was tending bar, could she pour me a drink?

"A ginger ale, if you have it."

"A ginger ale—I have it."

She personally poured my ginger ale and presented it to me over her sleeve, wiping off the drips on the bottom, and then suddenly broke into Mae West. As Mae she circled the table of guys, making snappy repartee, taking drink orders, laughing boisterously at everybody else's bad jokes and encouraging everyone to relax with her. Then she turned her attention back to me.

"We'll go swimming at six, so if you're up that early, come join us. I've ordered breakfast for six thirty down by the pool."

And that was Judy #3: The perfect hostess, encouraging everybody else to laugh and enjoy life.

DIMPLES, BUT NO TAP SHOES

A few years later I met that other icon of my childhood, Shirley Temple. I was tapped to make a pilot opposite her at Twentieth Century-Fox called *Go Fight City Hall*.

The Fox lot was in an uproar of excitement. After all, Shirley had been their biggest superstar moneymaker of all time. They held a special luncheon, welcoming her back into the fold, complete with press and warmly nostalgic speeches.

Of course this Shirley Temple was not in long curls and tap shoes. She was a mature woman who introduced herself as Shirley Temple Black. Same adorable dimpled smile, so you knew it really was the same charismatic person who had danced and sung into your heart decades before, but after talking to her a few minutes you realized her concern for humanity had grown to a size that would dwarf any actress ego she might ever have had. On the face of it, it seemed perfect that she'd be playing a social worker trying to right the world's wrongs.

But the script was funny, and somehow the giddy, flip writing and Shirley's seriously concerned personal character didn't jibe. I asked the director why all her lines sounded like Judy Holliday doing dumb blonde. He answered, "Because the pilot was written for Judy Holliday! She couldn't do it, so they cast Shirley Temple and never changed one word of the script." The pilot did not sell. Wonder why.

SUSAN

THE GOOD WITCH

When I auditioned for *Passions*, NBC's witchy soap, I recalled my long and close encounter with Glinda, the Good Witch of the West, from the old story *The Wizard of Oz*. Billie Burke played the enchantress in the MGM musical-milestone version in 1939, in a huge pink dress that lives on in merchandise tributes to the movie. Billie had been a great star of the London and New York stage, famous for her comic timing and perfect beauty. When producer Florenz Ziegfeld married her, she was a much bigger celebrity than he, and quantities of her hard-earned cash went into creating *The Ziegfeld Follies*, those extravaganzas that deified the American showgirl. That's how Billie told it anyway, and she proved her love through ups and downs of infidelity, worldwide fame, and the stock market crash. She became a movie actress to pay off the showman's colossal debts and worked long after his death until every penny was returned.

By the early fifties she was remembered for the *Topper* movie series and, of course, *The Wizard of Oz*. Around my tenth birthday I was cast in a new play she hoped to take to New York called *Mother Was a Bachelor*, a comedy set on the Fourth of July, 1900, wherein the worm turns and flags are waved. Billie's role was a downtrodden maiden aunt, a baker of apple pies who hardly dared to dream of better things. I was Charlie, the smarty-pants kid next door in overalls, who incited her to bold acts of self-assertion. Charlie literally recited the Declaration of Independence while Miss Burke shucked corn. Trapped in aprons, the leading lady made a butterfly transformation in Floradora-Girl hat and parasol for the final curtain. Burke was adorable onstage, fluttering, fumbling, and flinging props about our single set, a kitchen porch in the great Midwest.

We opened at the Pasadena Playhouse in California, which was as beautiful an antique as Miss Burke. She was, after all, around seventy-four years old, and needed some extra support systems: a diet of lamb chops, Romaine lettuce and raw sugar, trunks full of personal photos, Christian Science literature and, best of all, the do-it-yourself face-lift kit. Arriving at the theater hours early to assure perfect privacy, she performed miracles before the mirror with surgical tape, rubber bands, and a length of kitchen string. Only once did I get a close look down through her curly blond hairdo to the bow in the middle that linked the bands that touched the tapes that held up the chins that Burke built. Over the footlight she registered about thirty-five. Occasionally in the heat of performance, when a rubber band would snap, her hand would fly to her cheek in girlish dismay and she would whisper, "The scaffolding is falling."

All this attention to beauty was not backed up by a firm grasp of the dialogue. "She hasn't learned a line since Flo died," my mother would say, but the star always came up with something, usually funny and not bound by the rather limited script. However inventive these departures were, eventually somebody had to return to the plot, and that was my job. We toured off and on over a two-year period, playing Palm Springs, Phoenix, and all of the East Coast straw-hat circuit. Box office was not boffo, and if the show wasn't quite a turkey, it certainly was a capon. Once, on Long Island, she was billeted in the chorus dressing room to accommodate her many trunks. It was a long, long hike to the stage. The management used a PA system for calls and would bark for her appearance repeatedly. "Onstage, Miss Burke! Miss Burke, onstage, please!" Finally she'd had enough and into the darkened backstage shouted, "I am not Miss Burke. I am Mrs. Florenz Ziegfeld!" Well, that shut them up.

This was the first time my acting had led to out-of-town travel. Seeing new places together was an adventure for Mother and me, bonding over historic Massachusetts hamlets or munching lobster rolls in Maine. We were both intrigued by and terrified of the fine-spoken iron lady, whose will to keep touring had put us on the road. Mother helped Billie with fast changes, tea and spirit gum. I encountered my first gay man, the juvenile lead, who could roll his mouth into double-decker lips as a party trick. Don, the character man, poured gin over his vanilla ice cream—a quart to a quart. I flew my paper planes into electric fans and had my first period. It was the summer of 1955, when pretty girls twirled their full skirts and petticoats while "The Ballad of Davy Crockett" played on every jukebox. I was twelve, the "old age of childhood," and I like to think the performing was polishing me up rather than wearing me down. Billie was proof that careers could go on forever.

With profits so low we never played New York, but we turned up for the show's last gasp on *NBC Matinee Theater*, the live midday broadcast of anthology drama and comedy designed to sell color TV sets in department stores across America. I did the show many times during its long run, but never more memorably than when I was united with Billie again in *Mother Was a Bachelor*. Executive producer Albert McCleary had created a system for shooting quickly and cheaply without sets, called "cameo technique." The backgrounds were black velour flats, and the foregrounds were just a few representational set pieces to indicate where you were: a branch for an orchard, say, or a mixing bowl on a table for our kitchen. The actors were shot in close-up for the most part, since there was nothing to pan away to. It looked pretty good on the tiny screens of the fifties, but it was a bit gloomy to work in for the actors. But, hell, they were lucky to have jobs. All the black velour must have confused Miss Burke, who went missing during the live broadcast, but some stage manager found her lost in the hall and dragged her back on camera for the happy ending. I twisted my ankle tripping over a sandbag myself and, as the only person there who actually knew what the show was supposed to be about, I had my first taste of creative stress. This was the-show-must-go-on experience writ large, and I learned the show is really unstoppable. Billie Burke did not continue on in live TV, but I'm still stumbling across that very stage at NBC today.

Jeanne Cooper got around a lot before she became soap opera's Queen Bee Bitch on *The Young and the Restless*. If you hit eBay you might find a copy of one of her nearly forgotten shows for sale. *Hawaiian Eye*, a formula detective series set on Waikiki Beach, starred her in an episode called "The Empty House." In crisp Warner Bros. black and white, Jeanne played a Lana Turner–type movie actress with a mixed-up daughter who craved her love. I played her daughter.

Jeanne had moxie and moves. She showed me how to saunter around her shoulders for a shot, a fancy bit of blocking the director had planned but couldn't explain. "It's like turning around the outside of a barrel." She demonstrated and I got it. The Cooper voice was husky and those Cherokee cheekbones made the camera fall in love. She was many cuts above the usual stable of television guest stars. One day together was enough to get my admiration going. I thought maybe short blond hair like Jeanne's would be the next thing I should try. I tried it, along with red, black and, in the end, broken-ends brown. But Jeanne's shade of cool blond was a state of mind and didn't come out of a bottle.

Dissolve to CBS in the late eighties, when I'm one of her cast mates on *Y&R*. She was delicious to be around, dramatic and open as a big French door. I happened to be in her dressing room running lines the day her first grandchild came into the world. Her joy was infectious, all mixed with tears at having to be at the studio when she wanted to be at the hospital.

My mother had been writing material for Kay Chancellor, Jeanne's character, for many years, and they had become girlfriends, linking up over long telephone conversations at all hours, when gossip was traded and trash was talked. The Cooper quotes were passed along to me every week by Mother, and talking about the powerful actress was one of the best connections she and I had.

I asked Jeanne to speak at Mother's memorial service. She certainly did, without notes, riffing on Elizabeth's acting technique. It was all funny and accurate and loving as a sister. Theirs was a real soap opera relationship, where the actor loves the writer because the words are good, and the writer loves the actress because she makes them live.

I was sitting in the second pew at that service, falling to pieces silently. When Bill began to sing "Panis Angelicus," tears welled up in my eyes and for a moment I couldn't breathe at all. Jeanne's hand dropped on my shoulder and held it tight till I took a breath and came back to where I had to be. She was sitting behind me. How did Cooper know? A great actress knows a great deal about the human heart.

The matriarch of *Days of our Lives* is Frances Reid, who plays Alice Horton, Julie's grandmother, among many other things. Alice is steady, forgiving and optimistic, all useful qualities on a drama that never ends. The characteristics closer to Frances's own personality are loving, beautiful and sharp.

She never suffers fools gladly and, as antiquity has been added to her frame, like nacre on a pearl, Frances may abruptly say to another actor, "Oh, you're not going to read the line like that, are you?" Artistic differences be damned, Frances speaks up for what is right as she sees it. When things go wrong onstage, as they have a few times in the forty years of *Days* production, it's Grandma Horton, the sainted lady of Salem, who will tell the stage manager, "This scene is f—ed up!"

When the show was smaller, and the Horton family was played by actors who were entwined offstage like a real family, Frances would give a great and welcoming Christmas party in her fine colonial house in Westwood. She always loved her Salem family, especially the daughters, and reached out to the cast with attention and encouragement even more than Alice might.

As youngsters, Reid and my mother were students together at Anna Head's School in Berkeley, California. There she is in an old yearbook photo, pretty, untouched by show business, but already nobody's fool. This coincidence always made me feel she belongs in my real family album, too, in one of those sepia pictures where the girls wore bobbed hair and bows and wanted to grow up into ladies someday.

As Alice, the nurturing matron related to or close friends with all the characters on the show, the woman had to reiterate exposition and list names in thousands of episodes. You know, those "someone's in the kitchen with Dinah" speeches: "Laura's in the emergency room and Shawn went to check with Abe about Sami because Marlena told Jennifer Hope can't find a parking place." Or, whatever. Frances didn't excel at these location lists, and hysterical outtakes of Alice in a quandary would be featured at the yearly cast parties. Reid laughed loudest.

Watching her talk to executives through the ages, I'd guess she never met a producer she really trusted. She takes the combative stance that producers always want more out of you than they are willing to pay for. Years of sitting in union negotiations fighting for a square deal for actors probably made her habitually wary of anybody with "producer" in his job description. This negative feeling has never colored the beleaguered producers' feelings for her, however. Ken Corday, the son of Betty and Ted Corday and now *Days'* executive producer, adores her and talks about her with a son's pride and warmth. But the guys upstairs all watch their step around Frances. Watch their step or else.

This tireless worker for all our rights lives alone in that pretty Westwood house. Reid remains the centerpiece of Salem. The crew is just as concerned about Frances's well-being as the millions of fans. When she enters the makeup room with a cane and perhaps a supporting sidekick, the whole place shouts, "Good morning, Frances, and how are you today?" She's great. Still acting after ninety birthdays. Still involved in politics, and art, and us. The heart of the show and the backbone of *Days*, she was, she is, and may she ever be. And that backbone is made of diamonds.

II

An Actor's Life for Me

BILL

OH, THE JOY

I can't believe my own career! Since 1947, when I got my first job as a professional performer, I've been thrilled by my work. Actually, it's never been work, but constant kicks. That doesn't mean I haven't devoted time to it. From getting up at four fifteen every morning all those years on *Days*, and putting in twelve-hour stints at the studio, to literally thousands of stage performances, I've sweated a lot. But not once have I wanted to toss in the towel. That's because it was six decades of *fun*.

And the people I've known! How many here have worked with Bing Crosby? Hm? Raise your hands. I sang "In My Merry Oldsmobile" with Bing Crosby and Patti Page! I've kissed Shirley Jones and played *Once Upon a Mattress* with Carol Burnett! Julie Wilson sang "Why Can't You Behave?" to me in *Kiss Me Kate*. I sang on the same stage with Al Hirt, the trumpet genius, and the Hi-Lo's, those fabulous singers.

Wait a minute! I did a show with Louis Armstrong—Satchmo—the father of jazz!

In 1954, I was on the biggest TV show ever staged: a tribute to Rodgers and Hammerstein airing *simultaneously* on NBC, CBS and ABC. Think about that! My costars included Mary Martin, Jack Benny,

Groucho Marx, Ezio Pinza, Gordon MacRae, Yul Brynner and Rosemary Clooney.

I did *The Tonight Show* with both Jack Paar and Johnny Carson.

I've worked with Cab Calloway, George S. Kaufman, Jo Stafford, Hoagy Carmichael, Barbara Cook, Billie Holiday, John Huston, Ann Blyth, Count Basie, Shirley Temple, Bill Haley and the Comets, Bobby Darin and Gypsy Rose Lee!

I've got to stop, my shoulder is out of joint from trying to pat myself on the back.

NEVER A DULL

I don't care how many times you play a show, the audience is different every time, so the show re-creates itself differently every time. It's like fingerprints or snowflakes. Also, especially in the theater, things *happen* when you're onstage and you have to find a way to deal with it.

One sultry evening while I was on tour with Lois Hunt in *Camelot*, the tent man had rolled up the canvas walls to catch a breath of air. Act two, scene six is a tender love scene for Lancelot and Guenevere, leading to Guenevere's song "I Loved You Once in Silence." As the lights came up a third character decided to join us onstage, a moth, with a wingspan of five inches.

This tattered soul made an entrance down one of the aisles, slowly thumping toward Lois and me. Everyone in the theater had to turn and watch. Lois and I noticed but continued to play our scene.

As the moth bumped into the pool of light onstage, Lois began her song. The moth, seeing the attractive white train of Lois's long gown, gave a mighty heave and landed smack on it. Singing angelically, Lois crossed the stage (the moth riding behind her, in full view), turned and sat on a low bench. The audience gasped, for the moth was no longer in sight.

Then suddenly Lois's long white gown began to move and flutter down around her ankles and calves. Her eyes widened as she realized what was under her dress. I rose, crossed the stage (in character), knelt, reached up under her gown and felt for the intruder. Gotcha! I took him out of his hiding place and threw him smartly down on the stage. He wasn't even stunned. He bounced, shook, and started bumping back toward Lois's gown. Trying to maintain the bearing of Lancelot, the perfect knight, I finally stomped on him. The audience burst into cheers and tumultuous applause.

"YOU NEED AN ACT"

Acting in a musical was one thing, but performing solo did *not* come easily to me. I was invited to do a single at the Blue Angel, an intimate nightclub in Manhattan, back in December 1950. I'd been working on *Your Show of Shows* for less than a year, and I had never even *been* to any nightclubs. Not having a notion about what a single act was, I asked Buck Warnick and Jimmy Starbuck what to do, and they said, "Just stand there and sing songs." Fortunately for the Blue Angel patrons, comedian Wally Cox was also on the bill. I sang, but I don't think I did much entertaining, if you catch my drift.

My next stint as a single was at the Chicago Theatre in the summer of '51. I still didn't know what I was doing, but by then the teenage girls liked whatever I did and yelled their approval. The next year, I sang at the Roxy, a huge, glittery movie palace in New York, with the same teenage-girl reaction. I was a success without having a clue.

I was booked to open at the Beverly Hills in Covington, Kentucky, the month of August 1954. We did two shows a night, one for the dinner crowd, families mostly, and a late second show for singles on the make and drinkers. A line of ten dancing girls, tall, zaftig and blond, did a flashy opening number, I did twenty minutes, and then they did a closing number.

The audience knew who I was and gave me a terrific welcome. They were with me through my opening number, "It's a Big, Wide Wonderful World." But I still had eighteen more minutes to fill, and I floundered in a sea of inexperience. Nothing I did worked. I tried "Rock the Joint." They didn't want to hear me singing rock. I sang "Kokomo." No response. Frustrated and concerned, and because there were children in the audience, I tried "I Know an Old Lady Who Swallowed a Fly." People turned to each other and began to converse. I tried "It's Nice to Get Up in the Morning" in Glasgow-burr Scottish. Four people applauded; the rest motioned the waiters for more drinks. Columnist Walter Winchell came backstage and told me that was the worst act he'd ever seen.

While I vainly tried to figure out how to be a nightclub entertainer, I stayed at Roland's Theatrical Boarding House. Room and board *and* laundry for $25 a week.

Roland's was a huge old mansion surrounded by big trees. All ten of the blond dancers were staying there. Mr. Roland, the owner, was tall and skinny. He regaled the boarders with off-color stories, pinched the girls, and pulled pranks like putting screws and condoms next to their places at dinner, like party favors.

The girls stayed up all night and slept all day. They'd haul out of bed around two p.m., lie out in the sun, then arrive for dinner in bathing suits or pajamas, barefoot, sans makeup, hair all afly. After dinner they would pad off to their rooms to get gussied up for the evening. One afternoon, about three thirty, I heard the ornate front doorbell twirled, followed by the delighted squeals of the girls. I found them all surrounding a smallish peddler out on the front porch.

The peddler wore a heavily starched shirt, tie, vest and straw hat. Meredith Willson might have known this fellow when he wrote *The Music Man*. Having unfolded and set up a sturdy stand upon which he rested his very large showcase, he was already into a well-versed spiel. The items were small, as were the prices, but I'd guess he sold a couple hundred dollars' worth in about forty-five minutes.

Most of his goods were gewgaws, quaint if not archaic, items your grandparents might have sitting on tatted doilies or in the medicine chest. Garters, buttons, hairpins, thimbles, ribbons, fountain pens, hankies, patterned silk hose, sequins, reading glasses, brooches, stickpins, butter molds and pocketknives with pearl handles. There was a toothpick holder, an ivory-handled straight razor, buttonhooks, buckles, collar buttons, skate keys, mustache pomade, watch fobs, a cloisonné bicycle bell, snuffboxes, eyecups, ukulele strings, banjo picks and little ornate padlocks. And when the girls would look away or talk to each other, he would wink at the men and say, ". . . And rubber goods for the gentlemen."

A few months later, I was playing a week at the Olympia Theater in Miami—vaudeville—with the old song-and-dance man Sammy Weiss. Sammy gave me my first piece of advice about doing a single act. "After your first song, *say* something."

I said, "Like what?"

He shrugged. "Doesn't matter. Say, 'Good afternoon, everybody. Thanks for coming today.' Anything at all. It'll make you a real person rather than just a singer. They'll like that."

The next show, after my first number, I said just what he told me to. And—lo!—my second number did better.

Then he said, "That was fine. Now say something after your second number."

Still clueless, I said, "Like what?"

He said, "Bill, it doesn't matter."

So, after my second number, I said, "Thank you. Glad you liked that one. Now here is my mother's favorite song." And—lo!—my third number went better.

I was sorry when the week was over and I couldn't extract more wisdom from Sammy.

Fortunately, I was booked to sing four long weekends at the Casa Seville, a dark and smelly nightclub in Franklin Square, on Long Island (where Mary and our four kids and I were living at the time).

Gene Seville, the frog-voiced owner, asked me to do twenty-two minutes, so I picked the songs that had done the best for me up to that point. After my first weekend, he called me at home. "Bill," he croaked, "this is Gene Seville. You ever woiked nightclubs before?"

"Almost never."

"That's what I thought. So, I'm going to do you a favor. To play clubs you need an act. I'm going to invite somebody Thoisday night that you should know. He writes special material numbers and acts for singas. His name is Bobby Kroll."

And so I met Bobby Kroll, who wrote for me for the next twenty years. He taught me *a lot*. Bobby wrote two very successful acts for

Florence Henderson and me to perform in 1958 and 1959. His material is timeless, and I still sing some of the numbers today.

ON THE ROAD WITH BIRDIE

Ranked just under playing the lead in a hit show on Broadway would be doing the show's national tour. So I was quite honored when director-choreographer Gower Champion asked me to take *Bye Bye Birdie* on its first major tour around the country, playing the role of Albert Peterson. When I'd seen the show, I loved the music, the fun, the dances, and especially the part of Albert Peterson, created by Dick Van Dyke.

Mary and I discussed the pros and cons. It would mean my being away from home for eleven months—the tour included two-month stops in San Francisco and Los Angeles and six months in Chicago—and that was bad news. But my folks lived in Chicago, and I could live with them and put the hotel money I was saving into a fund for the kids' college education—that was good news. With a sigh, we agreed I would accept the offer.

I loved the show, but being away from home all that time was a killer.

When we began our five-week rehearsal schedule, they hadn't yet cast all their teenagers. Marge Champion asked me if my kids could sing. I said, "Sure."

"Why don't you bring them in on Saturday and let them audition for Gower?"

Mary and I figured it might even help keep us together over the long haul if one or two of the kids were with me.

Saturday came and we took the older three into Manhattan. On the way to town I stressed that *loud* was good. They could all sing beautifully, but they were not ready for life on the wicked stage. First, Carrie (age thirteen) shyly sang "We love you, Conrad, oh yes we do." And then Billy (age eleven and a half) more shyly sang the same immortal strain, and Cathy (age ten) couldn't even stand and try. They all bombed out.

On the way home they sang "We love you, Conrad" at peak decibels. I said, "That's it! That's it!"

And they laughed and said, "Oh! Is *that* what they wanted?!"

The rehearsal period was a happy and creative time. Gower Champion was a sensitive, stylish director, and our cast was terrific.

The one out-of-kilter casting turned out to be Joan Blondell as Mae Peterson, my character's nagging mother. She was really too big a star to be billed under Elaine Dunn and me, and audiences didn't want to see this classy-dame movie star slump around in sensible shoes and complain: they wanted to see her stride onstage with that athletic 1930s star strut and a sexy twinkle in her eye. Joan and Gower tried to figure a way around the difficulty, cutting and changing lines. She was always funny, stunningly pretty, and always tried one hundred percent to give the audience what they deserved, but she remained frustrated the entire year.

Joan was one of the few in the company strong enough to withstand the gorgons and gryphons of being on the road. Playing a long tour—away from home and loved ones—is difficult! Our teenage girls were often in tears; some of the older members of the company partied too much. Apathy, depression and negativism always go along with a touring company, attacking the weakest like wolves chasing antelope. As the weeks unfolded I was to experience many sad times with my coactors. One of the singing ladies just flipped out one day, and she was discovered in the park across the street from the theater, seated nude in a garden, throwing sand on herself. One of our character actors looked to me to solve his loneliness, calling me late at night and asking me to talk him out of suicide. One beautiful young woman, the wife of one of our musicians, took a bottle of sleeping pills. Her husband and I carried her inert body down four flights of stairs to an ER.

That eleven-month tour of *Birdie* turned out to be the most difficult time in our whole marriage for Mary and me. During the run in Chicago, Mary joined me for a few days, we had a horrific fight, causing me to lose precious sleep, and I ended up with strep throat. I missed two performances—the only time in my entire career I've called in sick. Mary went home very angry. Touring's hard.

FOXY BOBS

The *Birdie* tour wasn't the only time my addiction to Broadway clouded my vision and put distance between me and my wife and children.

I spent the summer of '62 in Dawson City, up in Canada's Yukon Territory, playing the out-of-town tryout of *Foxy*. "Why?" you may well ask.

You see, the phone had rung. It was Bobbie Lewis, the famous director, with whom I'd studied acting for two years.

"Bill, how would you like to do a Broadway show with me?"

I instinctively said, "Yes, of course!" I heard the magic phrase "Broadway show," you see, and knew I wanted to do it.

Bobbie went on. "It's a modern farce-musical called *Foxy*, based on the Ben Jonson classic *Volpone*, and the star is going to be Bert Lahr. But your part is the lead, Bill. The romantic *lead!*"

I figured a romantic lead, even in a Bert Lahr farce-musical, should be a barrel of fun to play.

Bobbie added, "The score is first-rate: by Johnny Mercer and Robert Emmet Dolan!" I fell for it.

Two days later I received the script, written by Ian Hunter and Ring Lardner, Jr. The book was funny enough, but the part Bobbie wanted me for, Ben, had only twenty-two lines and portions of two songs. I called him and told him I couldn't do that part, that there was nothing to it.

He said, "All right, but at least come down and meet with me and the producer, Robert Whitehead."

I carried the script into town, gave it to the two Roberts, thanked them, and said I didn't want to do that small a part.

They said, passing the syrup ladle back and forth, of course they didn't expect me to play the part as written. But they had plans to really make something out of that role. The love story had to be beefed up—more music, more scenes.

Bobbie looked me in the eye and said, "I can't do it without you, Bill."

Bob Whitehead smiled and added, "Trust me."

I asked when and how this was going to happen. They said that fortunately the show was going to play in Dawson City, at the Gold Rush Festival, for seven weeks. During the regular rehearsal period and the seven-week out-of-town run all the changes would absolutely be made, so that when they came to New York (to Broadway—tadah!) everything would be all set. I foolishly believed them, took back my script and said okay.

Much about my *Foxy* experience was memorable. When we arrived in Dawson City, the sun shone twenty-four hours a day. The town is built on permafrost and the houses all settle and tilt toward the fireplaces (which melt the ice foundation). I saw the Northern Lights, huge pink salmon going upstream to spawn, moose and Dall sheep. I went fly-fishing with Bert Lahr many afternoons. The 350 townspeople came to *every* performance and gave cast members notes if we chanced to meet over sourdough pancakes.

But I slowly came to the chagrined realization that my part was not going to be changed, improved, or added to. Robert Whitehead had contractually given the final say-so to the two authors, who weren't about to change one line. Bobbie Lewis said, "Bill, there's nothing I can do."

Foxy did arrive on Broadway eighteen months later, with a mostly different cast, and it ran about a hundred performances. Handsome young John Davidson played my character.

Such was the mystical hold of Broadway over its dream-bound charges. I could see the perfidious lies only in hindsight.

Bobbie Lewis sent me a Christmas card every year till he died. Susan and I ran into him once in London, at a party with Claire Trevor. He was cordial and witty as ever, but I noticed he looked down into his drink a lot.

EXTRAS

Scene: Boston. I'm working on Otto Preminger's picture *The Cardinal*, starring Tom Tryon. I'm playing Tom's brother, and tomorrow we're going to be shooting a sequence in an old trolley car. I say to Otto, "My wife and five children will be here tomorrow. Do you need some extras to work in the trolley?"

He jumps at the idea. "Have them go to 'costumes' at four a.m. and be out at the set at seven a.m. I'll give each of them ten dollars. They'll be done by lunchtime."

I tell the kids, and their eyes widen with the wonder of working in a real movie and getting a whopping ten dollars just for sitting in a trolley.

Out to the location near the top of a hill. It is below freezing and the costumes, from the 1917 era, are not very warm. Each child gets a donut. The windchill creates ruddy cheeks.

The trolley car is an antique and has no power of its own. Gravity will be its power source. Windows have been removed to allow the camera to shoot inside the cab. A truck pulls the trolley up the hill, we ride down the hill playing the scene. When Otto screams, lines are forgotten. We get pulled up the hill, we play the scene going down the hill. Over and over. The wind blowing through the windows burns the ears.

Up the hill, down the hill. Move the camera to shoot from a different angle. Change the lights. Up the hill, down the hill. Preminger shouts for the last time, "Cut! Print!" and we're all released. We have our family photo taken in front of the trolley car. Some are not smiling. Strangely, after working this one cold morning with Otto, not one of my tyro actors was hot to go into the moviemaking biz.

CLEAR ACROSS THE COUNTRY

We've all seen the films where Mickey Rooney and Judy Garland and a gang of young hopefuls say, "Hey, kids, this may be a crazy idea, but . . . let's rent a barn and put on a show!" We all know it's impossible, but somehow the show comes together, the audience leaps to its feet cheering, and sheer audacity saves the day.

Well, you may not believe this, but . . .

I've been in a few situations just as crazy and audacious. It really wasn't going to be possible, but it happened anyway. And was a success.

While I was playing a revival of *Brigadoon* in New York, I got a call from Robert Cherin Productions to participate in a bus-and-truck tour of *On a Clear Day You Can See Forever*.

The tour was for twenty weeks. Howard Keel would play Dr. Bruckner the first five weeks, I would play him the next five weeks, John Raitt would come in and do five weeks, and John McMartin would play the last five weeks.

On a Clear Day was a Broadway hit, despite the fact that the script sent out by the publisher was never really finalized. The original show came in at four and a half hours, so drastic cuts were made. The result was that every production you saw was different from every other production.

When I met director Ross Bowman and my costar, Carla Alberghetti, in New York, to rehearse, we all had different scripts. The three of us couldn't even read through the play. We weren't really concerned, though, since we had an entire week to rehearse and decide which version we were going to do. And then the phone rang.

"Hello? . . . Yes, Bill and Carla are here. . . . (long pause) Howard Keel has no voice? . . . Can't go on tonight? . . . Well, just a minute. I'll ask him. . . . (with his hand over the phone) Bill, the company is playing San Diego tonight, and they want to know if you could fly out there now and go on for Howard Keel, who has severe laryngitis."

I thought a few seconds. "I could rememorize the version Shirley Jones and I played last summer. If they all want to follow me and take my version just the way it comes, I'm on my way."

Ross repeated what I'd said, nodded his head and took down some flight information. As I put on my coat, Ross was still holding the phone and scratching his head. Carla was sitting there with her mouth open. I ran downstairs and flew to San Diego.

At nine thirty that night, I walked in the stage door, out in front of the house curtain, looked into the pit and broke into a grin. The musical conductor was Gordon Munford, the same one Shirley and I'd had on our tour. We quickly ran down all our musical notes and changes. The audience, which had waited for my arrival, got a big charge out of this.

I told him, "I start at letter B in the verse of 'On a Clear Day,' I use the soft high ending of 'Melinda,' and I finish 'Come Back to Me' on the high G." Gordon relayed my changes to the orchestra, then turned to me and said, "We're ready. Are you?"

I hollered (so they could hear me backstage), "Hit it, maestro!" and waved to the audience as I slipped between the curtains. Huge excited applause.

The overture began, and I was behind the curtain meeting my co-actors.

"Hello. I'm Linda Michele. I play Daisy."

"I'm John Rubinstein. I play Warren."

That's all we had time for. We got into our opening tableau, the curtains parted, and we were into act one, scene one. But I was doing my version, and they had to watch and listen every second. We came together like we'd been playing it forever, and the audience rode high on the wave with us. The crowd gave us a standing O and didn't want to leave the theater. My heart does flip-flops every time I think about it.

WHERE THE NUTS COME FROM

But the wildest, most impossible of all was . . .

During the summer of 1960, while playing *Who Was That Lady?* in Ohio, with Jimmy Coco, I had a call from Bob Turoff. Bob and I had played *Oklahoma!* in Kansas City the summer before, and now he was directing shows in Rochester and Syracuse, New York.

He'd just had a star pull out of *West Side Story*, and the show had to be canceled. So he had all that cast ready to rehearse, and no show! He was scheduled to open two days after my play closed, could I please come do a show for him, opening with only one day of rehearsal?

I was game, but what show? I said, "How about *Anything Goes?*"

Bob said, "Nope. Just did that."

"*The Student Prince?*"

"Bob Rounseville is playing it for us right now."

Then I said, "You know, Bob, I've been wanting to play *Where's Charley?* for ten years, ever since I saw Ray Bolger play it on Broadway."

He immediately shot back, "Hey, me too! *Where's Charley?* will be perfect!"

Bob picked up scripts and scores and drove to Ohio, along with Roberta MacDonald, who would be playing opposite me as Amy Spettigue. I told Jimmy Coco what I was going to do, and he told me he'd played *Charley's Aunt*, the straight-play version, years before and he'd love to help.

So the next day, Bob and Roberta and Jimmy Coco and I blocked out the entire play, with Roberta playing Amy, me playing Charley and

Jimmy playing everybody else. Bob and Roberta got in their car and drove back to Rochester. Jimmy and I went over my staging, and I spent every waking moment for the next three days learning the role of Charley.

I remember asking Jimmy, "This line: 'I'm from Brazil, where the nuts come from.' What is funny about that?"

"I don't know, but it's funny. Just say it and whip open your fan in the middle of the line, and they'll fall down."

"You're kidding."

"No, I'm not. Just say, 'I'm from Brazil . . . ,' then snap open your fan, and say, '. . . where the nuts come from.' And then fan yourself. I guarantee the audience will think it's funny."

"All right," I said, wondering what had happened to Jimmy's sense of theater.

Forty-eight hours later I opened in *Where's Charley?* It was one of the greatest experiences of my life. I entered the stage for my first scene, and something magical happened between me and the audience. We sensed each other's excitement, relaxed into each other's arms, took off.

The audience yokked and snortled, chickered and hoo-hahed *without cease*! I could do no wrong. I blessed Jimmy Coco for telling me, "Just read the lines. They're funny," and double-blessed George Abbott for writing such surefire dialogue.

By the time I got to my eleven o'clock number, "Once in Love with Amy," it was icing on the cake. They applauded the song, applauded the first soft-shoe chorus, brayed loudly during the community-sing chorus, laughed at my interpolated old minstrel gags, applauded my fiddle solo, and then cheered my final song-and-dance chorus. Rochester and I were lovers that night!

Not only was *Where's Charley?* sold out, not only did we get rave reviews, but I've never had a better time onstage in my whole career. I've been thanking Bob Turoff ever since—over forty years now—for having the guts to do it.

So? Have I opened my heart enough for you to see inside? There you'll find all those characters, many talking in dialects, you'll hear those songs

and orchestras, see those love scenes and comedy bits, touch those costumes, smell that makeup, hear the echo of applause and laughter, and if
you touch my heart perhaps you'll feel all that crazy showbiz thrill. If
you do see and hear and feel that much, you'll know why I have these
tears of gratitude when I think about it.

"Hi-diddle-dee-dee! An actor's life for me!"

I 2

Those Crazy Guys

BILL

LENNY

"Places, Mr. Hayes," the stage manager announced. "Oh, and by the way, Leonard Bernstein is in the house tonight."

I pushed aside the curtain that was my dressing room door and looked him in the eye.

He nodded. "It's true, and he's in the front row." Holy cow! The front row at Music Theater, Highland Park, Illinois, was so close some leggy patrons rested their feet on the lip of the stage. Front-row sitters could easily be seen in the spill of stage lights.

"You couldn't put him back a few rows?"

"We're sold out tonight, and Mr. Hutchins gave up his own seat. Anyway, 'places' is called." Frank H. Hutchins was the producer.

"Thank you," I said, two-blocking my neckerchief, pulling down my swabby cap so it covered part of my right eye, and stepping out to the top of aisle one. Downbeat.

The show was *On the Town*, book and lyrics by Betty Comden and Adolph Green, music by Leonard Bernstein. We were a huge hit, sold out the whole two weeks that summer of 1956.

On the Town opens with a workman waking just before six in the morning, yawning and singing "I Feel Like I'm Not Out of Bed Yet." A momentary lull. And then, at exactly six a.m., a loud bell rings and three World War II sailors on a twenty-four-hour liberty come bursting out the gate singing "New York, New York, a hell of a town!"

The Highland Park Music Theater was a 1,750-seat circus-striped tent, a theater-in-the-round with a nine-piece orchestra in the pit.

Performing in the round is very intimate. Because there are only a dozen rows of seats, the audience is so close they feel like they're onstage with the actors. Sometimes, when there's a hot love scene or a physical piece of business, you'll see them lean back in their chairs. They don't even know they're doing it, but their body language says they're too close for comfort.

We three sailors charged down the aisle and exploded onto that stage with shot-from-guns energy. Jimmie Komack was Ozzie; Jimmie went on to write and produce *The Courtship of Eddie's Father, Chico and the Man* and *Welcome Back, Kotter*. And Tom Williams, who was later to produce *Adam-12* for several years, played Chip. I was Gabey. The three of us were pumped, striding around that stage like we owned New York, singing at the tops of our lungs. The audience was so elated they applauded through much of the number.

And there he was—Leonard Bernstein in the flesh. The renowned composer of the piece was sitting right in our laps. And what an audience he was! Obviously enjoying the show, he laughed out loud at the jokes, cried at what we did with "Lonely Town," observed and appreciated all the nuances of the show. And I was born to play Gabey. I hit a ringing high A in the last phrase of "Lucky to Be Me," got all the laughs, and danced the "Gabey the Great Lover" ballet, dressed only in my white bell-bottoms and sailor cap.

After the show, who was the most vocal person backstage? Leonard Bernstein. As I took off my makeup and got out of my costume, I could hear him going around to all the dressing rooms excitedly congratulating and kissing everybody in the cast, saying, "That's the best *On the Town* I've ever seen!"

Flipping aside my dressing-room curtain, he grabbed and hugged me, kissed me on the cheek, looked in my eyes and said, "You are a beautiful Gabey." Then he started to leave, stopped, and turned back. "I'm conducting at Ravinia tomorrow night and have to make an appearance at some patron parties right now—they're waiting for me. Would you care to join me?"

I said, "I would," and, noticing that Bernstein was wearing a summer tux, I added, "Mr. Bernstein, I'm not very dressed up."

He said, "It's Lenny, and you're fine, just the way you are." We piled into his limousine, the driver checked his itinerary, and off we went. "Lenny" raved about our production all the way to the first of the five patron parties. Backers of the magnificent Ravinia Philharmonic Orchestra get a few perks, and one of them is to meet the stars who appear in concert.

The patrons at each of the luxurious private homes were all Bernstein fans. Lenny graciously met each one, introduced me, we'd accept a glass of champagne, he'd schmooze with everybody, play a little something on the piano, wave a cheery good night, and off we'd go to the next party. Same routine each place.

Two glasses of champagne was enough for me, and after several I was buzzed. Giddy, in fact. As we departed the last elegant soiree, I told Lenny I was going to take a nap either in my dressing room or my car, as I didn't think it wise for me to drive until I floated back to earth.

He asked, "Why don't you stay with me? I'm in a guesthouse near here. You can watch my rehearsal tomorrow morning, and then my driver will whisk you back to the theater." I was a pushover. The driver took us down a tree-lined lane to a turnaround at the rear of a huge mansion, where there was a small guesthouse.

Lenny gestured at the single bed, said, "You get the bed," took off all his clothes, leapt onto the billiard table and went to sleep—on his back.

I stripped down to my shorts, turned off the light and slipped under the sheet. Two things became immediately apparent. Lenny was a champion snorer, and he was in an extreme state of arousal. Moonlight flooded in the window, spotlighting his erection.

I closed my eyes and told my revved body to shut down and go to sleep. But there was this trombone blast of snoring that occurred at odd intervals, and every time I opened my eyes his moonlit baton was beating time.

I heard a clock chime five a.m., then finally drifted off. At eight thirty, Lenny, already dressed in his rehearsal clothes, woke me and said breakfast was being set out for us. Two antique chairs in the brilliant morning sunshine. Pink tablecloth and napkins in rings, silver service, scrambled eggs and bacon, freshly squeezed orange juice, hot rolls with strawberry preserves, butler and maid in attendance.

Breakfast over, I was given a brand-new toothbrush and toothpaste, and we were back in the limo. It was a six-minute drive to that beautiful outdoor amphitheater called Ravinia; the orchestra was tuned up and ready. Tossy Spivakovsky was the violin soloist, Byron Janis the concert pianist.

I had seen Bernstein conduct several times and had always figured him for more of a showoff than a conductor, really a flake. But he was magical. Within minutes he had those seen-it-all musicians laughing and interested and keeping their eyes glued to him. He conducted without a score; he corrected the second drum part from memory; he demonstrated to Byron Janis what kind of triplets he wanted ("It's between a classical triplet and a jazz triplet"), explained fully what each of his conducting movements meant ("Violins, I will bring you in at letter A. Then you go on, but I'll be with the oboe, who has a solo. I'll join you again at letter B"). He snowed me. Leonard Bernstein was truly a genius.

Lenny "the Man with the Baton" Bernstein, thanks for the vivid memories.

SUSAN

ZIMBALISTIC

I was on the lot at Warner Bros. Studio using the pay phone to call my mother when Efrem Zimbalist, Jr., the god of my idolatry, stepped into the sunny street sensuously sucking on a fine cigar. I hung up on Mother and left the phone booth to get a better look.

I was wearing a sexy black cocktail dress with rhinestone straps for my appearance on *Surfside Six*, a fun detective show set in Miami. Efrem was the star of *77 Sunset Strip*, a fun detective show set in Hollywood. Immediately Zimbalist walked to my side, removed the cigar and planted a deep dark kiss right down my throat. "You're Efrem Zimbal-ist," I squeaked. "Yes, I know," he suavely agreed, and walked out of my life forever. Damn, it was hot.

A year earlier, when 77 premiered, I'd become his panting fan over-night, writing to Warners and receiving a signed eight-by-ten glossy. He was smoking a pipe in that picture. Zimbalist was in his forties, with regular features, a perfect Semitic nose, baritone voice, and a nice head of hair. He was the son of a famous violinist father and an opera so-prano. He was classy. For worldly charm and come-hither intellectual appeal, nobody on TV touched him, except maybe Lenny Bernstein or Alistair Cooke. Those were my pinup boys.

"Why not write directly to the show's producer, what's his name, Howie Horwitz?" my mother suggested brightly. It was a great notion, because the crew-cut Howie actually answered. What a thrill to receive mail with a big WB on the envelope. The bemused producer agreed with me that his star, who had appeared on some New York soaps, was remark-able, but he probably wondered what a seventeen-year-old saw in Efrem.

After exchanging many funny letters, Horwitz had me come to the studio to meet him. He wasn't surprised to learn I'd been a child actress, and swore that when I turned eighteen and could work a full eight-hour day plus overtime, he'd see that I got an acting job on the lot. He kept the promise, and that's how I began my adult career and happened to be chatting excitedly to Mother in that studio phone booth. When I got a part on 77 I worked with Roger Smith before he married Ann-Margret, which wasn't bad either.

I doubt Efrem had left his soundstage to come looking for Seaforth to give her a thrill. I believe it was momentary madness and just good luck. Zimbalist's luck ran on for years while he played the buttoned-down star of WB's *The FBI*. So, my fan letters had a payoff: that kiss from Zimbalist by the soundstage. Forty-four more years of getting to be an actress was the bonus.

WE'VE GOT BADGES

On radio more than fifty years ago a cop show aired called *Dragnet*, set in Los Angeles and starring Jack Webb as Detective Friday. The show had a flat, underplayed style that translated perfectly to television. Jack was small and gimlet-eyed in person; he had conceived the show, then produced, directed and starred in it for many seasons. Harry Morgan, the memorable character actor with a flat nasal voice, like a Grant Wood painting come to life, was Webb's on-air sidekick. Each week these two deadpan faces under hats drove around the smoggy streets of greater L.A. investigating crime and demanding "just the facts, ma'am." Every comedian of the era spoofed it, and Jack Webb was practically a poster boy for the LAPD. *Dragnet*'s afterlife included a movie in the nineties and another TV series in the twenty-first century.

Jack was mighty strange in person. It was impossible to imagine him married to the luscious, warm singer Julie London of "Cry Me a River" fame, though he had been. I made five episodes of *Dragnet* and never saw him smile. Webb didn't want you to play the scene, but read it. The entire script was on teleprompter, running under the camera lens on a bright white screen. Even though everybody had memorized the dialogue, he demanded the actors use the machine because he ran the roll at superhuman speed. We all sounded like we were chanting a teletype. Well, it was stylish.

Jack didn't give director's notes to your face either. After rehearsal on camera he'd look at the words racing through that teleprompter and address your performance. "First page was okay . . . you popped your eyes on the third word of the second sentence. Don't. Second page, pick up the pace. Hold your prop up to your chin so we see it in the close-up, then lose it out of the shot. Don't smile." The last person I'd seen work that way was directing a chimp in a Tide commercial. It was a bit creepy.

I must have read at a fast enough clip to suit him because first I was playing a police academy cadet, all in uniform; then in another show I was a porn queen all in, uh, a bathrobe. I'd never seen a porno flick when I shot with Webb. If I knew then what I know now I might have attempted some acting twists. As it was, I just banged away as usual. No pun intended.

BILL

THE MAN WITH THE MANSION

Hard-core? With Jack Webb? Well, I can't top that, but I can come close. In 1962, I played a quick week at Chicago's Drake Hotel. My Bobby Kroll special material was working beautifully. On opening night I received a telegram from Hugh Hefner, inviting me to drop by the Playboy Mansion following my second show.

Did I know Hugh Hefner? Did he know me? How did he know I was opening at the Drake? Would there be Playboy bunnies in attendance? I was intrigued.

I walked over to the mansion and entered through the open front door. Though it was teeming with bodies, no one seemed to notice that I had arrived, so I just wandered in. The first thing I saw was a hot-and-cold buffet running the length of the ballroom-sized living room. A gigantic stereo was playing jazz. Groups of young men and women were gathered here and there, eating and laughing. Encountering a fire pole that descended to the floor below, I slid down.

I discovered I was in a comfortably cushioned cocktail lounge. The dim light came from one wall, which was in fact a big window looking into—underwater—the lighted swimming pool. Now and then a bikinied youthful body would plunge in from somewhere above and paddle by, followed by bubbles and flowing hair. I was in a James Bond movie! By the light of the pool I recognized, entangled on several pillows, Burgess Meredith and Kaja Sundsten. Kaja had been a dancer in the *Carousel* I'd been in fifteen years before. We greeted each other warmly; they went back to business, and were married soon after.

Back upstairs, I filled an oversized dinner plate with curried something, and sat on the grand-piano bench to eat. Then my handsome host, Hugh Hefner, made an appearance. It was a hot night and he was in low-rise slacks and a sport shirt open to the navel. We introduced ourselves, I thanked him for his invitation, and he asked me if I played the piano.

"Only for very loud community singing," I replied.

"Show me," he said. So I did.

He turned down the living room stereo, came back and sat next to me, and we began to sing "Shine on, Harvest Moon." Soon the piano was surrounded by a crush of A-rack girlies and a few boyfriend types. I would bang loudly on the keyboard, start a song, and let them take over, Hef singing lustily, with the girls pressing so closely around I sometimes forgot what key I was in. At four a.m., I begged off. Hef and a bevy of centerfolds saw me to the door and waved good night.

A respectful host, guests who were sober and kept their clothes on, and a nice old-fashioned songfest . . . *not* what I'd expected of the den of iniquity!

SUSAN

TESTOSTERONE

The Travels of Jamie McPheeters, a Pulitzer Prize–winning novel about wagon-train westering, was a truly wonderful book. In the era of television Western overload the title was transformed into a weekly series that hardly resembled its origins. I was in a segment featuring a tribe of imaginary losers "headin' for Californee." My pa, played by David McCallum of *The Man from U.N.C.L.E.*, in heavy makeup, was a looney-preacher stereotype with beard and Bible. I played the prophet's stressed-out daughter in a sort of nun's habit, with loose hair, and vulnerably barefoot. Leadership figures for the wagon train were Charles McGraw and Charles Bronson. My recollection of the plot is cloudy, but two shooting days remain vivid in memory.

Bronson boasted that he was involved in a ménage à trois with a compact blond actor and his wife. He volunteered this while chasing a nineteen-year-old me around the back lot location trails. Though I was curious enough to listen, I quickly became reluctant to participate in any romantic activity with the dark and broody Bronson. When we wrapped the segment I was still one jump ahead of him. Believing I'd never see him again and wanting to exit without a scene, when he asked for my phone number I made one up.

A couple of days later my grandmother, Jessie, answered the phone at home and a voice that sounded like Bronson's asked if Susan Seaforth lived there. "Yes," Jessie responded, "and who is calling, please?" The caller hung up. I gulped to imagine him persistent enough to track down my real number (he could easily have gotten it from the second assistant or the production office, I then realized). I'd handled myself very badly, but tra-la. I was on Alvarado Terrace, and the perturbed actor was in Beverly Hills somewhere enjoying his ménage. If he had two already, wasn't that enough?

A month or so later MGM called to book a day of retakes and added scenes for *The Travels of.* . . . I opened the pink pages Wednesday to see lots of dialogue for the preacher's kid, who becomes hysterical and gets slapped into sensibility. The slapper was to be . . . Bronson. The added scene was scheduled for the end of the day Thursday. No wiggle room for Seaforth.

Back in my habit again, I hid out in the dressing room all afternoon. The director had fallen way behind schedule, so when we were called out to block, he cut the camera moves and just stood us on "the trail." Charles McGraw, an upstage bush, a couple of horses, Bronson and me. This was emotional stuff, but really pretty static talking, so the director decided to save more time by going for a take without rehearsal. Okay. One horse sighed.

When the lighting director stepped in to take a meter reading, Bronson pulled out his Colt .45 and began to twirl it over my feet. He dropped it straight down, and blood spurted out of my bare right foot. "Oh, look, I dropped my gun," the rough-hewn actor said and gave me a killing look. Charles McGraw said nothing. Silence from the director and the crew. I was more than ready to burst into hysterics then. And, "Action!" Dialogue, dialogue . . . "Oh, Papa, oh, Papa," blubber, blubber . . . *smash!* Charles Bronson punched me a good one in the face and I fell straight backward. Smooth as a dancer, he caught me inches from the dirt we were all standing in and propped me up for the next line, which was mine. I got out the frontier equivalent of "Thanks. I needed that."

"Print! That's a wrap!" screamed the director, relieved, no doubt, and I limped off to my dressing room alone. Seconds later, as I was feeling my jaw, Charlie pulled open my door and said, "I hope it hurts like hell. Don't ever lie to me again." I think I wound up apologizing to him.

BILL

ROSEBUSH

You can't explain a rosebush, so don't try. All you can do is enjoy the perfection of its blossoms, sensually unfolding, and a scent that must be the foretaste of heaven.

Even more remarkable is the bush's reaction to being cut back. Something at its core says, "Oh, you thought that one was pretty? You ain't seen nothin' yet. How about . . . *this*?" And four more stems will pop out and surge up to replace the one that was clipped off. Not just once or twice, but all year long. A rosebush is a gift that keeps giving.

I have a friend like that. His whole life has been one "Oh, yeah? Watch *this*" after another. He never stops producing beauty.

Robert Clary was born into a Parisian family with so many siblings they could field a soccer team and still leave most of them back at the dinner table. Was he lost in the anonymity of little-brotherhood? Oh, no. As a precocious adolescent, he found his way into the spotlight as a singer and dancer.

But that was just at the time when it was unfashionable to be Jewish in Hitlerville. Robert and nearly all his family were sent off to the infamous camps of Germany, Poland and Eastern Europe. Though his parents and many siblings did not survive, Robert did. He'd made himself too valuable to exterminate: cobbler by day, singer to the troops by night. They loved his "Bei Mir Bist Du Schoen."

Liberated, Robert arrived back in Paris to no home and no family. But, like the new roses, he began popping up in little nightclubs all over France.

Film star Eddie Cantor picked up on his talent and featured Robert on his television specials in the fifties. Robert flowered for two years on Broadway in *New Faces of 1952*, and then created the unforgettable LeBeau in TV's *Hogan's Heroes*.

In 1972, he came into my life as Robert LeClere on *Days of our Lives*. Our characters, Robert and Doug, sang and danced together for the next fourteen years.

During those years I came to see that Robert Clary is much more than just a performer. He's a mensch.

He's a lover. His wife, Natalie, and he remained deeply in love and best friends, adoring each other, for forty years, until she passed through the door of eternal life. She's gone, but not from his heart. Susan and I treasure the sweet times we shared with Robert and Natalie, at philharmonic concerts, dining in each other's homes. Natalie had a sweet way with chocolate desserts.

Robert is a friend who goes out of his way to create and maintain close relationships. A dozen years ago he started a spurious "club" called THURSDAY, an acronym for Thirsty, Hungry, Unemployed Remnants of Show business, Don't Ask whY. He invites a dozen friends, all over sixty-five, to join him for lunch every Thursday. The group includes performers, writers, directors and producers he worked with all through his career, many of whom are now retired. And Robert takes it upon himself to prick them to stay alive in mind and spirit. He sasses them, berates them, carps and criticizes, constantly acting as thornily as he can, but it's evident that he deeply values their friendship, is sensitive to their needs. I've been a member of that gemütlich group for ten years now, and I hate when I have to miss the bad jokes and the good camaraderie.

He is a painter. Every day of his life he has devoted some time to painting people "in their natural habitat." Challenging himself with difficult perspectives and an inordinate amount of detail, he brings out the beauty of his subjects' souls. Susan and I happily own three of Robert's paintings.

Robert and I have a special friendship, which has grown close over thirty years. Singing duets first brought us together; working as actors in the same plots for years tied us even closer. And, though we grew up in two different worlds, we somehow understand each other and appreciate each other's strengths and failings.

Humor is a part of our relationship. We both imitate Geneviève, when she was on *The Jack Paar Show*: "No, Jacques. Is beautie!" We still laugh about Bill Bell and Bill Rega trying to write lines for Robert in a stilted parody of a French accent: "Thees ees 'orrible! We 'ave too many customer and not enough chair!"

I went to see Robert perform at the Jazz Bakery, and he came to see me in the *Palm Springs Follies*. We've attended funerals of best friends together. We've pondered life's mysteries.

And, if you didn't know, Robert is an impeccable musician. Listen to any of the eight CDs he's recorded in the last decade. They impressed me so much I got him to produce my latest CD, called *This Is Bill Hayes*. He made a great contribution.

Where does it come from, this need to continuously produce beauty? I don't know, but it's been a part of Robert Clary's whole life. He's like a rosebush, and I love him.

SUSAN

MAC

When *Days of our Lives* was looking for a commanding actor to play Dr. Tom Horton, patriarch of the core family, Macdonald Carey, the movie star and family man, was looking for work. For twenty-eight years Mac was our sweetheart, as consistently loving and fair to the *Days* gang as a perfect father is supposed to be.

His fame helped launch the show; his was the first big name to appear in a soap. When the Television Academy decided to acknowledge daytime achievements, they came up with one and only one category: Best in Daytime. Mac was nominated along with news, and interview shows, maybe even Julia Child. Eventually this impossible single category morphed into the Daytime Emmy Awards. Mac, however, remained in a class by himself.

He was a fine, realistic actor with a mellifluous bass voice. Sometimes his grip on the lines was a tad loose, and then the red light of the camera's all-seeing eye would bring on an attack of nerves that made him shake. Once the boys in the control booth realized this was the problem, the red light was shut off. Mac's trembling instantly stopped. We all have our quirks.

For many years Mac fought the battle of the bottle, never enough to make him incapable of performing, but enough to blur the edges of his usual sharpness. Then AA entered his life, and he returned to his Catholic faith. He thrived, working his twelve-step program to the desired effect. He then apologized, one-on-one, to each of those he had worked with through the years for ever being tipsy onstage. Rare humility.

As horizons cleared for Mac, he began to write verse and took much pleasure in being a published poet after the age of sixty. He had the capacity to listen to the longest and dullest tale with interest and sympathy. He wore cashmere sweaters and always smelt of a wonderful woodsy scent. Carey had the rare quality of growing more open-minded with age and seemed to enjoy doing *Days* and being with people more and more as seasons passed. Mac took Holy Communion to his fellow parishioners, where it was most needed, and kept the faith.

In 1979, Hayes and Hayes talked head writer Ann Marcus into writing in a telethon for Salem's University Hospital so the whole cast could do variety material, and the fans would see us in a new setting. Mac was center stage in all the bits. The opening number was "Comedy Tonight," our spoof of hospital life. Bill was a crazed surgeon, I was a groggy patient on the operating table, and Mac, in a huge fright wig, pushed the gurney. As Dr. Tom, he made such a moving pitch to raise funds for University Hospital to buy a CAT scanner that NBC got calls from viewers wanting to pledge real money.

The big number was Mac tap-dancing and singing "We Gave 'Em the Old Soft Shoe," which begins: "When me and my Alice was playing the Palace. . . ." The old smoothie crooned while Bill, Wesley Eure (playing Michael Horton), Eileen Barnett (as Stephanie Woodruff), and yours truly soft-shoed upstage. He kept one eye on the cue cards and was easing around on two artificial hips at the time, but he sang and danced with the grace of a star.

Macdonald Carey died in 1994, at the age of eighty-one. His last appearance on the show was just a few months before. His funeral was in Beverly Hills at the Church of the Good Shepherd on a gorgeous California day.

The sanctuary overflowed with people. Up front a big contingent from the Knights of Columbus, in black velvet robes and Vasco da Gama–style hats, added a colorful note. Mac had chosen a fellow student from his poetry-writing class to give the eulogy. This would-be poet took the opportunity not so much to eulogize Mac as to speak warmly of himself. That set off Susan Flannery, seated behind us: "Jesus Christ, where did they find this guy?" Fortunately, Cardinal Mahoney in the pulpit couldn't hear Flannery. The cardinal had given Mac's last Communion, and he reported the frail actor's last words: "Wow, that sure doesn't taste like tomato juice."

Then it was time to say good-bye and we were all dismissed, a row at a time. I watched the dear friends of our daytime years walk up the aisle. "No more cashmere hugs," whispered Maree Cheatham. Denise Alexander, Wes Kenney, Pat Falken Smith, each slowly passed by. So many hearts united again for a last moment to love Dr. Tom. I cried then, for the *Days* I'll always treasure . . . and days gone by.

BILL

ARCHIE KNEW

On December 16, 1954, at eight thirty a.m., the phone rang.

"Good morning, Bill. It's Archie Bleyer. Hope it's not too early."

"Archie, I've got four kids."

"That's what I thought. Bill, when you were in my record store in Hempstead last month, did I hear you right? You're finished recording for MGM Records?"

"You heard right."

"Then you're free to discuss making a record?"

"I am. What's up?"

"I've got this song. How soon can you get to my office?"

"Twelve thirty."

"I'll be waiting for you."

Indeed he was waiting for me, and I could see he was excited. He ushered me into his little office and closed the door.

He said, "I heard a song on a TV show last night, and I know it will make a hit record. I called the publisher, Disney, and there is no record out on it yet. I think, if we move fast enough, we can have the inside track." He unfolded a long lead-sheet, sat down at the piano, squinted through the bottoms of his bifocals, and said, "Here, read through this, see what you think."

He played *ump-chink, ump-chink, ump-chink, ump-chink*, and I sang, "Born on a mountaintop in Tennessee, Greenest state in the Land of the Free. . . ."

By the time we finished running through it, the funny little chorus already had the feeling of familiarity all songwriters hope for but few successfully create.

Archie turned to me. "Well? Do you like that?"

I said, "I love it! It's a crazy little song, and I think it's great!"

He looked at his watch. "You want to record it?"

"Yes."

"Tonight?"

"You bet."

He jumped up and left the room.

For years, arranger-conductor Archie had led the CBS staff orchestra for Arthur Godfrey's radio and TV shows. And, one day in 1953, Godfrey—believing they weren't showing proper humility—fired Julius LaRosa, the Chordettes . . . and Archie Bleyer. Archie, having confidence in himself and the others, immediately started Cadence Records and began turning out hit records. He had a magic touch. It meant a lot to me that he had chosen me to do this song.

Coming back in the room, he said, "RCA Studios on Twenty-third Street, ten o'clock tonight. I'll write the arrangement this afternoon." He grabbed a different lead-sheet. "And here's another song from the same show, words by Davy Crockett himself. I think we ought to put this on the other side." So we ran through "Farewell" once.

"I agree. It's the perfect flip side," I said.

He hustled me out the door. "The Disney people think 'The Ballad of Davy Crockett' is just background music, but I know better. See you tonight."

While I went home to study the song, enjoying the simplicity of the melody and chords, and the old-time country-folk speech of the lyrics,

Archie knocked out the orchestration and called the guys. His arrangement was perfect, utilizing only half a dozen of the twenty-two verses, just enough to tell a story of heroism and love of country.

The musicians arrived and the engineer placed us in a small circle. I was facing the two (seated) guitarists. The acoustical bass was on my right, facing across to the Jew's harp player. The three boy singers were slightly behind, on my left.

Archie asked the Jew's harp player, who looked anything but Jewish (I think his name was Buster), to file down the little twanger on his instrument to raise the pitch from E-flat to E-natural, and while he was filing, the engineer set out five microphones. He had each of us play or sing a few bars to set his levels and place the microphones to advantage. Then he had us all try a few bars together, made a few final adjustments, and said to Archie, "Okay, I'm ready."

I remind you who are used to today's multitrack soundboards that in those days our equipment was capable of recording only one track at a time.

Archie said, "Let's try a take."

The engineer started all his recording machines and then slated it from the booth, " 'The Ballad of Davy Crockett'—take one."

We went through it—one time.

Archie said, "Let's listen to it." The engineer played it for us. Archie cracked a smile, said, "Play it one more time, and let's hear it." The engineer rewound his two-inch tape and cranked it up. Archie was grinning at the group. "That's good enough for me. Let's do the other tune and go home." It was eleven thirty. One track, one take, and we had done it!

We polished off "Farewell" by midnight.

After the musicians left, Archie and I sat and listened to both songs one more time. He grabbed me by the arms and said, "That's a hit record!" Archie was such a conservative suit-and-tie man—always wore a hat and carried a briefcase—that for him to grab my arms and get that excited was out of the ordinary. I quit for the night, and he stayed to have the engineer make him a couple dozen dubs.

Incredibly, it all happened in one day.

The next morning Archie okayed the masters and placed a staggeringly large original order of copies to be pressed: 750,000 78s and 250,000 45s! That was his own money he was putting on the line, too! He was so sure.

Two days later he mailed copies of Cadence Record #1256 to disc jockeys and radio stations all over the country, as fast as he could pack and ship. And everywhere the record was played it became an overnight smash—a hit with every kid from age one right up through high school.

Two and a half weeks after the session I made an appearance in Boston at a teenage ballroom called The Totem Pole. They had a small band that played for dancing, and I'd brought a few charts with me— maybe twenty minutes of music.

I sang my opening number—a medley of "My Song" and "Lady Be Good"—and, while applauding, the crowd started to shout, "Davy Crockett!" I did my second number and the same thing happened. So I turned to the pianist and said, "Give me a B-seventh, please," and I sang the song a capella. And those blasé teenagers sang the chorus with me every time.

I whipped home and called Al Coliaco, asking him to make me a band arrangement of the song. I was going to need it—soon.

Bang, it was on the charts! And I suddenly was getting calls to appear everywhere: the Copa in Pittsburgh, *The Perry Como Show* on CBS, *The Milton Berle Show* on NBC. It was a skyrocket.

I was featured in *Cashbox*, *Billboard* and *Variety*. "The Ballad of Davy Crockett" was the fastest-selling record, the record most played by disc jockeys, and the record most played on jukeboxes, all over the U.S.A. My record quickly rose to number one. And stayed there.

After the horse had left the barn, Disney released a record of Fess Parker singing the song, but—as Archie Bleyer had surmised—we had the inside track. We ruled for months. And Crockettmania merchandising— T-shirts, puzzles, powder horns, canteens, moccasins, anything with the name Davy Crockett on it—generated $300 million in income in 1955.

Booked to appear at Willow Grove, a theme park just outside Philadelphia, I performed for several thousand in a huge auditorium. I did maybe twenty-five minutes of songs, and then finally donned my buckskin-fringed jacket and coonskin cap. Applause, excitement, cheers! I said, "Okay, you want to sing it with me?"

"Yes," they all screamed.

"Well, come on up!" I said. And about two thousand children flew up onstage to join me. When they all crowded into place, the shorter ones in front, I started, and they all sang the entire song with me. Not just the chorus. Every word, every note. I realized those kids were serious. It was a song that moved them. Part of the reason might have been the political mood at the time. The Russian bear was as volatile as ever and the A-bomb was always menacing. It was a fearful time, and patriotism kept the flag snapping in the wind.

I thought of my own ancestors, who were American pioneers, following the frontier from east to west.

My great-great-great-great-great-great-great-great-great-grandmother Penelope Stout was shipwrecked in the lee of Sandy Hook in 1639, scalped by warring Iroquois and left for dead. Friendly Delawares, however, found her and cared for her until she was well enough to return to her friends in New Amsterdam (now New York City). Penelope and her husband returned to the Jersey Shore, bought land from the Indians and stayed. Their homestead is now called Middletown, New Jersey. When she died, in 1732, at age 110, her children, grandchildren and great-grandchildren numbered 502. That's a pioneer!

My mother's great-great-grandfather, Rev. John Mitchell, who fought in the last year of the Revolutionary War, was present at Surrender Field in 1781, following the Battle of Yorktown. Family tradition reports that eighteen-year-old John climbed a tall tree to witness the handing over of General Cornwallis's sword.

Personalizing it this way, the "crazy little song" became a lot bigger and less crazy to me. It had brought my sense of family and pride in pioneer ancestry closer to my heart. And I was proud that I had been a conduit through which children of the country could believe in truth, honor and patriotism.

I have my gold record on the wall now, I have the memory of that streaking ride across the sky, I'm happy my recording touched so many lives and received all those "Best Record of the Year 1955" awards. And I can still see Archie Bleyer, wrinkling his nose and grinning, as we listened to the playback on that night when he was so sure.

Today, fifty years later, whenever I sing a verse of "The Ballad of Davy Crockett," every child in the audience (now all over fifty-five years old) sings the chorus along with me. For a moment we remember together.

SUSAN

SOAPY HEROES

"Take the work seriously, and yourself never," said Spencer Tracy, a pretty fair movie actor.

Being a leading man in soap opera isn't all beer and skittles. Modern daytime action calls for nearly nude fights as well as frolics. You need to be fit enough for stunts, charismatic enough for love scenes and glib with tons of dialogue.

When the villains in daytime drama are under contract they never seem to go to jail. A super-baddie will exchange sneering barbs with the hero during interrogation, but somehow he never gets detained because the chase is the fun part of this storytelling. The villain has to get away so the adventure can continue. "Playing out a story," it can be called. Each week the hero resolves, swears, vows and assures the victim that "Whoever did this will pay." But whoever did . . . doesn't.

Where does that leave the actor cast as the hero? He may be playing a cop, a secret agent, or just a wronged and righteous husband in search of his wife. I'm speaking of essence here, not specifics. Is the actor gloomy? Resigned? Or does he go nuts? Does he feel like a jerk when Mr. Baddy blasts off like Brer Rabbit back to his briar patch yet again? Instead of singing "(I Can't Get No) Satisfaction," the champions of sanity I've worked with on *Days of our Lives* leave the strife at the studio.

It's a real test of talent to carry on in these roles year after year and still be trusted and even loved by the audience. A district attorney at election time points with pride to the criminals he's locked up, but soap opera cops are awash in unsolved mysteries.

Drake Hogestyn plays John Black on *Days*, appearing opposite Deidre Hall as Marlena in every situation known to man. Earlier in life he once played professional baseball. "He sure got his money's worth out of the thirty-seven dollars he spent on acting lessons," a prop man used to kibitz behind the scenery when Drake was getting to second base in a suspenseful scene.

"I'm the luckiest guy in the world," Drake says simply, then smiles.

The Hogestyn dressing room is fixed up with gym equipment so he can stoically pump iron every morning before taping starts. I've never seen him throw a tantrum or a curve at another actor, but he will engage them in long bouts of storytelling. He's had the sportsman's many interesting physical mishaps and grisly medical treatments. Hogy describes each with relish. There's an ongoing foot story that will make you limp just to hear it. His sense of fairness and fun may come from sports or some inner calm, but it's been a godsend to the soap opera set, where raging egos waste everybody's time.

A while ago a thief was loose at NBC Burbank. Our dressing rooms are off three different corridors, and during the day actors, messengers and wardrobe personnel are continually in and out. In all the bustle, doors are rarely locked. Security guards are there all the time, too, but on this occasion the light-fingered one had gotten into lots of pants pockets and wallets. He was just helping himself to a Hogy twenty when Drake opened his dressing room door. The thief fled down the long gray hallway, and Drake chased, tackled, and pinned the dude until security dragged him away. Our hero.

This year Drake's battling gophers on the home front. He can give you every gopher statistic imaginable, including the depth of their tunnels and the height of their chews in ratio to his newly planted hedges. He's droll.

I watched a still-boyish Hogy patiently explaining a simple acting concept to a manly yet inexperienced newcomer to the cast. "Finish that line before you turn away, so the camera gets a clean close-up for the edit." Why didn't the kid know? Probably because he was cast for his great looks and acting "potential." The experience of working with pros like Drake is supposed to enlighten youngsters and get that potential on a fast track. Directors are shooting over a hundred pages of show a day now. You can't stop a cavalry charge to coach one private. Drake takes on responsibilities, like speaking to the manly one, with courtesy and clarity. So the new actor probably got his clean close-up that day, and in a few months he will think he's picked up all the senior cast mate has to teach. Doubtful.

In the 2004 story line Marlena literally shut the door on John to pursue her career as a murdering maniac. John was bewildered and destroyed by her rejection. He had the line, "I love you, Marlena. Does that count for nothing?" Drake made it so real, the true soap opera "moment" that rips you up and keeps you caring. It was an acting home run.

Drake has an unflappable optimism that's unique. It has been a big factor in keeping his troupe of actors productive and relaxed. "I suppose you think you're holding up this tent," Chico says to Harpo in *A Night at the Opera*. Harpo, embracing a tall pole, nods and smiles but never says a thing. When he steps away, by golly, that tent flops down. On *Days*, John Black has been a tent-pole character, straight and strong. Like an American hardwood, he stands tall and casts a cool shade.

Now to me Peter Reckell, who plays Bo Brady, has that wild-man-of-the-wilderness quality that women go dippy for. He appears out of the frightening forest and . . . will he rescue the girl . . . or ravish her? "Here comes trouble" is what Bo's character was created to provide. The actor playing him must have an edge.

Bo's daily state of edginess can be checked by studying Peter's beard and haircut history. Sometimes he broods behind a mustache, threatens through a goatee or just takes off into the jungle to sprout a face full of mysterious fur. Peter looks intriguingly good, razored or hirsute.

"He will rise to every challenge," producers say, meaning they are about to dump the actor in a tank of ice, or keelhaul him under a flying clipper ship. Peter's great with stunts and, more interestingly, is an all-around performer.

When the supervillain Stefano had a computer chip planted in Bo's brain, Bo became an accomplished mime in whiteface and gloves. (I guess Stefano planned to irritate mall shoppers to death.) The last remarriage of Bo and Hope featured Peter doing an Irish jig with the Brady men. Frank Parker, as father Shawn, just stomped around and shouted a lot, but rhythmic Peter turned into the Lord of the Dance. Josh Taylor, as Roman, clicked his heels off, too, but it was Peter's show. When the character actress couldn't remember her scene with Bo very clearly, Peter ran lines over and over again. His show babies were sometimes played by screaming brats. Reckell would gently coo and carry the babes round the sets until the piercing shrieks stopped and his shoulders were covered with spit-up.

One of the best acting experiences Bill and I ever had was a day of scenes with only Peter and Kristian Alfonso, as Hope. The full crew and just the four of us had a mess of pages to tape. That day was more like a vacation with your beloved grown-up kids in Paris, which is actually what the scenes were about.

The hero in a cliff-hanger moment I remember best is when *Days* had Peter bound and gagged, then suspended by his feet from a long rope over a fiery cauldron. If this made our boy grumpy, he had no chance to say so, because producer-director Steve Wyman was in charge and seized the occasion to stroll over to the cauldron to say in his professorial way, "Of all the situations we've put you through, Peter, this is probably the worst! Ha-ha-ha! And on behalf of the show I just want to thank you for being such a good sport."

Part Three

13

Now Appearing in the Role of Mother

BILL

TABLE FOR SEVEN

January 12, 1956. Our fifth treasure was given to us at Mineola Hospital, on Long Island. Name: Peggy. Now we were complete, a family of seven.

Seven, the sacred number of ancient cultures, the symbol of perfection, abundance and completion, the luckiest number on life's whole crap table.

When we moved farther out on Long Island, my parents gave us their beautiful maple dining room set. My happiest memories in that house are of our family of seven crowding around that big red table. Breakfast and lunch were mostly fend-for-yourself in the kitchen, but for ten heart-filling years we had dinner together.

During the years we surrounded that table, Carrie, our oldest, tried out for every extracurricular activity offered at school—cheerleader, variety show, whatever. Naturally, she didn't get every office or a part in every play, but not for lack of trying. She put her hair up in curlers every night, carefully wrapping her head in toilet paper to hold everything in place. Her clothes, schoolbooks and papers were happily strewn all over her room up on the third floor. Because she was innately gregarious, Carrie's girlfriends and boyfriends filled her life.

Billy's little room on the first floor was neat. He would be up early in the morning, heating the iron to press the wrinkles out of the shirt he planned to wear that day. He practiced the piano and consistently brought home the best grades of all five. Billy was mechanical, a natural athlete, thought nothing of climbing out on the steeply canted roof of the Garden City Community Church and crouching there, listening to his parents practice with the choir. He saved his money and bought only meaningful things: special toys or mechanized gadgets.

Cathy, our redhead, who was born two months premature, was always different. She never understood the art of teasing, which her two brothers were so slick at. She was instinctively caring, wanting to instruct and protect younger children. Her good-night kisses were always passionate. Probably a holdover from her incubator days, she needed a light in the room to go to sleep by.

Tommy, our clown, our pixie, was good in math and even better at schmoozing adults with his charm. We'd come home from an evening out, and the babysitter would report, "They were all fine, but oh, that Tommy!" His sense of humor was delicious, and from an early age he could make the best French toast. His favorite times were when Mary and I were affectionate with each other. He'd smile and say, "Busy-busy!"

Peggy was affectionate and exuberant. Until she became a teenager, her greeting to me was to run at me full-tilt and jump on me. She was always adventuresome. Once she opened the car door to step outside, while the car was moving, and popped right out on the road. She was generous with her things and couldn't keep a nickel for five minutes.

That beautiful decade was so fleeting! Did any of us appreciate what our togetherness meant? We were all so caught up in the moment: the dishes, the laundry, the book reports. Those were their formative years, and I wonder what Mary and I were giving our fabulous five. We wanted to give them meaningful lessons of life, to prepare them to fly on their own. Did we give them sufficient love? Did we nurture their inner wounds as well as applying iodine to their scrapes?

The parenting I learned came from Mother and Dad and assorted elders. Grandma Mitchell and Uncle George could be very blunt. I shied away from being blunt. Mother and Dad parented with directness, but lots of love.

Mother taught by loving example and by encouragement. I probably tried to emulate her.

Mary was quick to scream, "Stop that!" and then warn the kids, "You do it again, I'll tell your father." I was more likely to say, "Here's a better way."

Oh, there were times when quiet direction didn't work. I remember driving into New York one day when Billy and Tommy were teasing and tussling and being extremely distracting. I asked them to stop. I *ordered* them to stop. Several times. Finally, I pulled over to the curb, got out, crawled into the backseat and bopped their heads together. They stopped fighting.

Usually, all I had to do to control their activities was just to look at them and speak softly. They could tell when I was serious and meant it, or when I was pliable. Peggy was an expert at waiting for the moment of distraction. The phone would ring, and just as I was saying hello, she would gaily skip out the front door saying, "I'm going out!" Cute.

Our meals were basic middle America: hamburgers, frozen peas and corn, pork chops and applesauce, beef stew, mashed potatoes with gravy, Shake 'n Bake chicken, tuna casserole. But that evening meal was the core of our home life.

In storage boxes I have five large envelopes crammed with the kids' first attempts at printing, writing and drawing, and piles of photographs from our vacation times and special moments. I could use those memories instead of sugar for the rest of my life.

Of course, parenting also includes days of pain and tears. Our most spectacular event occurred in 1959, when Tommy was five. He was playing with matches and started a fascinating little blaze in his dresser drawer. The fire grew to where Tommy couldn't put it out. The firemen afterward told us that, at this point, children usually go hide in the closet, with disastrous results. But Tommy went downstairs to tell his mother he'd done something bad and to come quick. She went up, felt the heat of the door, told the kids to get out of the house, and called the volunteer fire department. They arrived, sirens blaring, in three minutes.

I was a block away, at a church meeting, when my next-door neighbor burst in, saying, "Bill, everyone's all right, but it's your house!"

I sprinted home, seeing flames shooting out the upstairs windows and up into the night sky. All we could do was hold each other and watch as the firemen chopped and sprayed until it was out. Oh, boy! Fire is quick and thorough. The next morning we walked through the house together, happy we were all alive, but understandably gloomy at how nearly everything was gone.

Our Cathy was the most sensitive of the group. My guess is she knew our marriage and family stability was in trouble before I did. She was the only one of the five who ever ran away. Once, when she was thirteen, she just left the house and set out walking into the cold night, to who knows where? Mary and I frantically drove around until we found her.

She began to correspond daily with her cousin Linda. She became withdrawn, enjoyed her classmates and teachers less, entered adolescence with a chip on her shoulder. More and more she felt Linda was the only one in the world who liked her and understood her. Young adolescence is a hard go.

At age sixteen she ran away for real. We were living in Chicago, where I'd taken a staff job at a local TV station. She, with her cousin Linda in tow, just left. Her note said she couldn't take any more of this school-church-and-rules life, not to worry, she could take care of herself, good-bye.

It was 1967, when all social traditions were being tested. The news was full of violence, drugs and catastrophic change. In my personal experience of parenting, this was the absolute nightmare.

I found a scrap of paper in her wastebasket with a number on it: 35.99. That was the price of a one-way bus ticket to New York, so I guessed they'd gone to Greenwich Village. I flew to New York and scoured the Village, located the "flower children" area—and *found them*! Cathy had used pliers to pull off her braces and had rubbed her gorgeous Titian-colored hair with carbon paper, turning it jet black. But I knew my own child.

Bringing her back, I released her from her "bondage" of school, church and rules in exchange for staying home with us. Was I an enabler? Was I too soft? As a parent, I couldn't let my barely sixteen-year-old daughter rot in that rat-infested, condemned building a thousand miles from home. Couldn't do it. Sometimes parents' decisions come out of dilemma, where the lesser of two negatives is the more desirable. To this day, I can't listen to the Beatles' recording of "She's Leaving Home" without my eyes stinging.

The point of all this is: I knew that by marrying Susan I would be combining two distinctly different worlds. We were on shaky terrain. The kids knew I had loved Mary, and they knew they'd been created by that love. They certainly would have preferred to have our lucky-seven unit all in one piece. It's natural for children of divorce to say, "Hey! Let's get back to the way it was!" All the kids wanted Dad to be happy, but it's another thing to surrender your primary rights to an actress who has only played a mother on TV.

And, though Susan wanted to take me and all that came with me, she couldn't have been prepared for the meaningful bonds that tightly held me and my children, who are—and always will be—my life's treasures.

One by one the kids have come to see what I saw in those deep blue eyes. And, over the burnishing years, Susan has come to see my treasures as hers. Ours. Now, when they hurt, she hurts. She has become— a parent.

What I've just described was not an easy or quick transition, and there is much gratitude in my heart that it has happened.

Susan's heart is filled with reverent recollections of life with her mother and grandmother, but there's still plenty of room there for our snapshots, too. And, I'm happy to say, she now sees the value to me of all my memories, even the ones that picture me with Carrie, Billy, Cathy, Tommy, Peggy—and Mary—all of us glowing with young life around that old maple table.

SUSAN

There have been two clouds drifting across the sunny landscape of our marriage. One I created, and one I inherited, but both stayed around long enough to cause showers of tears before I grew into being a better wife.

The combination of racy Doug and reckless Julie had reached a noticeable status in daytime. Nobody said "supercouple" though. That term was created for Luke and Laura on *General Hospital* in the late seventies. Yet I think we were a touch extraordinary, if only for falling in love in public. The networks like duos. "Who are the couples?" they would ask writers in brainstorming sessions. So, most characters are born to be paired off. Ultimately, a Tweedledum will be written to match your personal creation of Tweedledee.

Actors usually see themselves as strong individuals who don't need a partner to be fascinating. May I say, actors don't know everything. Our casting had been so good, life itself was following along. I had been partnered with a winner and my soul mate. As a bride I wanted everything to be as perfect at work as it was at home.

Our agent said to me this year, "Is there anybody in show business who doesn't like Bill Hayes? I want to meet the guy who says, 'I didn't like him thirty years ago and I don't like him now!'" No such person lives. My sweetie is a team player with no visible ego. He's good, enthusiastic, pleasant and prepared. This combination is more rare than you might expect. With directors or producers he chooses his moments to ask for time-outs, a line change or even a lightbulb in his dressing room. Bill is not by nature a fusser and rarely looks for trouble ahead. Well, I do.

My mistake was assuming that my partner on-screen, who was now my partner in life, would want me to speak for both of us. I spoke constantly. I was the type-A person, or control freak. However you picture the person in a room who thinks their idea is caviar and yours is chum, that was me. It wasn't very pretty.

Mrs. Hayes, formally just Susan Seaforth, AFTRA member, was driven to share with the crew and directors any imagined slight to Bill and complained about it. Was he asked to stand behind someone in a scene? Was one of his lines cut, God forbid? If the costumer put Bill in gray and another actor in red, I would hustle into wardrobe and demand a change of shirts. I felt I was a wary tigress protecting my endangered cub. Bill was no cub and I was just a pain in the ass.

Bill understood all this fussing was based on my love for him and concern about our appeal as a couple, but he never asked for my micromanagement of his work. In fact, I saw him wince many a time if I got some suggestion in before he could shush me. Even knowing this "stage mothering" disturbed him most of all, I didn't stop.

He may have had thoughts of murdering me once we drove through the NBC gate each morning, but he never admitted it.

Being in a long-running soap is a lot like being shipwrecked on a desert island. You have to make the best of whatever the casting department washes onto your shore. Whoever the actor is, you have plenty of concerns in common, like getting your contracts renewed. There I was with the partner of my dreams, but I roiled around in my own insecurity and refused to relax and enjoy it.

In 1982 the network chose to present less of our characters on-screen and emphasize younger ones. I ranted to Bill at home and sulked at work in the studio. Thus, I succeeded in making an uncomfortable time of transition much harder on both of us.

When *Days* wrote us off the show in 1984, I probably had done plenty to make that decision seem like a relief to the writers and producers. Then I had several years to regretfully replay scenes in my mind. In them Susan was telling everybody how to do their jobs. Why oh why couldn't I have given those dear people a break? In 1990, Al Rabin, *Days'* executive producer, reopened my theatrical trunk with an invitation to return to the show. Much chastened, my first words were, "I don't want to try to direct or stage-manage anymore. You are the producer. I'll be very happy just to act."

Since then I have watched other soap actors coupled as spouses or lovers work effectively at making their team a hit with the producers and the public. Kevin Spirtas and Patrika Darbo tirelessly promoted "The Wesleys" on *Days* in the 1990s without making enemies. They remained professionals.

During an out-to-pasture period—that is, between engagements on *Days*—Bill was cast in *Sweeney Todd*, Stephen Sondheim's dark musical of social and actual cannibalism, as the evil Judge Turpin. The show was in Fort Lauderdale, Florida, and I stayed home during his rehearsals and flew in for opening night. We'd talked every day on the phone, and he praised the company and director, as he usually does during those busy rehearsal days.

Curtain up, I was really enjoying Bill's performance and looking forward to the big barber-chair scene where he'd get his throat cut. But, first, on comes the full company for the orgy scene.

They are dancing in masks and bondage attire, making ooohs and aaahs when the victim is dragged in all in white. Bill strides on from stage right in judge's black robe, swings down center as the guests spread-eagle the soprano. He turns upstage facing her, then lifts his robes and—Say, those are pretty close-fitting tights, I think. Holy mackerel . . . no tights! The Hayes posterior in all its peachy perfection is *out* and riveting as he pounds into the soprano. Wait a minute. I realize the whole company must be seeing the one significant item hidden from the audience. Wifey was stunned. There he was, elder of First Christian Church, grampa to an even dozen, my beloved partner and sainted husband . . . bare-assed in operetta.

Now if he had shared this staging with me in advance I certainly would have advised against it. But he didn't. One, to surprise me, and two, because he was following his director's vision. As an artist, I applauded this frisky choice. As an audience, I screamed. As a wife, I was learning he did great performances full of courageous stuff without my input. As a woman, I couldn't wait to get him back to the motel room.

Bill returned home to California with a Golden Buns Award in his suitcase. "From the company," he said. Or could it have been the soprano?

THE FAMILY'S VALUES

I had married into quite a mob. That was part of Billy's mystique for me, his large and warmhearted family. There were two brothers with four children each, his completely loving and supportive parents and a passel of cousins as close as kin can be. They all sang, played musical instruments, taught school or were in some way perfectly responsible. Not a wormy apple in the bunch. "Those Hayeses stick like glue," Jimmy Starbuck, Bill's choreographer buddy from *Your Show of Shows*, warned me. Jimmy was gay and had spent forty years loving Bill from afar. The family was straight-arrow and loved him from a-very close. I liked that. I was ready for group good times.

Bill's children were another matter. When Bill and I wed I became their stepmother, but only their spouses introduced me that way. The

(from l to r) Phil, George and Bill posing as angels in 1935.
BILL HAYES

Susan, Elizabeth and Jessie: grandes dames in 1948.
SUSAN HAYES

With (from l to r) George, Dad and Phil as George leaves for active duty in January of '43.

BETTY HAYES

Aviation Cadet William F. Hayes, USN 7566785.

UNITED STATES NAVY

Bill's parents, William and Betty, waltzing on their 50th anniversary.

BILL HAYES

1353 Alvarado Terrace.

SUSAN HAYES

Facing glamour with Loretta Young.

SUSAN HAYES

Supporting ever-bemused
Billie Burke.

JOHN E. REED

Bill tries pre-Rocky
beefcake in 1958.

JOE ABELES

Susan serves cheesecake on hay, 1962.

ALLIED ARTISTS

With Sid Caesar and Imogene Coca
on *Your Show of Shows.*
BILL HAYES

Nightclub headlining with
Florence Henderson.
BILL HAYES

The biggest TV show ever, 1954's
A Salute to Rodgers and Hammerstein.
In addition to the honorees, in front,
there were (back row) Tony Martin,
Rosemary Clooney, Florence
Henderson, Gordon MacRae, Mary
Martin, Ezio Pinza, Patricia Morison,
Yul Brynner, (middle row) Jan
Clayton, John Raitt, Bill, Janice Rule,
Charlie McCarthy, Edgar Bergen,
(front row) Ed Sullivan, Groucho
Marx and Jack Benny.
BILL HAYES

Stepping out with Hubert Humphrey and Judy Johnson at a 1952 movie mogul roast.

MIKE ZWERLING

With (from l to r) Tommy, Carrie, Billy, Cathy, Peggy and Mary on location for *The Cardinal*.

BILL HAYES

Davy Crockett's chief balladeer.

JOE ABELES

With Richard Rodgers in 1967. You sang his songs *exactly* as written!

BILL HAYES

With Denise Alexander in 1970
on our very first photo shoot.

With Betty Corday, *Days'*
producer and real matriarch.

In 1971 *Days* hits its
stride with our 1500th
episode.

The Marx Brothers sketch: Groucho (Frances Reid), Harpo (Susan) and Margaret Dumont (Jed Allan).

GARY NULL, NBC

At Doug's Place with some familiar-looking extras: (from l to r) Peggy, Kathleen, Cathy and Tommy.

GARY NULL, NBC

Representing the art form of the Soap.

© 1976 TIME INC.

Three weddings (clockwise from top left): at home for real (1974), at NBC (1976), and Descanso Gardens (1981).

An actor's life (clockwise from top left): *Where's Charley?* (1960), *Mass Appeal* (1985), *Amadeus* (1985) and *1776* (1972).

GARY NULL, NBC

KEITH CRARY

Musically attuned (clockwise from top left): Curly and Ado Annie in *Oklahoma!;* as tramps clowning for the Rose Parade; telethoning vigorously with the Tea-for-Two Cha-Cha; and Fagin and Nancy in *Oliver!*

GARY NULL, NBC

GARY NULL, NBC

GEOFF SINCLAIR

Returning from Tahiti in 1973.

In front of the Taj Mahal, 1986.

Pure joy in Venice in 1995.

With Elizabeth on her birthday.
BILL AND SUSAN HAYES

"Da Doctah" at Oxford.
FRED SHAUGHNESSY

(Clockwise from upper right)
Cathy, Peggy, Carrie, Billy and
Tommy today.
SUSAN HAYES

The Hair Years: Bill in mustache,
Kristian Alfonso in maximum fluff.
GARY NULL, NBC

Some of the *Days* family: With
Suzanne Rogers (top) and Mary
Frann (left).
GARY NULL, NBC

With "Wonder Woman" Deidre Hall.
BILL HAYES

The Williams–Brady family: Bo (Peter Reckell), Hope (Kristian Alfonso), Shawn (Jason Cook), Julie and Doug.

JEFF KATZ, COLUMBIA PICTURES TELEVISION

With Robert Clary during the recording of Bill's CD *This Is Bill Hayes.*

SUSAN HAYES

A black-tie *Days* anniversary with Ken Corday and Thaao Penghlis.

BILL HAYES

80's: Chuckling on the cover
of *Soap Opera Digest*.

GARY NULL, NBC

70's: Choosing an imaginary palomino
at Pueblo Los Angeles.

YANNI BEGAKIS

Home for Christmas
in the 21st century.

MIKE LARSON

young Hayeses just called me Susan, respectfully. "I'd like you to meet my dad and . . . Susan," they would say. It was fine with me. After four years of acquaintance I knew this was a volatile bunch.

Carrie, Bill's first daughter, was only five years my junior, already married to her college sweetheart and gone from the nest. She was everybody's dream, pick a role: sister, mother, wife. Carrie made everybody happy and had been an unfailing joy to her dad through all the tough times. I wished I'd had her as handy as next door, but her home was in Effingham, Illinois. I should have clung to her for advice in my early bridal years, but distance meant only rare opportunities to meet.

Bill's eldest son, William Foster Hayes IV, was handsome as a movie star, a Navy ensign, pilot, athlete, and most important freshly "born again." His search for God began with a visionary experience of Christ that changed him from a prime college-boy party animal into a reflective young man. Ultimately he left the Navy for the seminary and a lifetime commitment to missionary and Christian counseling work. His feelings for his dad were loving, but clouded with old angers over the many times Bill was away somewhere working while he was growing up. He became a husband just a few months before his father's remarriage. Bonnie, the bride, was delightful and dedicated, too, but they both were out of state and emotionally elsewhere when I became a Hayes.

But there were four teenagers living with Bill when I set my cap for him. Chronologically there was Cathy, his redheaded daughter, who enjoyed taking responsibility for helpless things and was devoted to her cousin Linda, Mary's niece. The girls had shared a magical mystery tour of the sixties hippy world since age twelve. They were former runaways, and Bill was letting them nurture their spirituality, Beatles songs and around seventeen cats. School had been abandoned as irrelevant and stressful. They created a little nest of their own in the guesthouse, where the air was funky with the odor of cat box and the smoke from all kinds of plants. Cathy cared for her father's home in her own style, and being a protective soul, she probably resented my intrusions.

Linda, the cousin, had a frailty of looks and manner that showed a troubled grasp on the nuts and bolts of survival. She was simply too much for her parents to handle, and Bill had taken her on as a bonus child when Cathy made Linda's life her responsibility. They were always a team. Linda gracefully accepted everyone's care and seemed to need lots of it.

Tommy, Bill's fourth child, was a golden-haired tennis-playing life of the party. He obviously adored his father and deeply missed his mother. His budding masculinity coincided with Bill's new bachelor status, but Tommy had more dates. He had a taste for wine, women and song from his fifteenth birthday and didn't appear to let anything bother him.

Peggy was Bill's baby, and a sweeter, sadder little thing you can't imagine. She had such low self-esteem a limp would come and go in her walk. The slender blonde looked like a young Catherine Deneuve, but she didn't have any sense of herself. The cousins and Tom seemed to dominate the air of Hayes House. Peggy looked used to living on scraps of love. Her father was painfully aware that she had missed out on mothering just at the most crucial moments of a girl's life. She plodded through school and hung on to her family by her fingernails. She made friends with the neighbor boy across the street, who had more problems than she did.

Bill had custody of them all. His domicile was full of furniture Mary had abandoned, hundreds of pictures of family friends and old times, a failing collie called Smoky Hayes and those nearly formed kids with their self-protective ways.

While Bill tried to keep a tightly disciplined schedule for rest and work, the kids kept hours to please themselves. He had purchased a house within walking distance of high school and middle school for Tommy and Peggy, which worked well. Cathy was the housekeeper and might emerge with Linda in the middle of the night to do laundry and general cleaning while Bill was trying to sleep.

To my eyes Bill's home looked dirty and disorganized. I had never kept house for teenagers or even known any. I grew up with adults. Now, those adults were often odd ones, but they were adults. In the workplace I took orders all day. That's what actors do: show up at their call times, cross right, cross left. Orders were easy to follow. Why wouldn't kids want to take them? Only Smoky the dog struck me as obedient at Hayes House. I didn't get what the kids were going through. The unwanted divorce, the uprooting across the country far from friends, the general struggle to plant themselves anywhere, were not meaningful to me. They all had Bill, what more could they want?

My grandmother believed a clean house and hard work were the answers to most of life's problems. At that point I had no reason to doubt her theory, so I applied it to this home Bill was trying to create for his children. His concern for them was so enormous I feared I'd lose him if I let go with a broadside of advice, but my disapproval was as obvious to the junior Hayeses as a pimple on the nose. I'd come over and rearrange furniture or do some tight-lipped tidying up. I never praised anything I found there. Having no idea how to talk to the kids, I never offered any practical help or got to know them well enough to establish trust. I did nothing beyond suggesting a change of wardrobe. Not a good issue to build on. I certainly wasted a great chance to have genuine input in their troubled lives. They all needed so much it scared me.

One day Cathy and Linda took off in Bill's old green station wagon for the Midwest, a parting agitated by style of outlook, not lack of love. Minutes after the good-byes, Peggy and I were wielding brooms together and sweeping out for a new era. The cousins made a living for themselves delivering newspapers on the rural routes of Michigan. It was a stress-free life they craved. Cathy loved her father, but felt more needed by Linda, and I imagine my hovering around cued her it was time to vacate the premises. The cats left with them, smoke cleared, and the guesthouse began to air out.

Tommy went off to Bill's alma mater in tiny Greencastle, Indiana. Maybe he was too much of a big-city kid for the place, but he blew off two expensive years enjoying dorm life and a C-minus average. After a financial reshuffle with Bill, he paid his own way at Wayne State for a while, working at responsible jobs. He became a man, away from California for years, but always stayed in close touch with all branches of his family, never neglecting his mother or his dad.

Bill took Peggy to various colleges to get a feel for them when that time was upon her, but she chose beauty school in L.A. and the gratification of an immediate career doing hairdressing in the studios. At her best she worked with a will for it and was always mischievous and fun to have around. After the neighbor kid broke in to trash her room in jealous rages a few times, she moved into an apartment with a born charmer named Shannon. He was into drugs but loved her; the diploma from beauty school got tacked up on the wall, and she was suddenly gone. I gave her my old Toyota. I also forced clothes on her she would have never picked out for herself—"You must take a straw hat to England, Peggy. Here, take this one"—things she smilingly accepted from me, but lost immediately. They never suited her anyway. I meant well, but couldn't even guess who she was or where she was heading.

Back in Salem, Julie's teen son David was being played by a very gifted young man named Richard Guthrie, who had limited experience as an actor, which is to say he was scared and insecure coming in to work. One director remembers the boy wet his pants his first day, doing a beer-guzzling scene. Personally, I didn't see it, but that just goes to show the things you get remembered for.

Julie was having lots of emotional struggles with her son's growing up, like most mothers, and Pat Falken Smith wrote many shouting matches for us. My overbearing assurance around Stage 9 probably set Richard on edge, and when the inevitable slap scene appeared in one script, I expected sparks from him.

Given that I'd been slapped soundly myself in a scene with Loretta Young on her anthology TV series when I was fourteen, not to mention getting walloped by Charlie Bronson, you would have expected me of all people to be careful of the fledgling actor. But I just played it full-out and whacked him a good one upside the head. Richard screamed, cried for a doctor and refused to go on. Of course. Wes Kenney had a few good words for both of us. In the weeks that followed, Pat wrote plenty more savage dialogue for mother and son, but the scenes were thereafter slapless. I was indignant that anyone might imagine I would hurt another actor on purpose, but if I wasn't secretly irritated at poor Richard, why did I hit him so hard? Did Susan, like Julie, think a good smack would knock some sense into him? Was that what I yearned to do to Tommy? I really can't say, but I knew Richard was frightened going in, and he had a bad day doing a good scene because of me. Here was an example of my lack of finesse at handling the young. After a few years I was pals enough with Richard that when he was beaten up for real, in an altercation with a heavyweight Hollywood type, he asked to recuperate in our guesthouse. At least I was able to pay him back with four days of TLC when he really needed it.

In real life my stepsons never got slapped by me or even yelled at, which was fortunate for us all.

The refrain of my song to myself for years was, "These kids don't appreciate their father, they think only of themselves." Well, was there ever an adolescent or young person not guilty of such sins? But I thought it was all unique and hostile stuff. I wasn't jealous; I just wanted them to grow up into adults worthy of their wonderful father.

After we married I felt too busy with *Days* to start a family of our own. Daytime stars who produced children and five shows a week amazed me. Who did they give their attention to? Besides, Bill had so much family and so many children he hardly needed additional responsibility. That motherhood might be a joyful life-expanding experience for me never crossed my mind. I doubted my gifts at parenting, for good reason, and honestly wanted all of my husband's attention I could get. Bill had been a dad since age twenty-two. I figured just being a husband might be light duty. Only he can say if it was so, but we've had sweet years and were never but a phone call away from crisis or good moments that required Papa's presence.

Peggy embarked on a long rough trip through chemical dependency that lasted for decades. The results were classic, wreckage at every turn. Her marriage to Shannon was a battleground, and we would get those three a.m. calls when the cannons roared: "I just want you to know your daughter is . . ." "Dad, come and get me! Shannon is . . ." After having two beautiful children, and two interventions, our sweetest girl was lost in an unhappy life. I was sad to the bone. Bill never stopped being there for her, but I came far too close to giving up. Then, after twenty-five years of riding the chemical carousel, Peggy bravely jumped off. She taught me the big decisions in life have to come out of our own hearts. Shannon, who had been a wild card, disengaged from those painted ponies before she did, but stayed loyal to his wife and children. He's a skilled carpenter and we've worked together on a dozen projects through the years. Some of my happiest moments have turned out to be riding in his pickup with the two-by-fours, or slicing up a grandchild's birthday cake. Very late in her marriage, Peggy fell in sober love with her husband and has made the most of it. Their combined work ethic would have made my grandmother proud. I admire her capacity to always expect great things of tomorrow because she's doing her best with today.

Those clouds over my marriage have lifted and drifted away; there are no more tears over teenagers anymore. And how did those junior Hayeses turn out?

Carrie became principal of the Carolina Friends School in Durham, North Carolina, a K–12 Quaker institution founded as the first integrated private school in the state. Carrie's eldest son is a business genius who closed a $300 million deal on his twenty-ninth birthday. Her two other children could be on *People* magazine's list of the twenty most beautiful faces in America.

Bill's eldest son produced William Foster Hayes V, plus three wonderful girls. He has traveled the world for more than twenty years, doing his best to spread love and understanding. He's marvelously wise and strong in his faith.

Cathy is driving another rural newspaper route, in North Carolina, and remembers Linda, who joined the angels at last. Another cousin shares her quiet life and keeps her happy company.

Tommy, now mellow, divorced and reflective, works hard at sales and stays close to his two sons, trying to be a good father every day. He's still smiling.

Peggy works in Hollywood as a top hairstylist at all the studios. She's won three Emmy Awards—so far. Her career is exciting and exacting, and I get a vicarious thrill hearing about it. She's raising a teenage daughter and helps out with her four grandchildren.

All Bill's children are worthy of him and they always were. I was nuts to think they had to become more extraordinary. All people are extraordinary from time to time. You just might have missed seeing them rise to an occasion. Being the child of an artist is exciting but uncertain. They all suffered his absences and flourished in his love. I didn't raise them, but as I grew into marriage I've tried to ease the channels of communication they'll always need to have with their dad. You never outgrow needing a father like Bill has been.

Nowadays I'm a step-great-grandmother. I feel remote as planet Pluto from them sometimes, and other times I listen to Carrie enthusiastically teaching a roomful of excited adolescents or watch Tommy hosting a family dinner that never leaves anybody out, and I think, Stepmothering was the mothering I got to do. It's turned out exactly like life, with some great days and most just fine. I'll keep on loving these people to my last breath, because they are his. And now, mine.

14

If Only

SUSAN

The death of a young woman has always been the ultimate tragedy in film or fiction, song or story. Annabel Lee and Madame Butterfly are famous names, but soap opera fans will remember the beautiful Brenda Benet.

My mother was head writing *Days* in 1979. Her copious plotting and dialogue talents had landed her the job. Our presence was probably more of a liability than an asset, but we were not in on story secrets and prayed for her success from afar. The head writer plots it all, and with that kind of responsibility, you would assume creative control is part of the package. For Mother the crown of power had more thorns than roses. She had a staff of one, not even an office at NBC, and a terrible tendency to rewrite all the scripts from top to bottom. Soon her eyes glazed over with fatigue. She wanted to prove she could swing this big job with impartiality; what better proof was there than sacrificing her son and daughter?

Mother believed Doug and Julie as a couple were less interesting than Doug and Julie apart. It had taken seven years of intrigue to get us to the altar on-screen. Her plan was to stage a disfiguring accident for Julie, followed by mental instability, followed by a Mexican divorce from her amazed husband, followed by another woman snapping up the discarded Doug. Producer Al Rabin was not comfortable with all this, but NBC loved it.

There were many memorable moments in this story line. I got my face blown up in an oven, then wore a plastic omelet of scar tissue glued on by the makeup man for six months before the plastic surgery sequence.

Bill got to play his own older brother, Byron (separated at the orphanage and lost for a lifetime). This character was soon to die from his evil wife's conniving, and not a moment too soon, since the white wig and mustache made my darling boy look a bit like Mark Twain. I got to play depression. That was easy. Seeing Mother give my husband away to a new actress was more than depressing. This new character, the brother's widow, was going to be sexy, sly and scheming, with a rich Southern-belle accent. Many actresses read for the part of Lee, the temptress in Mother's triangle, and when Brenda Benet turned up, my red flag did, too. "Anybody but Brenda," I told Mother. Mother cast her anyway.

The girl was ravishing, with an oval face, perfect features, velvet brown eyes and shining cascades of dark hair. One look and you never forgot her. We had been Deb Stars together in 1962. Before the Motion Picture Academy gave awards to makeup artists, the struggling Make-up Artists and Hairstylists Union drew attention to itself by putting on a kind of Hollywood Debutante Ball, where studio-contract actresses of promise were "presented" to the industry. This was all for publicity, but such stars as Raquel Welch and Linda Evans had done it. You received a cute little "Debbie," a chrome head of a starlet type about as big as a dumbbell. Brenda and I had posed in our long gowns and white gloves through many photo ops, and our friendship flowered. I had not plunged into steady soap work yet, but she was dancing on variety shows and had appeared in the Elvis movie *Harum Scarum*. Later we worked on *The Young Marrieds* at the same time, and later still our friendship soured over my mistake in judgment.

She had a hillside apartment in the Cahuenga Pass I admired excessively. I was welcome to drop by, and in my moments of girlish emotional crisis brought on by clashes with my mother (who wanted more input in my life), Brenda would listen in her cool way. A couple of times I had fumed and slept restlessly on her couch. Her rules forbade extra visitors, however, and my married men friends were verboten. The concept of home as sanctuary hadn't crossed my mind. I thought her "no man" rule was just territorial. When Brenda went off to ABC to tape one morning, I called my smarmy male friend, who I usually met with in an office closet. Brenda walked in on me in a most compromising position with this tired old Republican she detested. "Susan, how could you?" Now Brenda had known all about this guy, but she made me feel dirty as a dump truck. She was right. How could I? I was ashamed of myself and furious at her for making a scene. The Republican era ended then, but I barely apologized to Brenda and saw no more of her until the day she sauntered onto Stage 9, as Bill's new love interest.

What a mess. I hated the situation and made it worse and worse by being cold and wretched to Brenda. I actually criticized her to her face onstage in front of cast and crew. "Oh, yeah, twirl your hair around your finger. That's terrific—that's acting." I was saying such things to Brenda while she was trying to do scenes. I'd gone completely crazy with jealousy and old regrets. I couldn't seem to get past myself, and I don't know how Bill stood it. After just a few weeks I owed her so many apologies I should have stopped coming in to work.

Meanwhile, the Lee character entraps Doug with her helpless femininity, and he marries her. My Bill was not exactly thrilled with playing such a sucker and begged Mother to wise him up, but to no avail. She was working night and day (didn't I say head writing is an awful job?) and barely took our calls. Further disaster for Julie. If Susan didn't like it, well . . . hard cheese.

Brenda's life centered around her husband, actor Bill Bixby, and their son, Christopher. She was charming and fresh, and everybody loved her but me . . . and I had no excuse not to. The story rolled on to the next chapter, when Julie emerges from her mental crisis and skin grafts to reclaim Doug. The "fight-for-your-man stage" was juicy material. Bill the actor stayed focused on the job, but Susan the woman began to fall apart.

The show had taken total control of my life. Everybody I knew either watched it or was on it. Everybody I loved had a big stake in it. My mother and husband were disagreeing over the story. All the cast seemed to be coming to me to give Mother notes, or their thoughts, or complaints. Some of the cast were jealous that Mother was in charge, and became positively strange. Every word I reported back to her sounded so critical, she frequently hung up on my calls. My feelings were perpetually rubbed raw, but this was Elizabeth's day in the sun, after all. Bill and I prayed for her success, but what was happening to us?

I was booked on a red-eye flight to New York with Deidre Hall. Sitting up in first class, we got to talking while Bill dozed. Wrapped in airplane blankets like two squaws around a campfire, we gossiped and exchanged guesses about future plots, just like viewers. Dee knew plenty about how to do business in the world. She also was canny about "our world," the Corday universe, where crazy artists made *Days* flourish. The blond goddess of the small screen was full of insight. The Susan-Brenda pot was a-bubblin' and she saw my finer points were melting down. Dee talked about the makeup room, our personal snake pit of unguarded emotion, and how amusing it was to watch Brenda and me.

My demons and distress were transparent to the *Days* cast and crew? They found it all pretty funny? *Funny?* The thought of being laughed at deflated me.

Hall understood what a mess I was making for the whole company. That mystique of the wise woman isn't just scripted for Deidre. She really does have healing ways. This foundation of substance has always made her acting real as well as stylish. I believe if circumstance had put her in politics instead of performing, she would have risen high and done much good. Anyway, she did me some good when I was beyond taking advice from the usual sources. Our candid relationship continues to this day, and no friend of mine cuts to the heart of the matter, or makes better sense, than Miss Hall.

I began to get a grip on myself and stop thinking about Brenda every moment. By 1980, my mother was no longer head writer, but the Doug-Julie-Lee story was still strong. The pressure was off me, but Brenda's life was starting a downward spin. Her marriage slipped away, and the work on *Days* grew harder and harder. She was doing big scenes now, hysterical scenes with nothing but naked anger to play. The delicate brunette threw herself into acting at the studio and mothering little four-year-old Christopher at home. He was her joy. *Days* was her job. She was never confused about what was most important. Mommy

and son built a sandbox together with trips to the shore to collect exactly right, clean, pure sand to fill it. She cooked wonderful treats,
danced with him, adored him. They went off to the mountains together. "The sandwiches are made. We're committed!" she said and
laughed on a Friday afternoon. On Saturday her boy was dead. He was
stricken with some raging virus that closed his throat, and despite the
emergency hospital's treatments and surgery, he choked to death.

Brenda's character was immediately written out while she mourned,
as we all did, for the child and his parents. All too soon she was back
with us, very quiet and brave. This loss was a blow no mother ever re-
covers from, but she managed to show up, knowing her lines and not
letting Corday down. At what cost? By now Lee and Julie had scenes together, and one of them went so well I sent her the most beautiful or-
chid plant I could find, with a note enclosed to praise her wonderful
acting. I knocked on her dressing room door. She had candles burning
and a soulful bit of violin music playing on her little tape deck. And finally, finally I found the words to apologize. She was gracious and wist-
ful, looking like a watercolor of a woman in her soft silk kimono. She
was with me but not quite with me. The one-year anniversary of
Christopher's death had just passed.

The triangle story line was drawing to a close. Doug was set to remarry Julie, and all Lee's hysterics and murderous plans for killing Julie
had failed. Brenda was growing thinner and thinner, more and more
fragile. I'm told she was drinking then, but it's hard to imagine. The day
of our lavish second wedding, viewers saw Lee turn up to stop the ceremony, but Doug locked her in a closet. The vows and love songs followed, bride and groom rode off in a carriage to their honeymoon, and
Lee was left alone.

We got a call from producer Al Rabin late one evening. "I wanted
you to hear it from me first: Brenda has killed herself." She had locked
herself in her bathroom, put a gun in her mouth, and pulled the trigger.
Al was trying to control his shock. We were all stopped cold with sorrow and denial. How could she do it? Al said it was as though she chose
the moment when it would cause the least trouble to the writers of
Days to make her exit. Lanna Saunders, who played Marie Horton
then, held a private memorial at her home, where the cast and crew

could express their feelings and pray for Brenda together. We were devastated and so sorry . . . how had we missed her signals? What should *we* have done?

BILL

Ruggiero Leoncavallo, in 1892, wrote the words and music of what is arguably the most famous opera of all time: *I Pagliacci*, the clowns. It's a melodrama about strolling players, set in southern Italy in 1870.

Canio loves his wife, Nedda, so fiercely he doesn't want anyone to come near her. She becomes so afraid of Canio's jealousy that she plans to run away with Silvio. Just before the actors begin the play, Canio hears Nedda promise her lover to elope with him that night.

The play-within-the-play deals with a similar plot of jealousy and betrayal, and Canio is so distraught he can't perform without brooding about his real-life situation. When he hears Nedda utter exactly the same promise of elopement in the play, he goes berserk and kills her.

Actors are human beings. We the audience empathize with Canio in his situation, trying to make people laugh while his heart is breaking. We've all been put into the position of having to carry on while we're churning inside.

Such was our predicament when that really lovely girl Brenda Benet joined us. As head writer, Susan's mother was under the gun to create conflict between Doug and Julie. And she cast perhaps the one person Susan had had an unfortunate history with to play Lee, the character who would come between them.

Elizabeth, naturally, cast the best person for the role. Brenda, with an exquisite face and figure, was a very realistic actress. She said she'd completely forgotten the incident Susan recalled with shudders. But it was large in Susan's mind.

The closer Brenda and I got in the script, the more difficult it was for Susan to do her job. It was *Pagliacci* all over the TV screen. How did Susan learn any lines, go to work, act in front of the camera? I don't know. Brenda was aware of Susan's discomfort and must have felt like one of the clowns in *Pagliacci* herself.

Lee's actions and dialogue in the show escalated to where the only way Brenda could play them was to believe that Lee had gone off the deep end, that she was not just a gold-digging villainess but a round-the-bend cuckoo. She began to play Lee really mad.

Brenda had serious problems to deal with—her divorce from Bill Bixby and the tragic loss of her little boy—but I believed she was strong enough to handle them. The last time we sat next to each other in the makeup chairs, like two clowns getting made up, she was hilariously recounting her previous night's dinner, and it was a laughing moment.

I have to believe that something else, something we don't know about, must have angered her, saddened her, depressed her beyond caring. The decision to take her own life somehow didn't ring true to the Brenda I knew. I loved working with her, and I miss her terribly. She was with us, and then suddenly it was as if Canio had appeared and pronounced his last line in the opera: *La commedia è finita*. The comedy is over.

SUSAN

The complete departure of Brenda from my life meant there would be no chance to take up our old friendship, and I'd made our experiences as actresses together a trial instead of a joy. Perhaps I could have helped that little part of her life. Instead . . .

What did I learn? Be quick to forgive, and hurry to make peace. Don't let the sun go down on anger. I thank God I voiced my feelings of admiration and affection before she was gone forever. You never know what tomorrow's going to bring. Or take away. The cast from those years moved on, but never forgot the loss and waste of her suicide. New actors came along, other friendships and scenes were played out, but, personally, I never dared to take a story line so seriously again. Had I not been so focused on those scripts I might have seen the real drama in the girl's life. I might have helped.

God grant Brenda is with her Christopher now, in a special corner of paradise for mothers and sons.

15

All Fired Up

SUSAN

When an actor is cast in a play or movie, the entire script is on the table. He prepares for a certain character, and the producer hires the best talent to fit that character's description. Serial storytelling expands this situation way beyond a single plot or set of circumstances. That's the charm of an open-ended story. New stuff happens every day. Say the show needs an ingénue, some girl who looks vulnerable and beautiful, but not a whit glamorous. She should be a good actress, but shorter in stature than the leading lady playing her mother. Let's assume the right girl gets the job. She's just eighteen, she's great, and everybody loves her, but to advance a fast-moving plot her character grows older at a superhuman rate. After a few seasons she's produced a baby, who morphs into a teenager over the Easter break. Wow, the girlish actress has become a leading lady, too. The audience accepts this amusing time warping in soap land, but it's always a bit unsettling to the actress. She enjoys the added sophistication of makeup, wardrobe changes and sex scenes, but she's perhaps twenty-three now and suddenly "parenting" an actor of twenty-two.

Julie's little son David went off to summer camp, an adorable Cub Scout of ten, and returned in September a six-foot-two lantern-jawed man of thirty. I had just turned thirty myself that year. Head writer Pat Falken Smith assured me I was being paranoid when I complained. My "son" was recast with a better, shorter actor of . . . twenty-five.

BILL

On a soap, *story* drives everything. The birth of a baby is exciting, but changing diapers and giving bottles is not, so baby characters don't stay babies very long. They become children who can talk. Child actors old enough to learn lines and take direction are hired, and they serve their purpose for a while.

Doug's daughter Hope, for instance, was briefly a gurgling pink face in a portable crib and then suddenly—voilà!—a little girl. She was supposed to be about four years old, so Natasha Ryan was cast. Natasha was actually six, but she was small and lovable and played Hope for the next six years. Natasha's Hope, never involved in a major plot, perched cutely atop the kitchen counter and put away cookies and milk while Doug and Robert (Robert Clary) sang to her.

Decisions were made that Hope was to become an eighteen-year-old, recast with the enchanting Kristian Alfonso. The story called for Hope to now be a leading lady with spunk, libido and brains. And Kristian had the acting chops to play whatever the producers and writers threw at her.

SUSAN

So, as life changes every day in a soap, what you were originally cast for, or that quality that drove a story, may no longer be needed. Meaning you aren't either. Millions of viewers may love you and associate you with the show, but your charms are old news. Tomorrow's plot might call for as many action sequences as *Die Hard*, and the producer notices you puff getting up the stairs to his office. The character you perfected has left the soundstage. Your physical presence doesn't fit in, not to mention the nuisance of your two-appearance-a-week contract guarantee.

Every time a new head writer climbs aboard the show ship, the cast and crew look over the side with apprehension. Will we be deemed fit to sail by this fresh new captain? Where's the voyage to go, and can we get a peek at his charts? How's he doing with the admirals from network up on the poop deck? What's the scuttlebutt? Will other stars be shanghaied from other shows? Will the ship sail away without us, or worse, throw us overboard into the dark depths of . . . unemployment?

This flow and, more frequently, ebb of fortune is a good thing. Change is good. If the cast of *Days* hadn't changed and been refreshed by new faces, it would have nothing to recommend it save antiquity, and nobody would be watching. Yes, the audience always complains about changes for a few weeks, but then adopts and adores the fresh talent. Networks are devoted to capturing a new young audience that's going to stay loyal all its life. Everyone over thirty who has tried to have a meaningful conversation with a teenager will tell you they don't like old faces. Styles of daytime dramas also change constantly to reflect our American jet stream of social transformation. Here's to the writers, producers and actors who have never been left behind or canceled because they didn't stick to an outdated concept of what a show is about.

In my opinion, *Days of our Lives* has had more course adjustments than most soaps. That simply reflects the numerous head-writer and executive-regime changes in its history. Originally a homey show, planted in a small town of the great Midwest, populated by doctors and lawyers in suits, it's been gradually transformed into the lair of continental villains with global influence, a nesting spot for devils, and once an interstellar landing pad for pod people. In the day-to-day course of things it all seemed pretty normal, too.

To be competitive all soaps must now tell stories that include high-quality action as well as snappy dialogue and plots. The art form has changed from modest romantic canoe to atomic submarine. Leading men must be more than officers who look smart on the deck in their dress whites. Today those men are Navy Seals, stripping out of wet suits with deadly knives clenched between their pearly teeth.

Days has lasted forty years with only a tiny portion of cast constantly in view. Most of the players from the past were jettisoned when a lighter cargo and spiffier crew was required. It's all okay. It's natural. It's healthy.

To the actor tossed over the rail with a hearty "yo-heave-ho" and a piddling splash . . . it's exactly like drowning.

Early on in the eighties, NBC embraced the idea of being a young viewers' network, and *Days* was one of several shows with too many character actors on the roster. Kristian Alfonso became Doug's daughter,

Hope. She was perfectly lovely inside and out. Peter Reckell was cast as Bo Brady, a rebelish motorcycle-riding hunk. Peter and Kristian both had masses of curly dark hair, and could have posed for portraits as Romeo and Juliet. Hot new team, young people in conflict! All this was great until it appeared the conflict was to be with us. Suddenly Doug and Julie, the savvy, hip, romantic couple we had played for years transmogrified into conservative nay-saying grumps. We became the parents from hell, reactive and awful.

I seriously doubt the producers or fans even noticed, but we were deeply disturbed. I couldn't accept finding myself upstage and out of focus in the dark while Kristian turned downstage into her key light with the last close-up of every scene. Were we being classified as over because of our many birthdays? Not much we could do about that. Bill's hair was silver, but thick and curly, and his face was handsome as ever. I lived on diets and didn't feel jowly, but I was nearly forty. More than the physical-decay issue was the temporary transformation of our characters to give Bo and Hope something to play against. We felt betrayed. But the head writer was just following a master plan to make youth more heroic in general.

It's plain as pudding now, but at the moment we believed a sit-down with this writer might change things. So, for the one and only time in our careers as a couple, we went upstairs to directly supplicate the reigning pope of the plot, Margaret DePriest. I nearly swooned as we approached that conference room. Feelings of doom and helplessness dropped over me. Dizzy and sick at my stomach, I dragged in behind Bill. My husband had lovingly, supportively and faithfully parented five children. He was cringing over the fathering Doug was providing Hope in the scripts. He pleaded for a change of tone. I listened to Margaret put down every suggestion Bill made, then finish up by telling him he didn't know beans about being a father.

You couldn't miss the handwriting on the wall: "This way out." NBC wanted to negotiate a new deal with a 50 percent cut in guarantee and lots of vacation options. We kept returning in our heads to what the characters were doing and ignored the good side of NBC's offer. "You're talking about apples and oranges, guys," Al Rabin kept saying. "Don't you want to travel more, enjoy life?" But we wanted what Al couldn't give, to keep the characters as they had always been. Then the local NBC News interviewed us, and I mouthed off about wanting "better story." My God, what an idiot! From then on Margaret DePriest preferred not to write for us. No more *Days of our Lives* for Doug and Julie. We cleaned out our personal wardrobe and left. I remember the vivid moment when I took my old patchwork quilt off the wall of our dressing room. As I carried it past the security desk to my car, the guard said, "This can't be happening." Security was out of the loop.

The lesson here? Do not take the show so seriously, ride out this head writer's term of service and stay on board. Indeed, Ms. DePriest didn't last long.

It hadn't been fun to be just ballast in the hold after a dozen years of being on the deck of our dear good ship, sailing into the wind, drenched in story. Well, we swam ashore and investigated life on dry land. *Days* became a dot on our horizon, far off as a star, shining brightly on without us.

BILL

I *loved* playing Doug! His joie de vivre was infectious and you never knew what he was going to do next. Bill Bell and I, discussing the character once, agreed that though Doug might be helping a lady across the street, he was probably unhooking her brassiere at the same time.

From 1970 to 1982, that was Doug. He had his serious moments, his love for Addie and Julie and Hope was steadfast, but he always had a light spirit that could never be squelched.

Then, in 1982, everything changed. It did not disturb me at all that from that moment on the main stories were to be teen stories and young-twenties stories. Perfectly okay with me. I was fifty-seven and Susan was thirty-nine, and it was right for our prominence to adjust accordingly. But Doug was no longer Doug, and that had me shaking my head every day. The writers began to give him *old* lines ("Why, when I was your age . . .") and gripey parent lines ("Hope, I don't want you to see that Bo Brady with his loud motorcycle and long hair!"). I know I never should have let it bother me. I was just an actor, hired to memorize the lines written for my character, whatever they were. But it did bother me. A lot. I felt they had not only thrown away an exciting component of the show but were seriously cheating their fans by jerking Doug around like that. I muttered in my beard for two years and then decided I should talk to the writers about my concerns.

Yes, it was my error to ask for the meeting with the producer and head writer, and it was more of an error to voice my disapproval of the writing to Susan. I should have learned, in our decade of marriage, that when I get upset Susan *gets upset*.

The meeting was with producer Al Rabin, head writer Margaret De-Priest and co–head writer Sheri Anderson. I explained to them my feelings: "You've changed Doug into a negative, conservative, old parent, and that's not the character I've been playing for fourteen years."

It was no use. They were apparently acting on orders from someone. Doug and Julie were merely serving their purpose in the new young story lines. If we'd just shut our mouths and accepted the situation we probably would have stayed on the show straight through till now. But the prospects looked bleak in comparison to the tide of importance we'd enjoyed for so many years.

Tension eddied all around us as we were invited to be interviewed by the local NBC News and, though we were trying our best, it was hard to be up and positive in our replies to the interviewer's questions. Our head writer happened to flick on the program just as Susan was saying, "Give us good stuff to play and we'll play it." She dialed Al Rabin and said there would be no more scenes written for Doug and Julie. And that was that. The next day Al told me negotiations were over and they were taking their last offer off the table. The viewers, of course, were told nothing.

Following our final scene, Doug and Julie just disappeared. Pfft! Gone! Our characters' names were not even mentioned on *Days* for the next two years. Fans asked us why we left and it was impossible to explain.

We had met working on *Days*, had gotten up at four fifteen in the morning two thousand times and spent some twenty thousand hours getting made up and costumed and taped in the studio, often leaving home before dawn and returning home after dark. We'd made out in our dressing room while waiting for our turn to be on, eaten thousands of meals in the commissary. For fourteen years the studio had been more our home than our home. And for Susan it had been sixteen years! Being wrenched away from all we had known together was like being pushed off a speeding train. We hit the ground hard.

I was more concerned about Susan than I was for myself. In her mind her identity was being Julie on *Days of our Lives*. She was hurt to have been written out and jarred with insecurity about what our future held. I called some producer friends to let them know we were free to work in theater again.

So, suddenly, after fourteen years of staying at home, our new life involved travel. Now and then we needed to go off solo, but much of the time we did plays and musicals together: *Tribute*; *Same Time, Next Year*; *Harvey*; *42nd Street*; *Love Letters*; *Christmas Carol*; *Same Time, Another Year*; *Cinderella*; *Mame*. We did fine, but life was never the same.

SUSAN

Milwaukee was our first port of call. We were invited to do a two-week run of *Oliver!* at the big Melody Top Theater (in the round, three thousand seats). In red wig and beaky rubber nose, Bill was the archvillain Fagin. Back in Cochise-length wig and low-cut costume, I was Nancy, singing "As Long as He Needs Me," that codependent love song. When Dickens wrote *Oliver Twist*, the gang of little thieves-in-training was about a dozen strong. The producer raised that figure to thirty. Each child having parents and extended family, this alone would boost ticket sales. The mob of thirty little men just about undid the director, who had never raised anything besides pansies. He skipped blocking Bill altogether to drill his marching moppets. At five p.m. on opening night they finally set Fagin's big solo, "Reviewing the Situation." It didn't matter. Bill was wonderful, though the buildup of sweat inside his rubber nose drove him crackers. We recommended Peter Reckell to play Jesus in *Jesus Christ Superstar* at the same theater that season, and he sold out every performance.

I was twisting in the wind not knowing what to do with my life after household chores each day. Thinking a bold act was called for, this unemployed, uncoordinated woman decided to go look a horse in the eye.

Emile Avery was an old cowboy who ran a stable in Burbank, where I went for riding lessons. There was a ring, some ramshackle stalls and a little white house with his strawberry-blond wife inside. A canary cage sat by the sink. The wife was young, lovable and pert. Emile was seventy-two and extremely pert. He had been a stunt man in pictures and knew just about every actor and horse in the area. My spirits were pretty low then, and the sight of NBC, just a few blocks down the street, didn't help. I was a sad little sack, and no athlete either. Emile put me up on Ol' Bud, the leather-mouthed wonder-horse with the velvet canter. We picked our way up the trails into Griffith Park, greeting the passing riders, dogs and horses.

"I've got to be careful, Emile. I trip and fall down a lot."

"No wonder, you're always looking at the ground. Stand up straight, Susan, and be proud."

I was, by God, forty, and nobody had said such things to me lately. I needed to hear them. I saw the leaves on the trees, the sun on the hillsides, and came for lessons whenever Emile would let me. My self-esteem began to come back as I mastered the climb into the saddle. Those morning rides were quite a change from soap opera drama down the street. Be confident, be brave. He never actually said such things—our talk was about how to hold the reins, raunchy tales and stories from his other marriages—but I got the idea. By the time I learned to canter through the Burbank dust I was game for life again. A woman on a horse!

GARDEN VARIETIES

Unexpectedly, Bill Bell put me on *The Young and the Restless*, playing a powerful fashion maven in sharp shoulder pads. Joanna was mother to adorable Tracey Bregman, an actress who began in soaps on *Days* when I was younger and more charming. My mother was writing on *Y&R* then and scripted many of our contentious mother-daughter scenes. It all sounded like echoes of 1353, but this time we were getting paid for the backchat. I loved Bell for giving me a contract on his stellar show. Ed Scott, the producer, was great, the part was fun and glamorous, and I could even steal moments to shop for big crystal earrings at the Beverly Center after work.

Two years later Bill Bell needed to end the character. I begged him for a little longer run and we cut the appearance guarantee. Still the ax fell one day, and a farewell cake was ordered with my name on it. This parting was not so catastrophic as my *Days* good-bye, but I couldn't face that cake. Ed Scott understood and slipped me a Tiffany pillbox with the *Y&R* logo. I'm told Bill Bell came for the cake-cutting and said many nice things about me. It was a good time to exit the character, but I assumed age had reared its wrinkled head to spite me. I told Ed as much. "Why didn't you tell me?" he said and ordered the cameras to pedestal up for my last scene (creating a better angle for my droopy chin). Bless the man. He always loved my mother's writing, too.

Somewhere in all this I dreamed of Ken Corday, the owner of *Days* and executive producer. In the dream he was standing at the end of a corridor, curly haired and charming. He smiles toward me, then turns away, and walks around the corner. I rush up the corridor and call his name, but it's too late. He never comes back. It was all a bit too classic to endure. I would wake up feeling pretty sad. Boo-hoo, poor me. Out of work again.

One day in 1990 I was in the garden pruning bushes, an activity I heartily recommend for sublimating discontent. Every bush can have a name. Every branch can be shaped to your will. Chop, chop. Our agents had dropped us. "Here's one for the agents." Chop. My unemployment insurance had run out. "Here's one for the governor of California." Chop. I was just getting rolling when the telephone rang in the house. It was Al Rabin asking for a brunch meeting at the Sheraton Universal. Amazingly, every pivotal event of my career seems to have happened within a one-mile radius of home.

A strong older female was needed on *Days* to work opposite the strong older male villains and to mentor the fascinating ingénues. "So, how about Julie?" someone must have said. "She has historic value, and has gotten into manual labor in private life. Let's get her." But where was Doug? The writers were going to bring me back a divorcée, and the how and why of my marital breakup was not to be mentioned. Perhaps the characters had fallen so far off the map of the *Days* world the executives believed no one would care. I cared, but the show was loaded with those older men under contract. Whatever happened to Doug was not dealt with for the next three years. Al kindly asked if I could bear to come back without Bill. I was thrilled and disappointed all at once, but had learned you don't get what you want very often.

In a week I was back on board, literally, on "The Cruise of Deception," a colorful story line of shipwreck disaster and tropic islands. Here was action-adventure writ large and I was doing it every day. On masquerade night I wore a tawny Queen Elizabeth costume straight off a drag queen's back. The next show I was skeet shooting with a rifle in my hands. On wreck day I got to jump into a tank and yell, "Geronimo!" Once on the island I ragged the red evening dress to flattering tatters. I didn't mind Kristian getting all the close-ups. She was eight months pregnant with her first baby and working like a trouper. I was back in a group shot again. I did feel the absence of Doug's charming banter when I teamed up with John Aniston (Jennifer's father), who plays Victor Kiriakis. John was solid and powerful, but not my darling. I kept quiet about that and enjoyed playing castaway with the young and beautiful actors. Kristian went off to have her first son, Geno. I stayed on to mentor other girls.

The little blond ingénue the Fates gave me to work with next was playing a sassy bitch, but the writing never matched her natural talent for being hateful. After an unforgettable run she left *Days* to do more of the same on nighttime TV. At her farewell party the cake had a picture of her face on it. I remember nobody took a slice of her mouth.

Another regime change. Julie is selected to say adios again in '93. Head writer Sheri Anderson hired my mother to script my farewell scene, a sweet one where Doug reappears and sings "The Most Beautiful Girl in the World" to me. He looked particularly handsome and sang particularly well as we glided off into the soap opera sunset. Tom Langan, the current producer, joined Ken Corday in giving me a beautiful diamond-and-ruby bracelet from Tiffany. The jewelry gift made it feel final. At least Doug and Julie were together, where they belonged. I felt the audience had never warmed to me without my sweet husband in sight, too. So I was blue on blue, especially to leave the cast and crew I enjoyed so much every day.

In those three years I'd worked hard to create a fan club, personally answering every letter and publishing a little journal four times a year. Some strangers turned into close true friends. That was why I felt so sorry to dissolve the club, but they wanted Julie and I wasn't Julie anymore.

I kept the diamond-and-ruby bracelet in a safe and, following the principle of locking the barn door after the horse has escaped, booked a face-lift. It turned out well, and I was doing some housework at home when a freelance tabloid writer I'd never met called to ask all about my surgery. I was shocked. She gave me twenty-four hours to consider giving her an interview. The next day I said, "Thank you, no."

"Really?" she said. Five weeks later the *Globe* ran a front-page story on my little face-lift with a candid photo of me taking out the garbage one morning. "Surgery fails, career in tatters. 'Hollywood is a sausage-factory,' declares former soap star." I hadn't realized I was well known enough to rate all that. Ah, shit.

Just when my face was looking better than it had in years I was off camera for a long time. But Hayes and Hayes were together behind the footlights doing *Oliver!* again, this time in Sarasota, Florida, at the Golden Apple Dinner Theater. Bill played Fagin without a rubber nose, but producer Bob Turoff, our magnificent director and friend of the heart, demanded red hair. Bill's platinum glory and fresh goatee were dipped in temporary henna rinse for our nine-week run. I was delighted with my gypsy wig and earthy brown cheeks. Mid-run Bill had to go to Morgantown, West Virginia, to play Emile de Becque in *South Pacific*, and rinsed over the Fagin hair with a sort of game-show-host brown. After that the hair began to fade into a shade of lilac that's hard to describe. The show was booked next in Singapore and Kuala Lumpur. I feared the audience would never respect a Fagin with lilac hair, and talked my darling into a beauty salon to strip the color mess off completely. Bill submitted to the bowl of bleach for about thirty minutes. When his hair was the color of summer corn, he announced, "I'm finished." "Oh, no, not yet, Bill," I sputtered. "I've had enough," he said, rinsed off and swept out. So that's how a golden-haired Nordic Fagin, who could have been named Swen, came to headline in *Oliver!* It was certainly like nothing Dickens had ever imagined.

The hardest, most gratifying experience of my stage career took place in Birmingham, Alabama, when I slammed into *Gypsy* as Mama Rose. I rehearsed for five long weeks without Bill, roaming the city and vocalizing with the conductor every day. My mother and Bill flew in for the opening night. Bill was more than pleased and my mother even liked it, too. I felt like an actress.

As the twentieth century wound down, we worked steadily doing plays and traveling. The First Christian Church of North Hollywood put me on the board as property chairman, and I learned about keeping up a fifty-year-old building every single day. As my handyman José used to say, "It's always something." I painted, carpeted, lifted and lugged, enjoying sprucing up God's house on the corner of Moorpark and Colfax. A full three years of volunteering.

The Autry Museum of Western Heritage had a great nine-month docent-training program. I joined, learning about the west in order to lead children through the museum on one-hour tours. L.A. school kids are nothing if not multicultural. I began to realize how many languages other than English fill today's classrooms. One summer project at the museum was to tape a little Western movie on the premises with children under twelve. I wrote, costumed, directed and edited the effort, along with a jolly team. We had a stagecoach robbery, a saloon siren and a kick line dancing to Willie Nelson. Lots of wahoos for me.

During those happy times, my job hunting in Hollywood was not fruitful. The day I failed to get Second Caucasian Victim in a police-file show, I thought of turning in my union cards and not bothering anymore. I had been an actress; now I was a housewife, a docent and a property manager.

In 1998, Doug and Julie were recalled to life yet again. Hope was having an identity crisis—amnesia, why beat around the bush?—and she needed her daddy. "Ken, if I return my bracelet, can I have my contract back?" Uh, no, this was a limited run, but we had a good time admiring our grown-up children, Peter and Kristian. We even got to be in a pretend plane crash, evacuating on the rubber slide together. This time we wound up on a tropical island with the whole Horton family.

When Aaron Spelling's *Sunset Beach* came on the air, it was so hot and spicy I was not suitable to even audition. No old faces were wanted. But toward the end of its run, producer Gary Tomlin made me the district attorney. The role was created for a guy, but what the hell, the show was circling the drain. I had a good time doing scenes in mannish suits around the police station for fourteen episodes. This time being fired was a generalized disaster, as the show was pink-slipped. I didn't take it personally.

In October 2003, we were in Xian, China, relaxing at the hotel after a day of touring the Terra-Cotta Warriors. The phone rang. It was Ken Corday. "We need Doug and Julie starting in December, but . . ."

"But, what?" We knew older, established characters—in other words our old friends—were being wiped out in the new serial-killer story line. "Are you bringing us back to kill us?" I ventured.

"Well, yes." My heart was sinking all the way from China through the earth and back to Burbank. Ken couldn't assume we would agree to come back if we knew what our fate would be. "That is, Doug. If you don't want any part of it, the part will be recast." One way or another, Doug was toast.

One consolation through all the years of off-again on-again, work with *Days* had been that nobody ever suggested just killing us. Well, this was the moment. Bill reflected on what a great run it had been. What a noble soul my husband has. With a smile and never a second of hurt feelings, he said, "Sure, Ken, I'll be glad to die for you." I could hardly believe what I had heard. You have to keep reminding yourself that it's only a show. Bill and Susan were going to be okay, but what Doug and Julie were facing was sad indeed.

BILL

When I heard Ken Corday say Doug was going to be killed, my heart stopped for several seconds, the way you feel when you hear about the death of a loved one. The character was that close to me. As Ken talked on, I quickly traversed the stages of grief—denial, anger, bargaining, depression, acceptance—and then I realized it couldn't be any more difficult than our abrupt detachment from the show back in 1984, the one that had stripped away my royal medals and dumped me in the alley along with my early seventies costumes. Then, as if I was sinking into a warm bath, I felt peaceful. I'd lived Doug's life through nearly two thousand episodes, and there aren't many in the world who can better that.

All the while Ken was explaining how Jim Reilly was a great storyteller, like the Irish of old. Then he asked me if I had any comments or requests, and I answered, "I'd like to see Doug go out as a hero, not a wuss."

"I'll tell Mr. Reilly what you said and I'm sure he'll do his best to write it that way."

We hung up and I stared at the phone, thinking, Well, here we go on another life's adventure. Susan gave me a nice long hug and a sweet kiss. I was amazed at how dear to me the character of Doug Williams had become. I mean, it's only fiction, yet oh so real. *Days* viewers will understand.

SUSAN

To put this moment in perspective, in 2003, we were losing something much more precious than a character on a soap opera. My own mother was in the last stages of bone cancer.

Mother's long writing experience on *Y&R* had ended in the nineties, but she watched the show like a hawk every day, as though her critiques still mattered. She stayed in touch with Jeanne Cooper, the show's matriarch, and Jack Smith, her old pal, who was now writer-producer under Bill Bell. In spring, the *Restless* duo took her out to lunch. Plenty of laughs and celebration at that table, I'm sure. Afterward, Jack decided to write her into *Y&R*. Mother was to be an actress again, after decades at the typewriter. Her character of Charlotte was a drunk with a secret, in scenes with Jeanne and Jess Walton. The woman was in her mid-eighties, full of chemo, and she hadn't worked in soap since she appeared as a patient of Dr. Tom Horton. (She remembered he called her by three different names in a two-page scene.) No matter, everybody loved her so much they took a chance. True to form, she rewrote most of her dialogue and had lots of suggestions for the directors, too. I told her what to expect the day in the studio to be like, and for once she listened, and reported back that my information was accurate. All the pressure of learning lines and having to be sharp turned her into a vital magnetic woman again. More than ever before she was creating and living joyously in the moment. *Soap Opera Weekly* picked her as Performer of the Week, with a full-page picture in blond wig and witty expression. Mike Logan of *TV Guide* praised her, and fan mail arrived. "I'm good, really good," she confided to most everybody she met, but they could see that. What a flowering of confidence and ego, and it was all her own. "Charlotte" appeared in sixteen episodes. In soap that's a career!

While Mother was in the midst of all this, I was booked to do one scene on *The Bold and the Beautiful*. So we worked at CBS on the same day. Before taping I was called out of makeup to the soundstage, and there stood Tracey Bregman, Susan Flannery and Bill and Lee Bell, those beautiful faces from the past, to welcome me. I could hardly speak for feeling so much. In an hour I played my little scene with Leslie-Anne Down, who had been my favorite heroine on *Upstairs, Downstairs*. I heard Mother being called to her set: "Onstage, Elizabeth," then watched her wheelchair gliding through the soundproof doors. I got a snapshot later of the two of us in our ready-for-our-close-up moment. Mother was on her last journey but burning still like a fiery little ember.

Our church was full for her funeral on January 3, 2004. The morning was bright and breezy, like Mother. The writers she adored poured out words of love.

In her papers I found an old letter from Ken Corday. It was a reply to some unsolicited criticism, suggestions and plot twists she had offered *Days*. His response was just like Mac Carey's old warning to me: "You catch more flies with honey than vinegar." I had to laugh; had neither of us ever learned? She's drifting around heaven now, probably buttonholing Charles Dickens with some story ideas. For a long time I couldn't get past the bite in our sweet-sour relationship. Now that I can't thank her for my life, I remember so many sweet times. Elizabeth was a living index of wounding remarks, because she always had opinions and loved a good line more than people's feelings. Well, so what? The ideas and fantasies tumbled out of her to the very, very end. I was lucky to hear about them for sixty years. Take care, you daughters of brilliant women. It's hard being onstage with a queen of drama, but you'll be in a wonderful show.

On January 5, 2004, we began again at *Days*. Many of the actors we'd shared dressing rooms with for years had already been swept away by the Salem Serial Killer. Gore had run deep and the mood on the set was low-to-lower. This unprecedented violence had driven ratings up. Bill's one request was to die fighting. So he became the first victim to face the killer eye-to-eye. It turned out to be darling Deidre Hall, the show's biggest star and loveliest character. This daring story was the talk of the industry, but we, like the fans, couldn't believe it was happening. Dee urged us not to be afraid of her offstage, but behind the laughs and the good acting she was not having fun doing in her soap family.

Bill's death scripts arrived. Doug realizes the killer is his favorite blond psychiatrist, and after a gallant fistfight, she stabs him in the throat. This happens on the steps of the Salem church. Hope finds her dying father, and he expires in her arms. Simultaneously, Julie has a vision of his departing spirit while she's praying in the church.

Bill threw himself into the fight sequence. I'd never seen him do that kind of action before. I was shocked at his quickness and the power of his punches. The stunt woman doubling Dee praised him. I knew he was a dancer, but I had forgotten the Navy trained him in hand-to-hand combat. Evidently he hadn't forgotten. That was the good part. Deidre pulled her knife and dealt the lethal blow. Special effects secured a blade to his neck before dribbling Max Factor blood all over him. I shot a picture for our scrapbook. The image of my darling skewered on the ground was more horrible than I had expected.

BILL

I loved the fight sequence. Stunt coordinator Spice Williams was brought in to stage the action and double Deidre Hall. Her character, Marlena, tricked me into falling into the open grave, momentarily stunning me. When she leaped into the grave, that was the only time Spice doubled her, as Deidre could have been seriously hurt doing that stunt.

Then Deidre took over again and we had a knock-down-drag-out in the dirt on the floor of the grave. She landed on top of me, but I struggled out from under her. As she rose I knocked her flat with an elbow to the face. She was out for a moment as I scrambled out of the grave and ran to the sanctity of the chapel. But she came to and followed me. The chapel door was locked and nobody came to let me in. That's when she brandished a long, deadly letter opener. Though I hit her with a roundhouse right, she gave me the coup de grâce right in the side of the neck. I bled profusely and slowly sank to the chapel threshold.

Deidre and I worked the action together like tango dancers. Deidre, always a lady in real life, played Marlena like an animal. It was beautiful!

Head writer Reilly had granted my request, had Doug go out fighting for his life heroically. As Doug expired, his last thoughts were of the two women in his life, Julie and Hope.

SUSAN

The transfiguration scene came next. Julie turns from her prayer to see Doug standing in a shaft of blazing white light. The lines were perfect: "Don't leave me . . . we have so much more of life to live . . . how can I go on without you?" All the things those left behind have always said. Loving Bill as I do, I can't imagine a life without him, but for that scene I did. My very recent loss was always in my consciousness, too. It was wrenching to imagine and impossible to rehearse. We were both in another reality, where there was no acting, just each other and that infinite promise that love is eternal.

BILL

The moment Doug died, the camera cut to Julie praying in the chapel. A bright light appeared and Doug walked out of it. Julie could see him, and they had a two-minute good-bye scene, superbly written.

How Susan got through the scene I'll never know. Her mother had just died, and Susan was at that time going through her mother's belongings.

And, since there are so many similarities and parallels between Susan/ Julie and Bill/Doug, Susan can't have been acting. If it rent *my* heart, just think what the scene did to Susan.

SUSAN

There was more. Five episodes of Bill as a corpse, cold on the ground, then stretched out in his coffin for Doug's wake. He held still as, as death I guess, and I kissed him in that coffin. I was numb as any new widow, pushing the real emotion down so I could get the acting up.

At last Doug's body wasn't on camera, and the farewell party for Bill Hayes took place on Stage 4. My sweetie had asked for a chocolate cake. Ken Corday presented an hourglass, the show's logo, and said some kind things. He seemed as depressed as a producer can get. The cast for the day stood glumly around. Most of the cake went untouched. Bill made a speech about being a ghost now and how he would be watching *Days* from the spirit world. He named the dozens and dozens of wonderful actors, writers, directors and crew that had served *Days* so happily in by-gone years. He said they were all still there, the spirits that love the art too much to ever leave. He said when those still to come would do something wonderful, the dead would know and cheer. It was the most selfless good-bye I have ever heard an actor give on his last day. I went to our dressing room and cried and cried for a very long time. Ken came in and embraced us both, telling us to remember it was just a soap opera. But, of course, it was our life.

On April first, we taped Doug's and Alice Horton's joint funeral. The Salem matriarch had choked to death on her own homemade donuts. Feisty ninety-year-old Frances Reid, who still played Alice Horton, was not pleased. Even Deidre, the Serial Killer herself, was scheduled to die. John Clarke, an original Horton who played my uncle Mickey, had chosen to retire. You could say the survivors were shell-shocked. Julie had become Salem's chief mourner. I soldiered on in black, thinking of my pension.

Bill was booked to headline at the *Palm Springs Follies* for seven weeks. It was a classy venue and he was pleased. He was rehearsing his upcoming songs, but aside from the tunes at the piano, he had become very quiet around the house. I guessed he was saving his voice or down in the dumps.

On this latest funeral morning an announcement from the Corday office went out for all cast and crew to assemble on Stage 4 at one p.m. There was a large turnout, with executives all over the place. I stood back from the crowd, behind the electric bull on the big new Western bar set. Ken Corday had a speech to deliver, but first he set a candle on the bar and lit it. "Thaao Penghlis [one of the dead cast] brought this to me from Bethlehem," Ken said. "This feels like a good time to light it." The crowd was very tense. I figured the show was canceled. Pink slips all around. "Is everyone as tired as I am of death and violence?" Ken was raising his voice. Stunned silence. "I say is everyone tired of it?" A few yeses, a pause, then more. "Let me hear it!" Many, many more. Something was coming now. He announced there would be no more funerals after Dee's, but changes and surprises were im-mi-nent. "Ladies and gentlemen, meet the new cast of *Days*!" The upstage barroom doors opened and one by one the killer's ten victims walked out like Lazarus. Applause! Cheering! Pandemonium!

Now playing the MC, Ken introduced each actor: "The beautiful Suzanne Rogers!" Whistles and stamping from the crew and executives. (Her character had been cut to pieces with a whiskey bottle.) Matthew Ashford was introduced, Josh Taylor strode through the doors, and then Ken looked around the stage for me. "Susan, are you hoping?" "I sure am." "And now the nicest guy in the world, Bill Hayes!" And there was my darling, looking like the cat that lives on canaries. I was clapping and hyperventilating as Dee whispered in my ear, "Did he tell you?" "No, no, not a word." For two weeks Bill had kept the mass resurrection a secret. I wasn't mad and didn't care, because Doug and Julie would be back together someday. What joy. Sparkling with relief and happiness, the faces of the returning cast shone like jewels. "I'm so glad you didn't die," everyone was saying. A phrase you hardly ever get to use in real life.

BILL

Ken called me one day in mid-March and asked a peculiar question: "Bill, are we alone?"

I warily said, "Yes, Ken. I'm the only one on the phone, if that's what you mean."

He said, "Good. Please keep Thursday, April first, open, and come to my office at noon. You'll join all the others whose characters have been killed off, and we'll walk over to Stage Four just before a big company meeting. I'm going to introduce you all—one by one—as our new cast."

Much confused, I asked, "Ken, do you want to explain this?"

He said, "No, I can't now. But please don't tell *anyone* that this is going to happen."

"You mean anyone?"

"No one."

I understood that to mean not even Susan. So I didn't tell her, breaking our solemn promise to each other, and for two weeks I sat on my own tongue to keep from blurting out the big secret.

When we were introduced as the new cast, and I walked out, no one was more surprised than Susan.

As viewers now know, all of us who had been killed, laid out and buried *on camera*, waked, eulogized and mourned, came back as captives on an uncharted island that contained an exact replica of Salem! Unable to communicate with our loved ones back in the real Salem, who continued to mourn us, we pondered how and especially why we had been brought to this strange pass.

And somehow, in all this mad, mad story, Jim Reilly has caused people to examine death and resurrection, their own human frailty, the fleeting grasp we have of our own lives, the meaning of family and loved ones and the importance of telling the ones you love what's in your heart. Today. Don't wait.

SUSAN

America had watched half of Salem die. Now they were alive. How could such things be? Ken wouldn't tell, but he was smiling. "Remember, it's a soap opera!"

So it was the great firing that really didn't happen. Back on board the good ship *Days* actors could haul anchor and sing out, "Heigh-ho, me hearties. We're bound for . . . an island prison!"

Was being fired so many times a tragedy? Of course not, not compared to the engulfing awfulness modern life can dish out. We have had the golden moment, that passionate soap opera moment, more than our share. But being Doug and Julie is still our dearest treasure. Our hearts just feel so empty when they go away.

Much later, after everyone went home, I was crossing Stage 4 to my dressing room. Bobby, our prop man for twenty-five years, was standing by a silent monitor crying softly and saying, "Isn't all this news wonderful? Yes, the most wonderful thing."

16

In the Street

SUSAN

If you watch network television today, you will notice promotional "pop-ups" for other shows in the extreme corner of your screen while you are trying to concentrate on the program you tuned in for. Soap actors also "pop up" in unexpected places—like game shows, awards ceremonies and local celebrations—to cross-pollinate the viewership. This promotes an ongoing fantasy that the whole network is actually a family, and if you like our burgers, you will love our chips.

We were once invited to ride in the Macy's Thanksgiving Day Parade. The NBC publicity department that arranged our lives in those days happily advised us, "You each will have your own float." What a coup. "You two will be the tortoise and the hare." Costumes were to be provided by Macy's New York. We flew east with happy hearts.

The costumes turned up in our room at the Warwick Hotel. There had been no time for a fitting and fit they did not. Two little Tyrolean numbers with embroidered cotton shirts, short pants, too-large shoes and no socks. Maybe they would match the floats. We hoped.

Thanksgiving dawned freezingly. The parade assembly spot was mass chaos, and I was separated from my darling and his cold, cold knees immediately. A tall young man named Gray was in charge of wrangling Doug and Julie with propriety and tact. I couldn't have asked for a nicer guy to fall back on, as I struggled up onto the wide-bodied tortoise, which stood about nine feet off the ground, with a bicycle saddle on its slippery red back. I felt completely exposed, looking down on my plump lower limbs as they began to turn violet with chill. Bill's wild hare was much grander and taller. His saddle was twelve feet up in the air. Yes, he had a great view of Broadway, if he could see through the deteriorating weather and avoid being swept off his seat by the wind. I'd chosen to leave my glasses back at the hotel for the sake of glamour and was practically blind. The drivers propelling these things were not obliged to keep in touch with the actors on top. Big brass bands began to march and off we went.

"Hey, Julie, I watch youse guys every day!" "Hey, *Days of our Lives!*" Every policeman and fireman on the line of march gave us a great hello. "We watch you at the station, never miss it!" The crowds were good-humored and hardy. It was a big charge to see how many sophisticated urbanites loved our daytime drama of the heartland.

"Hey, New York!" I called, waving and freezing in my Katzenjammer costume. Then it started to rain something sharp from the sky. I yelled over toward Bill's merry hare, "What's this stuff?"

"Sleet!" he screamed and smiled . . . waving, waving.

Bill pulled farther and farther ahead. This did not seem quite fair. Wasn't the tortoise supposed to win the race? My float slowed to a creep. Strange bands were high-stepping by. At Forty-second Street I didn't hear the beat of dancing feet. In front of George M. Cohan's statue, the tortoise died. The driver crawled out from under his shell to say, "Motor's shot, you'll have to catch another ride." My God, in the middle of a downpour, in front of all these people? Mr. Gray, who had been patrolling the sidewalk and eyeing the situation, said he could take me back to the assembly area.

"No," I refused, "I'll never find my husband again. Can't I just get on his float?" The worried publicist guided me to Bill's unstoppable hare and gave me a mighty boost up. Bill dragged me onto his bicycle seat built for one. Ouch! We clutched each other, and waved no more.

"Hey, Jules, how's it going?" yelled a New Yorker. Slippery when wet, I can tell you. These were my years of short dark hairdos, heavily permed. The icy rain had turned my head to kinky stubble, and my eye makeup was running down in licorice streaks. We stayed astride the giant rabbit till parade's end. A freelance photographer who sold pictures to fan magazines and tabloids appeared out of nowhere, snapping candid moments, as we attempted to dismount with legs numb and spread-eagled from three hours on the frozen float. Gray was there with a stepladder trying to stay between us and the eager photog.

"Mrs. Hayes, try not to be photographed now. You're not at your best," he suggested. I'll say.

Back at the Warwick we dropped our yodeler outfits in sopping heaps, changed and beat it out to LaGuardia and a flight to Maine. Air New England was an optimistic little airline. A ten-seat plane with an unpretentious curtain separating passengers from pilots. We watched them pound on the control panel to get some lights lit, then they noticed us watching and remembered to close the curtain. We took off into black and stormy skies.

Our holiday destination was a Thanksgiving dinner in Waterville, where Carrie was living at the time. We pitched and yawed up the Atlantic seaboard through god-awful rough air. The pilot landed in Augusta, an unscheduled stop, and turned back to us. "I'm just going to call my wife. Sit tight." He scrambled out into the freezing drizzle.

Minutes passed, and a new face appeared at the door of the tiny cabin. "Flight's over. Everybody out." We found our luggage waiting beside a pair of taxis.

"Pilot's late tonight," the driver volunteered as we squeezed into the cab with all the other resigned passengers.

"Does this happen often?" Bill asked.

"Yup. This flight never actually gets to Waterville. We drive everyone there, only takes about ninety minutes."

There was crusty snow all over Waterville when we rang Carrie's bell hours later. Kisses and hugs, and then she asked what we would like for dinner. There was no turkey, no cranberries and (not to be critical) no heat. The hearty Mainers were conserving fuel and kept the thermostat on sixty-five degrees. "Dinner" was scuttling around the kitchen floor. Two live lobsters with claws wrapped in rubber bands were enjoying their last walk on the wild side. We tore them to pieces and ended the holiday under an electric blanket . . . thankful at last.

Those delicious lobsters reminded me of Peggy McCay. A fan had shipped two large live ones to the proprietor of Brady's Fish Market in Salem some years ago. Meant as a treat and a tribute to her chowder, I suppose, but a big mistake on the fan's part. The moment Peggy opened the package at NBC, she became an activist for lobster rights. The toothsome twosome were returned to the sea. Not the Pacific, which was handy, but the Atlantic and the homey waters of Maine. Those lobsters may have died or eaten each other up in their crate by the time they got to the state o' Maine, but Peggy's sense of justice had been served.

BILL

MY FOURTH OF JULY

When I was a little boy in Harvey, Illinois, the Fourth of July parade was a big deal. People applauded all the marching bands and used to take their caps off when the open touring cars holding the Civil War veterans drove slowly by. Sometimes there would be a horse-drawn wagon with a live Dixieland band. Veterans from World War I, many of them proudly wearing their uniforms, comprised a goodly group. And there were always "funny cars," the kind that were tricked up with gears and cams so they could rear back like Roy Rogers on Trigger.

Fourth of July was also fun for us kids, because that was before laws were created to protect us from firecrackers. Fireworks would be on sale everywhere, all made in China, and for a dime you could have a fine time. Cherry bombs were two cents, long strings of little tiny crackers that would go off in sequence were a penny apiece; skyrockets were way out of reach.

So I always looked forward to the Fourth; that is, until 1996. All summer long I was playing *I Do! I Do!* at the Mark Two Dinner Theatre in Orlando with Carol Lawrence. Producer Mark Howard threw a picnic in the park for the theater gang that afternoon. Games, deviled eggs, hot dogs, the works. Whoopee!

While driving out to the park, I noticed a police car following me. Then another behind him. Within a minute there were a total of five black-and-whites behind me, spread to cover both lanes. I thought, Wow! Something's going on!

Then, from the opposite direction, came another phalanx of five police cars, and as they rounded into view all ten police cars turned on their flashing roof lights at the same time. I started looking around to see what poor sap was in deep doo-doo.

It was me!

All ten cars converged and forced me off the road onto the gravel shoulder. I stopped.

As the police cars all rolled up, pointed directly at my car, their doors flew open. Officers spilled out, ducking behind the open car doors and aiming their handguns at . . . *me*! Holy mackerel, Andy, I wasn't going *that* fast.

A bullhorn blasted behind me, "Turn off your engine, remove the key, and exit your vehicle." I complied.

"Place the key on the roof of the vehicle." I did so.

"Lift up your shirt and turn around three hundred sixty degrees." I followed the order. I could see close to twenty pistols aimed at me.

"Back up to the rear of your vehicle." I backed up.

"Kneel down and put your hands behind your back." I knelt on the gravel, assumed the position. *Crunch-crunch*, I heard someone approaching from behind. *Clink! Clink!* I was handcuffed. All shapes and sizes of cops then began to leave their car doors and slowly walk my way, guns at the ready.

"What's your name?"

"Bill Hayes."

"Where's your driver's license?"

"In my wallet, right there." I patted my hip pocket. An unseen pair of hands removed my wallet and began to look through the cards.

"William Foster Hayes?"

"That's right."

"Is that your car?"

"It's a rented car."

"Where'd you rent it?"

"I didn't rent it. I'm working at the Mark Two Dinner Theatre, and the company rented it for me."

"Where were you going?"

"To the park. Company picnic."

"What do you do at that theater?"

"I'm an actor. I'm in a play there." I adjusted my position.

"Don't move." Several guns remained trained on me, while half a dozen cops examined my car—opened the trunk, looked in the spare-tire well, under the rug, beneath the car, even under the hood. Not finding what they were looking for, they shook their heads at the voice behind me.

Finally, the voice said, "All right, Mr. Hayes, it seems you're not the man we thought you were. You may get up." I stood up. Someone unlocked the cuffs; I rubbed my knees. Feeling a little weak, I leaned against the car.

The voice chuckled in a friendly way and said, "You all right?"

I turned to the man, looked him in the eye, and said, "It may be funny to you, but it was very frightening to me."

"I'm sorry. It was wrong of me to laugh. I understand how you feel."

I was not smiling. "You want to tell me what that was all about?" By this time all the other cars had left.

"Bad killer somewhere in this area. You fit his description. Fifty-year-old Caucasian driving a rented red Oldsmobile. Wanted in several states. Car's loaded with a regular arsenal. Just doing our job." He took off his hat, got in the police car and drove away.

Even being taken for a fifty-year-old didn't make it any easier. I drove to the picnic, but wasn't up to hot dogs and games. When I told people what had happened, they were kind of matter-of-fact.

"Oh, yeah, that was a 'felony stop.'" They seemed to know all about it.

SUSAN

ONE MORE TIME

In another decade NBC asked us to parade for Macy's again. "How would you like to do a number?" they teased.

"I'll write it myself," crowed Bill, taking the bait. He dusted off his

ASCAP card and produced "Here Comes the Macy's Parade," a perfect tune for the occasion.

We recorded it with full orchestra in Burbank, got snappily choreographed by Jack Bunch at the studio, and fitted in newsboy costumes by our own dear wardrobe department—who knew our measurements. The outfits were Norman Rockwellish knickers in orange and pink, with dashing little caps and scarves.

Hayes and Hayes would be float-free. Instead, we had a corner of Seventy-second Street to prance around on. Thanksgiving morning this time was sunshiny bright, with air as snappy as a candied apple. The whole parade was going to pause for our showstopping ditty. We were introduced by Regis Philbin, danced into position, opened our mouths and . . . nothing. Nada sounda. No music feed to the street! Technicians in Master Control heard the playback, but we couldn't. Regis hopped into the breech, apologized to the audience and us, and reintroduced us.

For a second time we went into our dance. "Here comes the Macy's Parade . . ."—only this time it did. The technical snafu had slammed shut our window of opportunity to pause the parade, so the biggest, brassiest band in New York trooped down the street right across our number. We could hear nothing but "On Wisconsin," and it all ended in confusion (a place I've often visited). The director came out of the remote truck, upset and nearly in tears.

"I'm so sorry. It was such a cute number, too," he moaned.

"It's live TV, buddy, we're used to this." We felt lighthearted, actually. The worst thing that could happen had. We'd made asses of ourselves at a harvest festival of epic proportions. Evening found us at Sardi's with Mother having a civilized turkey dinner.

In 2002, Kristen Storms as Belle and Jason Cook as Shawn rode for *Days* in the Macy's Parade, not singing a song of their own composing on a float that didn't break down. They missed a lot.

I7

At Home and Abroad

SUSAN

Bill is an artist, first, last and always. I am whatever is needed as long as it doesn't involve making change. Mostly I'm a homemaker. Bill's enthusiastic about our house and loves to tour people through it. This house is more than sixty years old and sprawls across the center of a deep lot with no coherent architectural plan. We've been here so long the old trees fell over and died, and new ones are just putting down roots. I've been tweaking this pile of stucco for three decades. Bill caught me up short one day by saying I was trying to turn it into 1353 Alvarado Terrace. True, I'd added some stained glass, but turning a one-story ranch house into a mansion is impossible.

Recently I happened to find the notes from our Italian honeymoon, and I got a look at myself as a happy bride in love with my groom and the sensual marble-halled rooms of the Mediterranean. Oh, how I wanted every beautiful experience we were having reduced to an object, captured in a suitcase and brought back home. And so . . .

In Venice we acquired a still life of tulips and peaches in the Dutch Masters style, and a gilded carved *putto* strumming a golden lyre. In Florence we added a wrought-iron mirror, a walnut mailbox marked *Posta*, a framed marble *pietra-dura* of the Duomo and an ivory miniature of "The Fair Lady." In Sorrento, only an intarsia-wood tray with brass railing, six ceramic fruits, and a necklace of coral strawberries. In Siena, two large majolica apothecary jars. Waiting for us in Rome, on the Via

Margutta, was a bronze statuette of a "Singing Mephistopheles" washed in silver, two large framed paintings of women, one nude, and a little Renaissance mandolin worked by jewelers in the stone called tiger's-eye.

Bill had mapped out excursions bursting with sights to see on foot. How giddy the real sunshine on the Grand Canal made us feel. We even caught a blessing from the Pope. I remember lying in our matrimonial bed at the Hotel Raphael in Rome, my thighs twitching involuntarily because I'd never walked them around so much in my life.

We loved the coffee bars, the vegetable displays, the cypress alleyways, the art, the sky, and each other so much there couldn't be enough souvenirs in the world to remind us of our bliss.

BILL

FIFTY-FIVE KILOS OVERWEIGHT

The curtain came down on our honeymoon fantastico on the Via Veneto in Rome, having dinner with Alan King and Jimmy Coco. We went back to our room and reviewed our 189 Polaroids, then finished packing our staggering stack of mementos.

We each had only one suitcase, but the six boxes of excess were elephantine. We paid the airline 332,600 lire ($200) for being fifty-five kilos overweight. Small stuff included: one set ceramic salt and pepper shakers, two wooden angel plaques, twelve miniatures, six mosaic hearts, one silk scarf, one tin of cookies (I bought those), one dozen museum books, carved saints, Florentine leather goods, cloth dolls, pairs of gloves, pen-and-ink drawings, a miniature Sicilian donkey cart, several religious medals (blessed by the Pope), Venetian-glass beads, silk flowers, posters.

We had spent 1,638,000 lire ($1,000) for all those items, gave most away as gifts, and adorned our home with the rest. We still look at them today, pat them, fondle them, and immediately get transported back to that dream time of romance and tuberoses.

SUSAN

HGTV

The House and Garden Network gave us a call a couple of years ago. They had come up with the title "Soap Pads" for visits to soap actors' digs. We had made the list of old favorites to be photographed at home. Exactly what our house looked like was unimportant evidently, because the planning was all done by phone and the producers didn't even ask for a picture to see what they might be getting into. "We'll get your interview over with first, then shoot a few rooms. Three max. Should take about three hours." It sounded like fun, and I was devoted to the network, where you could watch hours and hours of violence-free television (except for the occasional demolition).

The crew arrived, and instantly we agreed the exterior was off-limits. Brown spots in the lawn and a purple front door couldn't have been what they had in mind. Our producer for the episode looked fifteen, but assured us she had made forty of these spots all over the world.

On camera we thumped the piano keys, sang and kissed, and were finished in forty minutes, just as she had promised. I told the true story of our dining room set, how we purchased it in Italy, and how the ship transporting it sank in L.A. Harbor after ramming a tanker. "How exciting it is to buy things around the world for our home," I gushed.

Then the artsy-fartsy photography began. Slowly the camera panned the old velvet sofa, pausing at the Pierrot from Verona, Italy, caressing the dusty lampshade and gently going out of focus down the damask chair leg. That day it was 106 degrees in the Valley, and our place is the last of the un-air-conditioned homes standing. To block out ambient light, black plastic sheets were snapped over every window. We all baked like muffins in an oven. As the camera seemed to X-ray my kitchen counters, I saw with a sinking heart that my grout needed bleaching. After nine hours of fluffing and filming furniture, they left. The segment played and played. We looked a bit brightly lit and haggard, but the sofa, the damask and even the grout never looked better. Viewers echoed my words, "How exciting it must be to buy things. . . ." Sometimes I think it would have been a whole lot easier just buzzing down to the Ethan Allen store.

HAREM SCAREM

Take those carvings from Egypt in the dining room. They are herms, guardians of a house's exterior, fashioned to look like people holding up the roof. We found ours in the Khan el-Khalili Bazaar in Cairo our last night in Egypt, in October of 1980. We picked out a four-paneled, six-foot-tall carved wooden screen from the same dealer. The screen is of a style you've seen in a hundred movies, from *Casablanca* to *Zorro*. Spool carving was created to make a dense cover over harem windows, allowing ladies within to peek out but not get out. Every old exterior in Egypt had second-story windows onto the street, covered with this carving, in some degree of dusty decay. Bill enjoys exotic things, and I loved the cracking, dried-up old herms. The bazaar dealer was big-eyed and oily, trying to interest us in a life-size copy of King Tut's throne, but we were satisfied with our two very large and heavy items. "I'll meet you at the airdrome in the morning. We will fabricate packages for you. Not to worry." We gave him almost all our Egyptian pounds, a check, and put the rest of the charges on our American Express Card. Our three weeks of cruising down the Nile with a Los Angeles County Museum of Art group had been a tourist's dream. We hated to be leaving the Land of the Pharaohs so soon.

Our guide in Egypt had been a tank commander during the Six-Day War with Israel. His name was Afifi, and he had a political agenda to trot out under every palm tree. We debated heatedly, the only way to do anything in that Middle Eastern climate. I flaunted my free will by sunbathing topless on the aft deck of our Nile cruise boat. I shouted that he should be grateful to C. B. DeMille for putting his country on the map of the American imagination. "If it wasn't for Hollywood, why would the tourists come?" Yes, I was acting like an insufferable barbarian, but he kept fighting that war over and over. After two weeks in the sun our tour companions wanted to dump him down some well like Joseph.

Afifi just loved his country and wanted us to think it was the source of every good thing in history. His type of righteous guide appears all over the world and, bless their hearts, somebody's got to do it. We wound up liking him for his unflagging enthusiasm in all that shifting sand and stifling heat. Under his guidance we had purchased a little carving of a husband and wife, side by side, from an antiquities dealer in Luxor. Afifi gave Bill a parting gift of a snowy white galabia gown we'd admired on him. He probably thought Bill deserved a gift for being married to me. I got a handshake. This paragon of Egyptian hospitality had not supervised our trip into the Khan el-Khalili.

At the airdrome our gang was saying, "Till we meet again" and "En sh'Allah" to the old tank officer as a seven-foot crate, big as Seti's sarcophagus, rolled up to our side, pushed by the bazaar guy's flunky. "What's this?"

"Our antiques," Bill chortled proudly. In America, any object over fifty years old rates that distinction, I'd told him, and he unwisely kept using the word to the assembled multitude gathering around the crate. We were not in America, but Egypt, where an antique has likely been around since the Flood and where you need a government certificate to take one out of the country.

As the second crate was wheeled in, the disturbed Afifi lowered his head in his hands and muttered, "Oh, no."

BILL

SUSPECT IN THE THIRD WORLD

The tour of Egypt had been spectacular. All my life I had salivated over rotogravure photos of the Great Pyramids, the Sphinx and King Tut's treasures, and we had actually been able to see the real things, touch them, and feel their breathtaking ancient mystique. I rode a camel out into the desert to the Great Pyramid of Cheops. Susan and I crept into the dark airless center of Chefren's Pyramid, that 4,500-year-old pile. We took pictures of each other standing by the Sphinx. We entered King Tut's tomb.

I loved the unfolding panorama of the Nile: the cliffs, the donkeys, the women drawing water from the river and putting the jugs on their heads for the long walk home, workers watering their fields with oxen-powered wheels, palm trees, the feluccas languidly tacking upwind.

Then they gave us a "day of leisure" in Cairo before flying us home, and that was our undoing. In the Khan el-Khalili, that sprawling exotic bazaar, we entered an inviting shop called Babany, just to nose around their fanciful old-looking wares, and ended up purchasing two large wooden herms and one heavy four-paneled mashrabiya screen. The proprietor pronounced them genuine antiques, said he would crate them and meet us the next morning at the Cairo airport.

Afifi's face registered abject horror as he foresaw the trouble Susan and I weren't expecting. He accompanied the boxes to Customs, spoke impassioned Arabic to the young men in uniform, and returned to us with apprehension dripping off his usually unperturbable face. Looking deeply crestfallen, Afifi said to us, "I've done all I can do. But they're all young and don't know what they're doing."

Our group inched forward into the Customs area, jocular, everybody clasping passports, plane tickets and airport-tax-receipt exit cards (necessary to leave the country). I obligingly showed my receipt for our purchases. The young man scrutinized it a moment, shook his head and barked at an assistant to open the two big boxes. Oh, my!

The assistant very importantly inserted a knife under the lids and pried them off, tack by tack, exposing the wood carvings wrapped in cotton packing and the screen wrapped in brown paper. The Customs officer called over several associates, then asked me to open our suitcases.

SUSAN

We were pulled out of the check-in line. Way out. Officials in uniform with loosely zipped flies and red-rimmed eyes excitedly watched Bill open our bags. They went through my suitcase five times without finding the married couple demurely wrapped in dirty panties. I was shaking even though we had a certificate for the couple. The crates were torn open, and we were asked for those certificates of antiquity. We had receipts and even business cards from the bazaar shop, but no official papers.

BILL

The Customs man spoke in Arabic to our Sphinx Tours agent, who pursed his lips and shook his head. "You will have to stay here in Cairo." The clock stopped, and I was in a spotlight of disbelief.

"But . . . why?"

"If these pieces are authentic antiques, they are not allowed to leave the country without written government permission. This is a receipt, not a certificate of permission. Also it is possible, if they are antiques, that they have been stolen. This must be checked. You are involved. You must remain here until this has been investigated and the articles are checked for authenticity."

I said, "You keep the boxes."

The Customs agent shook his head. "No, that will not be possible. You are implicated. You must be cleared." He was deadly serious. (In retrospect, I believe I should have shown him a "certificate" of cash.) He continued, "Your wife will go with the group, and she may take your suitcase with her. That is all."

I gave Susan half the money I had in my pocket. The Customs man took my arm, pulled me from her, and said, "Follow me, please."

As I was led away into the harangue, the din, the Arabic cacophony that was the Cairo airport, a primitive place of stray cats and luggage wrapped in old tents, I was at the center of a tight group of uniformed Customs personnel, moving with purpose through checkpoints and barriers. Now under suspicion as a smuggler of stolen goods, I was conducted to the interrogation room, with its ancient office couch and a framed photo of Sadat. Perhaps a score of uniformed men brought the two big boxes into the room and crowded in to inspect the suspicious contents.

The Customs agent seated himself behind the desk, inserted three used carbon papers into an official document pad, and methodically filled out his report. While he was writing, another ten Customs men came into the room to peer at the screen, the wood-carved herms, and me, the perpetrator.

Customs agent number two, with a soft belly, curving mustache and generous nose, began performing an intricate task. First he took four lengths of electrical wire and wound them around each other, so that he had one double strand eight feet long. Then he produced an ancient hot plate and brushed off the dust. He bit the green rubber tips off one end of his newly made wire and (lovingly) attached the wire to the trivet coils. Next he fished the parts of a male plug out of his pocket and fitted them together. He connected the plug to the other end of his wire, rested the trivet on two bricks on the floor, and inserted the plug into a wall outlet. The coil turned red.

Nobody spoke to me. I observed three lean cockroaches zigzagging the floor near my feet.

The month before, Susan and I had seen the movie *Midnight Express*, which is based on a true story about a guy named Billy Hayes, who had been kept in a Turkish prison for nearly ten years. I began to think about movie rights to my own story.

Customs agent number two opened a filing-cabinet drawer and took out a length of string, which he wrapped around the boxes, and meticulously snipped off the leftover ends. He then took out a few pieces of some hard red substance, put them into an empty 7-Up can, and set the can onto the trivet. When the inner substance began to steam, he took the can and approached the wrapped-and-tied boxes. He poured the hot wax onto the knot of string, licked a metal doodad on his key ring and pressed it into the soft, hot, viscous red liquid.

At last I realized what he'd been doing. He was securing the wrapped boxes with sealing wax.

The Sphinx Tours agent arrived, bringing Susan with him. Her plane had been delayed, so they allowed her to come sit with me for a brief time. My stomach was knotted, my shoulders hunched, and my toes flexed in my shoes. It was unnerving to realize that these authorities were going to keep my passport, ticket and exit card until I was "cleared."

A tall, slender man in a green uniform entered. He sported glasses and a thin black mustache. He was with the tourist police. He told me, in Arabic, translated by the Sphinx Tours agent, that I was in luck, that the antiquities expert had been sent for and would be coming to check the items soon. Then he interrogated me, through the translator, writing down what I assumed were my answers. Finally appearing satisfied with his report, he asked me if I had anything further to say.

Through the interpreter, I made an impassioned statement: "For my wife and me, this trip to Egypt has been a life's dream. Our object in buying these items was not to rob Egypt of any of its treasures, but to have some pieces of art that represented the beauty of the country so we could always remember this dream we'd shared."

The tourist policeman, fixing me with a steely look, said, "That had nothing to do with it," and left.

My passport, plane ticket and exit card were then locked inside a cabinet.

Still another man arrived, tall, vigorous, handsome. This was tourist police chief Hamada, obviously the most important man of the more than thirty who had thus far been involved in my case.

Chief Hamada studied all the reports on the desk, then studied me. Appraising Susan, he offered her a cigarette. She was so distraught she *took* the cigarette and lit up, looking at me out of the sides of her eyes. I think she was doing Bette Davis.

The Sphinx Tours agent told Susan it was time for her to leave. I gave her the house keys, we kissed and said comforting good-bye phrases. Away she went to catch her plane and be consoled by our more fortunate travel companions, who might have lost only a watch.

Chief Hamada, followed by two soldiers armed with rifles (bayonets attached), had me brought from the Customs cubicle to his own office. Speaking in a cultured English, he began to question me in a totally different manner. "Where are you from? Do you have children? Do you live in a house? Ah, you have grandchildren? And what do you do for a living? You are paid to perform?" He ordered tea for me, and we talked.

He said, "I'm sorry for what has happened. I hope the objects in question are fakes. That way you will be free to go immediately. Oh, by the way, the antiquities expert had to go look into another crime before this one, so he won't be here for a few hours. If the articles are proved to be antiques, the seller from the Khan el-Khalili will be put in prison. And you . . . Well, it would be better for you if they are reproductions."

I asked to go to the toilet, and had to be accompanied every step by one of the armed guards. He even stood next to me at the old marble urinal. I was given a carton of food: two boiled eggs, cheese, dry cake. Time dragged on.

Six p.m. The tourist policeman unlocked the cabinet containing my passport and papers, then motioned me to follow him and the soldiers to a storage room. Twelve men were gathered around a makeshift table. Night had fallen.

A police officer sat at the head of a long table. My papers were delivered to him. Chief Hamada arrived, introduced the antiquities expert to me, and motioned to the police officer to proceed.

Five soldiers carried my boxes in and put one up on the table under the low-hanging pool-room light. They all inspected the seal, broke it and opened the box containing the mashrabiya screen. They pulled back the brown paper. The expert looked closely for no more than five seconds, chuckled, looked at me as if I was a stupid idiot, and said to me in English, "Forgery. What you pay?"

"Three hundred fifty pounds."

"Worth fifty," he snorted, and gestured for the other box. Same procedure. All five soldiers inspected the seal, watched it being broken, undid the lid with a crowbar, removed cotton to reveal the herms, and took one out. The expert looked at them for five seconds. Again he laughed and said, "Reproduction. How much?"

"Seven hundred pounds."

He shook his head. "Hundred fifty. No more. Do you like ancient Egyptian art?" I nodded. Pointing at the boxes, he said, "How do you like modern Egyptian art?" When I said nothing, he laughed at his own joke, lit a cigarette and signaled to Hamada that he was finished.

The policeman picked up my passport, plane ticket and exit card and presented them to me with some ceremony. "You are free to go. Boxes will be released to Sphinx Tours agent tomorrow before flight."

Hamada nodded his head and said, "Mr. Hayes, congratulations!" He left the room.

I stepped out of the storage room, clutching my passport, drenched in sweat. The Sphinx Tours agent said, "Be here tomorrow morning by eight o'clock, so we have plenty of time to get your boxes and arrange the flight. Oh, by the way, if you want to give the antiquities expert baksheesh, I could get it to him personally without anybody knowing."

With a little suspicion crossing my mind, I said, "Sorry, I don't have any more money."

He put me in a cab to the Mena House Hotel, where we had been staying. No rooms. Abba Eben walked by me with several men in suits. I considered asking him to use his eloquent, persuasive powers to get me a room, but didn't. Instead I convinced the man on the desk to call around and find me a hotel. He got me a cheap room on Pyramid Street in Giza.

It was a loud, low-class disco hotel all lit up with garish neon signs. I rented a room for twenty pounds, and was beginning to feel pinched in my wallet.

I figured out the time difference and asked the desk to put in a call to Susan in London, where the group was about to arrive to spend the night. The man shook his head, said no phone call possible, but they would try to get a radio call through. Around two a.m., the operator called me, said the London hotel was on the line—via radio—and I had thirty seconds to leave a message. "Tell Mrs. Hayes I called. Everything is fine. I'm on my way home." I thanked the operator.

"Don't forget to settle your bill before leaving," she snapped.

I went back to sleep, serenaded by the disco music blaring up through the floorboards. At three a.m., the disco music stopped. At four a.m., local poultry started to cock-a-doodle-doo. Breakfasting in the coffee shop, I gave three Lomotils to a man whose wife was upstairs "in great pain." I cabbed to the airport—in traffic choked with oxcarts, loaded-down donkeys, bicycles and pedestrians carrying goods on their heads.

The Sphinx Tours agent, not receiving any baksheesh from me, had written me off. I tried to phone his office—more than a hundred times—but the call never went through. I was getting frantic. I had no boxes and no reservation.

At eleven thirty, I looked for Chief Hamada's office. He greeted me with a warm handshake and asked me how things were going. I explained my sad story. He smiled and asked, "When is your flight?"

"One fifty."

"Don't worry, Mr. Hayes. You will be on that plane. Won't you sit down and have some tea with me?"

We sat together in his office, had a glass of sweet tea, and proceeded to have the most marvelous chat. We talked about jobs and families and differing traditions. He said he would love to visit the United States, but because he was an officer it was probably impossible.

One hour later Chief Hamada conducted me (ever accompanied by two of his rifle-and-bayonet soldiers) to the British Airways ticket counter, showed them my passport and ticket and *ordered* them to put me on the flight. Then he *ordered* the British Air luggage master to make sure my two big boxes were on that flight or the flight would not be allowed to take off. He roused the assistant minister of tourism out of her office and *ordered* her to arrange for the release of my boxes, then left.

The assistant minister of tourism was not pleased. It seems I had broken too many laws: (1) It was against the law to pay for something with traveler's checks; (2) it was against the law to take anything costing over a thousand pounds out of the country; and (3) there was no such thing as a credit card, so I must be lying about the whole transaction. She explained to me I'd have to stay in Cairo a few more days to clear up the whole matter.

Starting to hyperventilate, I shouted, "No! I have to be at work on *Days of our Lives* in Los Angeles Monday morning, and I am going on the one fifty flight—today!" Out of the corner of my eye I saw one of Hamada's soldiers do a leaping about-face and run off toward the chief's office.

Ms. Tourism and all her associates were nodding and agreeing with each other in Arabic, when Hamada strode into the room. "What is the delay?"

"It was an illegal purchase because Mr. Hayes paid with traveler's checks."

He drew closer to her. "That is the way they do it in *his* country! He was not aware of the law in *our* country!"

"It was also illegal because the items cost more than a thousand pounds."

He got closer to her face. "But his *wife* was here! There were *two* of them!"

"And we don't believe him about the credit card."

He was now three inches from her nose. "If the store owner accepted it, then he must know something you do not!"

Hamada gave the lady minister of tourism the signed release and sent her and me across the courtyard and up the fire-escape-type steps to the Official Customs Store Room, followed by two of Hamada's soldiers. The release was addressed to a man named Ahmed. Ahmed was not there. Three of his assistants were there, but they were not authorized to let any item out of that storeroom. Only Ahmed could do that.

Suddenly I heard a roar from below in the courtyard. Hamada had two more of his soldiers and the British Airways luggage master in tow, and he was ordering them to go upstairs, into the storeroom, and bring the two boxes down to him—*now*! The three men came flying up the stairs, past the assistants, and into the inner sanctum of the storage room. Ahmed's assistants screamed at them in Arabic, but Hamada's men reemerged from the inner room, lumbered with my heavy boxes, and bumped down the staircase.

Back in the courtyard Hamada ordered the soldiers to tie the boxes shut and affix my luggage tags. Then they picked up the crates and jogged off toward the plane. Hamada grabbed me by the wrist and started off at a fast clip. Time: one forty p.m.

We flew past all the checkpoints and bayonet-armed guards, with the minister of tourism clacking after us in her high heels, straight to the check-in counter, where they gave me my boarding pass. Hamada took me again by the wrist and off we flew, zipping through metal detectors, the waiting rooms, Customs, Passport, and Emigration. People gaped.

At one forty-six, we arrived at the boarding gate. Hamada finally released my wrist and smiled at me, as if to say, "Wasn't that fun?" The tourism minister clacked up, her face wreathed in wonderment.

Hamada beamed at me. "I said you would make the flight. And do not worry, your boxes will make the plane, too." Then he took my hand and said, "The antiquities expert told you those wood carvings are not worth much. Do not believe him. They are beautiful." I nodded. Then he gave my hand a smart shake, clicked his heels, and said, "Good-bye, Mr. Hayes."

SUSAN

While Bill was having these cultural encounters, I was in another time zone, wearing his overcoat and hat in a fit of longing and fear for him. I got through Customs at LAX, I paid the cabdriver at the door of our empty house, and I immediately called my mother.

She was home entertaining Frank Pacelli that night, the wonderfully creative director from *Days*. They came over immediately, laughing and asking about our trip. I was making tea when Frank said in passing, "Where is Bill?" I took cruel delight in blurting out, "I don't know!"

This was on Saturday. On Monday, Doug and Julie were due in Salem for work. I then called our producer, Al Rabin, to ruin his weekend. Sunday evening found me back at LAX hanging out at the international arrival gate on the off chance I could collect my husband there. Sure enough, Bill came swinging into sight, with a five o'clock shadow and the effing crates. I kissed him hard and wept. Driving home, he studied his lines. The next day we received a floral tribute at work from Al. The card read, "Greetings, Sahib. Welcome back from up the river."

FEZ

The old fake herms now hang on the dining room wall beside the table that sank in the harbor, above the handwoven rug Bill bought in India the day I was so sick with fever. But I'll move on.

In our garden there's a gurgling fountain, an anniversary gift from Mother to remind us of all our trips to Spain. We once spent a glorious night in the Granada *parador*. Around midnight we slipped out into the gardens of the Alhambra to make secret love under the roses and the moon. Close to the fountain is a table we had commissioned in Fez, Morocco. It, too, was a heavy purchase.

The Kasbah of Fez, the old inner city, is a world-heritage sight closed to auto traffic. We were there in 2001, with the donkeys and the sweet-meat vendors on another tour. At lunch that day we dined in a gorgeous restaurant tiled to the twenty-foot ceilings in turquoise-green and gold. After piles of couscous were set out, tribal musicians danced in, beating their drums, blowing their pipes, and whacking away on Moroccan noisemakers. The belly dancer, who had been yawning over an upper balcony waiting for her cue, twirled in and did the obligatory bumps and camel walks. She was listless at best. Yet to me the musicians sounded wild and magical, the light from the candles on the tiles was kaleidoscoping a rainbow in the air. The rose petals in the central fountain were so glamorous, I just had to rise into that dreamscape and dance. So I did, high on life and mint tea.

Coming down from the experience, with my mouth full of rose-flavored Turkish delight, I asked Bill if we could order an inlaid table from the tile factory we'd visited that morning. Like Herod, he could deny his dancing Salome nothing, and I went off with the guide to seal a deal by the city gate. Bill took a nap.

Stygian smoke rolled out of those factories, produced by the burning olive pits used to stoke the kilns that bake the rich enamel tile colors. I asked for a pattern featuring the Star of Abraham, eight-pointed, done in the emerald green of Islam. "How much?" I asked.

"Ordinarily five hundred dollars, but for you four hundred dollars. . . . Of course, for that there is a tip."

"How much is this tip?"

"One hundred dollars." The reasoning charmed me. The salesman wrote up a $400 invoice and made a date to meet me in our hotel parking lot later to receive his "tip." It all seemed straightforward. The guide was wearing pointy yellow slippers, and the four-star Fez toilets had rose petals floating in them. I was clearly not in Kansas.

On the way out I remembered to ask, "How much to ship?"

"Oh, you pay COD, it's practically nothing."

Two months later the package arrived at the LAX Air Freight Terminal. The charges to ship? From Morocco, by air? A tile table set in concrete? Five hundred dollars!

QUEEN OF ADELAIDE

The largest souvenir we ever brought home was a live woman. Our first trip to Australia was courtesy of a *TV Guide*–style magazine called *TV Week*. *Days* was very popular beneath the Southern Cross. Doug and Julie were mentioned in *Crocodile Dundee* like family.

The Aussie sense of populism is strong. There the viewers reward their favorite artists directly with an object called the Logie. It's like an Emmy from the fans, and gets its awful name from the gentleman who invented the television tube. Without a Television Academy middleman to make things stuffy, it's a mighty popularity contest, run by the magazine, with a big breezy broadcast, too. Hayes and Hayes were presenters at these Logie Awards a few times. Our pay this first trip was the journey itself, and a chance to be flown all over the country as guests of *TV Week*.

We were on our way to Ayres Rock, that huge monolith in the red center, now known by its Aboriginal name, Uluru. It was mouse season at this Gibraltar of the desert. There are two seasons there . . . mouse and fly. Mouse is the more pleasant.

The biggest Logie winner in Australia is Anne Wills, with nineteen accolades as most popular female. Nobody has ever won more. She was queen of television in Adelaide, the southern coastal city. Our flight went through Adelaide, so Anne asked if we could spare a few minutes for an interview while the plane refueled. Of course we could. That morning, Anne let it slip to her viewers that she was scheduled to meet us and where.

Australia has a small population for its size, and real crowds in the smaller cities are uncommon. We peeked out the plane window on landing in Adelaide to behold a scene on the tarmac that can only be described as a melee. Thousands of people were pressing against the chain-link fence by the gate to get at us. We hesitated at the top of the Quantas flight steps. Roses were flying over the chain link. Excited *Days* fans with dozens of toy koala bears were chanting our names. An airport official, mumbling about compromised security, tried to hustle us through the mob. I saw several boomerangs raised in greeting and thousands of grabbing hands reaching out to shake ours. We had never caused such a stir on the streets of Burbank.

We met a very embarrassed and animated Anne in the VIP lounge, where the noise level from the crowd outside was so loud we couldn't record a thing. Willsy is half Polynesian, half Aussie, and all personal magnetism. Her huge eyes, like black spangles, were dancing with fun at the unholy uproar she had caused. Strangely, I knew immediately this mischievous woman was going to be the greatest treasure we could find in Australia. We did the interview later, on our way back to Sydney, and planned how she and her husband, Michael, might lead a tour of Australian fans to California and the NBC Studios.

Six months later 140 housewives, carrying quarts of Australian champagne to give the cast, stood on the Salem stage and were once again delirious, but silently this time because we were taping. Then their buses parked by our brown and spotty lawn while we knocked them senseless with bowls of Fish House Punch served in our backyard. It was the strongest recipe for a group libation I could find. The Aussies as a group may not really be so crazy for shrimps on the "barbie," but they do love to drink.

Then, tragically, Michael crashed in his small plane and Anne became a widow. We asked her to come to America as soon as she could get away, to stay in our guesthouse for as long as she liked. It was a terrible time for Anne, but she could talk, and cry, and be out of the spotlight. We learned about her childhood on the Gilbert Islands, where she grew up speaking English and Pidgin. "Willsy, in Pidgin, how do you say 'piano'?"

"Him white teeth, him black teeth. You hit him, he cry out." She told us about the flock of sheep she had mistakenly purchased for investment and how they all had foot rot. We shopped, we cooked, we put on makeup together and became closer and closer. This lady was as famous as it gets back home, but in our house she was "little petal," the name she gave her dear ones. It all went so perfectly, she's never really left us alone since. Another husband has come and gone; she's masterfully interviewed every celebrity in the business on her show, including Kevin Costner and Robin Williams; and she's covered the Oscars live for Aussie TV for the last twenty-five years, bunking down the hall in our guest room each time.

"Tell us another Pidgin word. How about 'helicopter'?"

"Him mix-master goes up in sky like Jesus Christ!"

In the spring of 2004, *Days* sent me a script in which Julie showed travel photos to her little cousin Will and talked about all the journeys she and Doug had taken together. The stage directions for the scene said "ACTORS WILL SUPPLY PIX." So I filled a brown paper bag with pictures and went to see Steve Wyman, the *Days* producer, in his office, to select what might be usable.

While Steve talked on the phone, I drew out a dozen treasured pictures and set them gently faceup in their frames on his long mahogany conference table. The call ended, and Steve joined me. He saw Bill and me together in color at the Acropolis, Great Zimbabwe, the Taj Mahal, the Louvre, Evita's grave in Buenos Aires, the Temple of Heaven in China, and on the white deck of a cruise ship sailing to Antarctica. There was a moment of silence in the dark green room as he looked at each one. Then my boss, who has devoted over twenty years to *Days*, said, with a smidgen of envy in his gentle brown eyes, "What a wonderful life you two have had." How true.

18

Fans

SUSAN

SPOTTED WITH LEMONADE

"Are you Susan Seaforth Hayes?" My entire legal name hung on the lips of this strange woman, drinking a lemonade.

"Uh, yes," I replied.

"Oh, good, I thought I was hallucinating. I just got released from the hospital and they gave me some pretty heavy drugs. Well, have a nice day."

I was sitting in a food court in Stockton, California, chewing my way across a slice of pizza, when the lady with the withdrawal symptoms collapsed onto the stool opposite me and opened the conversation. Bill was up the aisle exploring his ice cream options.

We had coasted downhill to Stockton from Macalume Hill in the Sierra gold country, where the radiator of our old Mercedes had blown up. An antiques dealer who ran the only business in that remote ghost town had sold us an empty Sparkletts water bottle, with instructions to keep filling the busted radiator every mile or so. By topping the Sparkletts container with tap water and staying on a downhill trajectory, we tapped our way out of the mountains and into the only Mercedes repair shop in those parts. We had five hours to kill while the car was getting patched up, so we decided to catch *Top Gun* at the nearby Cineplex. We were on a USA road trip: no plans, no plots, no makeup, just Willie Nelson on the tape deck and an Auto Club map for guidance.

BILL

DEAD RINGER

Our driving trips are the best. Even if we have radiator trouble. They don't come often enough for me. At home, the list of things to do never gets shorter for either of us, but when we're driving someplace the list of things we *can* do is short indeed. Now and then we may get a cellphone call, but basically we're just jollying along on our own.

"There's a pretty farmhouse."

"Look at the beautiful horse!"

"Did I see a Cracker Barrel sign?"

Life is an adventure in the car. Always has been.

When I used to spend summer weeks with Grandma Mitchell, one of her pleasures was just to go for a ride in the car. She'd broken broncos but never learned to drive a "machine." So Aunt Nellie or Aunt Vera would take us for a wander through the Fox River Valley, out west of Chicago. Oh, I'd give anything if I could take the three of them for a spin today.

Not only do Susan and I get to talk to each other—not always possible amid the hustle and fuss at the studio—we get to meet friends of Doug and Julie. City folks are not as apt to say "Hello," but country cousins wouldn't think of passing up an opportunity to catch up on Salem news.

One time, I wish Susan had been with me. I was on a drive through West Virginia with my cousin Bob Smith. Bob was showing me places where our ancestors had lived generations ago and, mid-afternoon, we stopped at a roadside diner for a stretch and a piece of pie. We perched on stools, the only two customers in the place. The bustling lady behind the counter laid the tall lemon meringue wedges in front of us and said, "You know something? You are a dead ringer for Doug Williams on *Days of our Lives*."

Cousin Bob nodded his head and said, "That's him."

The waitress said, "No, no. But he sure is a dead ringer for Doug."

The next time she walked by, Bob said, "That's really him."

"Don't fool with me."

"I'm not fooling. He is Doug."

She laughed. "I know he's not, but he sure . . ." And walked away.

Fifteen minutes later, as we were leaving, she was still shaking her head, saying, "Yep, dead ringer."

Cousin Bob chuckled about it all the way home. Some months later he gave me a surprise gift. He'd gone to the glass factory and bought a delicate tall dinner bell, the kind you ring to let the kitchen help know they can clear the dishes. And, wouldn't you know? He'd had the little ringer removed from inside the bell. So his gift to me was . . . a *dead ringer!*

SUSAN

If we're together, even under the humbling circumstances of standing in line at a Burger King, somebody usually spots us. Perhaps 10 percent of the viewers who know us speak to us, and usually positively. Bill and I enjoy these greetings. *Days of our Lives* has been a key to unlock doors into people's hearts, and we step through them, immediate friends. This is a great bonus and a precious part of our public life. Assuming 50 percent of the public doesn't say hello, but just makes eye contact, it's wise to behave decently wherever you are. Unconventional behavior, if charming, is okay, even expected of a celebrity, but boorishness is unforgettable. Making a scene gets reported, too, among all the friends of the actual witnesses, and such stories beg for embellishment: "She threw her what?" So you risk being remembered badly forever by a slew of people who weren't even there. To avoid showing up in somebody's family folklore . . . be nice. Then there's the vast majority of Americans, who don't know us and don't care, God bless 'em. Yet, after so long on an old favorite show like *Days of our Lives,* Bill and I assume we are never really alone.

That lemonade lady in Stockton was unusual because she didn't ask, "And what's going to happen next?" Chalk that up to her being sedated. In her right mind she would have pumped me for plot twists. Sometimes the fan, who is so excited to see you in an unexpected place

(Home Depot?), and inquisitive as a bee, is a dear sweet lady, a lot like your grandmother, so you want to tell her something to make her day. "Stay tuned, a big surprise is coming up," we hedge. Well, there are surprises between commercials every day on the air. Soap opera actors only know a few days' worth of story more than the fans. Even with the Internet chat rooms going night and day, more rumors than facts get out. The writer and producers know the real scoop. If actors knew, they'd babble, so ignorance is us.

A generation ago, when Patricia Barry was playing my mother Addie on *Days*, she opened a script one day to discover her character had contracted leukemia. Nobody had warned her this was coming. She was married to Doug, and carrying a change-of-life baby around Salem. Probably the most popular character on *Days* that season, she wanted to forestall the terminal moment, so she called up Irv Kupcinet, the well-known columnist for the *Chicago Tribune* and a personal friend, to tell all and cry on his shoulder.

Now the mastermind head writer Bill Bell was more cunning than a serpent. After Patricia's news broke nationwide, he put Addie into remission. She delivered Doug's little baby girl (named Hope, for the actress's inner feelings, I suspect), bounced into motherhood, went out for a walk with the baby carriage and got hit by a car. Blindsided by a drunk driver—and Bell. Doug's heart was broken, Julie was in a position to make a new play for him, and Bell had struck a blow against drunks behind the wheel. Moral: the writer always wins.

To be a recognized soap opera actor in this country is not to be a celebrity like a movie star or a basketball god. Nobody bows and carries on, bearing bouquets or seating you pronto at Cracker Barrel. Folks treat you like family. Not all families are happy, right? Stars in film appear for a few hours a year on-screen, acting beautifully and looking amazing. Soapers are on-screen for months in an average year, acting their brains out and looking . . . familiar. We're the old shoes of show business. "I grew up with you, so here's my opinion," says a devoted fan. "You should lose weight." The longer they know you, the less mystique you can muster. For example . . .

Hayes and Hayes are driving again, this time through the home state of President Jefferson and Suzanne Rogers, Virginia. It's for lovers, the guidebooks say. Early one evening it commenced to rain as we stepped out of our rental car to refresh ourselves at a local diner in Low Gap. Slam went the driver's door, slam went the passenger door, and instantly we realized the car's lights were on, the motor was running and we were locked out.

Parked about five feet from the diner's front door, our lights are high-beaming through every window, and heads turn to stare at Doug and Julie banging on their locked car. The Low Gap eatery has a phone, but no kindly Auto Club office, no sireee. No locksmith either. The nearest was in Bluefield, in the next county. We cooled our heels and waited damply for his arrival while several folks sauntered up to whisper, "I know who you are!"

Rural darkness had fallen by the time our door was opened, and the gas tank was reading empty, so we put in at the closest motel. The storm had kicked up to a gale. When the travel clock was reading one a.m., a commotion began in the parking lot outside. We heard laughter, steps approaching, and a loud *rap-rap-rapping* on our door. "Come on out, we know you're in there." "Yeah, we watch you ever' dang day. You better come out!"

More pounding on the paper-thin door, the age and sex of the speakers impossible to guess. We stayed put in the dark. "Is this the right room?" "Yeah, that girl at the desk said Doug and Julie were in 106."

Bill and I couldn't believe it. It was dark and cold and pouring outside. The threats through the door became more specific, and no less enthusiastic, so we rang up the manager, who finally got the fans to go home. "Well, kiss my grits!" was their parting shot.

The locksmith from Bluefield had been our undoing. He told his wife, who told her sister, who told her daughter that some *Days* cast was actually sleeping nearby, and plainly they wanted to make sure it was true.

STORMY WEATHER

Lena Horne presented the most life-affirming, sexy, stylish and powerful one-woman show on Broadway I had ever seen.

Most onstage theatrics with music have the same general message: life is to be lived, make the most of it! Audiences feel lifted for a few hours, then get back down to their own very untheatrical, nonlyrical lives. Miss Horne's show came from a deeper place, where talent and beauty had not been fittingly rewarded because of the old American racial taboos. That was her personal story, but she had risen, really risen, above it. She embraced the audience with wisdom and ardor, as if to say in spirit, "Bad things happen but you can still be yourself and not surrender to despair."

Bill wanted to go backstage to say hello. I was hesitant to take the bloom off the perfect entertainment moment, but followed him into her dressing room. She greeted us with more than the usual performer's warmth. Lena Horne was a real *Days* fan and knew all about Doug and Julie. The exquisite woman reached down and embraced me. I felt the uplifting reassurance that comes when you get a flash of heaven through a stranger's eyes. "Oh, Miss Horne," I breathed against her shoulder, "if Brenda Benet could have seen you she would have wanted to live." Which, in my heart, I believed, and still do. Brenda's death was recent, and Lena, the fan, felt the loss. She hugged me tighter in jasmine-scented arms. We were in that moment each other's fans, united in the real opera of life.

HOPI SPRINGS ETERNAL

"Everyone gets to pick a tribe and present a written report," announced dear Miss Emerick, my white-haired second-grade teacher. She was the daughter of missionaries and had grown up in India, so she knew people made great topics. Mother dug up some old issues of *Arizona Highways* with wonderful pictures, and we quickly zeroed in on the Hopi to be my Indian tribe of choice. Thus began my lifelong admiration for that nation of Native Americans. A peaceful history, a spiritual outlook, and an isolated location atop Arizona mesas had helped preserve much of their traditional Pueblo lifeways, but by the time Hayes and Hayes visited, even these extraordinary people had become soap opera fans.

After the hit-and-run sheep incident, I'd been wary of another drive through Indian Country. In the 1980s a motel was built on Second

Mesa for tourists as a tribal enterprise, so we booked it for one night. The Four Corners road trip we planned was still taking shape when a letter arrived from Bonnie Secakuku, a Hopi girl, saying she had noticed our reservation for the reservation and would we care to stay an extra day for some escorted touring?

NBC was the only television network reaching "The Nations" at that time, and Doug and Julie turned out to be as popular as canned tuna. People even watched *Days* in Walpi, the oldest continuously inhabited village in North America. Walpi is a rocky, desert outpost that was established in the twelfth century. Electricity is on-again, off-again out there, and sometimes a TV was juiced up off the family pickup truck.

Bonnie Secakuku had four sisters. Kim, the quiet and most beautiful one, had been on the cover of *National Geographic*. "The Hopi are matriarchal," their handsome father, Ferrell, explained to us. He had a college degree in urban studies (of all things), and in later years would become tribal chairman. He also was a member of the Snake Clan and, in kiva ceremonies, danced with rattlers. On our daylong tour we drove up and down all three mesas, laughed and joked, met folks in the midst of their daily activities, and even stirred up corn pudding. In every direction the red and golden Hopi lands, "the center of the universe," stretched below the spring-fed mesas. Hopi belief says their origin is in the Grand Canyon. These days the tribe is short on material goods, but fabulously wealthy in human connections and a rich ceremonial tradition.

Smiles and open doors greeted us in every village, because the whole tribe recognized Doug and Julie. The Hopis certainly didn't need soap opera characters to identify with. Each person has family, clan and tribe identity that goes back to the creation of this world. We were dazzled, yet the people seemed as pleased to meet us as we were to meet them.

We watched the moon rise with the whole Secakuku family in Polacca after a great dinner of, you guessed it, sheep stew and corn on the cob. "Want to see a Kachina dance tomorrow?" God, yes! Ferrell loaded us into his truck at sunup the next morning. This was to be a religious event that blessed the watchers as well as the dancers, who had spent the night before in the kiva, purging themselves and preparing to take on the spirits they represent in the dance. Ferrell drove like mad up to First Mesa, parked, then hurried us up a ladder leaning against a wall to the roof of a mud-brick building. We peered down on the village plaza. Forty Kachinas were dancing in the pearly dawn while the whole tribal community of hundreds surrounded them in a great circle. A wonderful sound, like nothing we had ever heard, filled the sharp clear air. It was the deep, chanting voices, amplified by the painted wooden masks of the Corn Boy dancers. Blue spruce boughs had been woven into thick collars for every neck; red body paint, ankle bells, white kilts and deerskin boots disguised the identically dressed men. We probably had met many of them the day before. Here was my report for Miss Emerick at last, in the splendor of Technicolor and wraparound sound.

Who says there's no mystery in life? Bill and I had climbed up a ladder into the spirit world of ancient America.

MAIL

Fan mail can be categorized thus:

"Please send me a photo immediately, at your own expense."

"Please send me a photo immediately, at my expense, envelope enclosed."

"Send our organization a piece of clothing to raffle off at our next fund-raiser."

"Write me your life story, starting with your favorite color."

A form letter requesting friendship and devotion based on intimate interaction, and sent to the entire cast.

Praise.

Blame.

Birthday cards.

That about covers it. Then, when the moon is blue, a letter of understanding, sensitivity and humor turns up in your mail slot. The kind of letter you want to answer from the kind of person you want to meet.

Twenty-odd years ago, intriguing letters started arriving from Akron, Ohio, and signed by a Brother Raphael. They were copious and clever and mentioned keeping Hayes and Hayes in his prayers. A telethon appearance took us to Akron eventually, and we called up the brother from our hotel room. A refined voice answered and said, "Wait a moment, I'll summon him to the phone." A pause, then sounds of a receiver being placed on a desk, sounds of steps, and then a deep *ding-dong-dong* that had to come from a belfry. Brother Raphael turned out to be a real monk of the Order of the Annunciation of Mary. He worked in hospitals, teaching, caring for new immigrants, and praying all the time for the intentions of others. The gregarious monk said talking about *Days* was a great way to start up conversations with strangers, and he had seen how much the show meant to people whose lives were short on hope and family. He had taken his vows at eighteen, and evidently they didn't deny him television, because I'm sure he was our biggest all-time fan. We met that very day. He looked like an Italian Friar Tuck, bearing gifts of delicious home-cooked foods.

He used to laugh over the nuns of Salem, Sister Marie and her daughter Jessica, the now-and-then cloistered novice. "They didn't come out of any convent I've ever heard about." When the Hortons became so Catholic all of a sudden, in the nineties, he wrote some professional suggestions to the head writer. The response was, "Thank you for your comments, Brother, and stick to praying." He did that indeed, and, sure enough, *Days* is still on the air. When his order was working near Toledo, we paid him a visit. The next morning he was to say his first Mass as a priest. We had a sweet time, and it proved to be the last one we would have with him in this life.

Before we drove off, one of the monks suggested we should make a little detour around the cows and cornfields to see the Shrine of Our Lady of Consolation. "It's miraculous, you know." We didn't know. We are Protestants, but happily took off for Carey and a peek at the beautiful edifice.

Bill's daughter Peggy was in the deepest days of her drug use. He placed a paper with a prayer for Peggy's life in the hands of the

Madonna. It was a serious prayer, but we had begun the trip just planning to see our dear friend and fan. Our letter to the Madonna was answered. Peggy's turnaround began from that moment. So you never know what's going to happen when you answer a fan letter. Blessings may result.

TELETHONNING

Green Bay, Wisconsin, was the location of perhaps our sixth telethon for the March of Dimes. Doug and Julie were happy to fly off after work on Friday, or first thing Saturday morning . . . go on the air at six p.m. Saturday . . . work through till six p.m. Sunday, then catch the last plane to LAX and show up for work on Monday. Our break came between two and six a.m., Sunday morning, when it turns out absolutely nobody is watching, but the show must go on.

We did more than twenty of these regional shows for the March and other charities. We flew to Perth, Australia, one year, and joined in the conga line that formed every time a thousand dollars was pledged, singing, "Thank you very much for your kind donation, thank you very much for your kind donation, thank you very much for your kind donation. Thank you very very very much!" You hardly forget something like that.

After the Macy's Parade where my float broke down, we got a call to do a telethon in Abilene, Texas. Shari Lewis, the winsome puppeteer and creator of Lamb Chop, had also been in that parade, riding the Mother Goose float. From the cold and sleet she developed an ear infection so severe she couldn't do her usual appearance for the West Texas Rehabilitation Center, and she recommended us as replacements. Twenty-nine years later we are still making the trip each January to that windswept old cattle town, where the people are the salt of the earth and treat us like family. It's a wowie of a show and, thanks to those Texans, I can say I've appeared on the same bill with the Dixie Chicks, the Judds and even Ricky Scaggs.

Telethons are old-time TV's gift to charity. They work when folks are trapped at home in bad weather and turn on the set. January and

February usually guarantee miserable snow somewhere, so add travel dangers and delays to the package. Bill would bring his music charts and hope the local musicians could handle them.

In Albany (pronounced al*BAN*ee), Georgia, the bandleader looked at one arrangement and said to Bill, "Three flats, don't tell me. Don't tell me . . . that's the key of E, right? Why don't you folks come down to the lounge and catch our act? Do you know 'Jelly Roll Rag'? We play that one real good."

In San Jose, California, an accordionist had been hired to play piano and sat sidesaddle at the keyboard to get his bearings. In Possum Trot, Mississippi, the local producer had hired a man with a rubber left hand to accompany us. His bass notes were few but steady. Or the blind pianist who made beautiful music but, of course, could not see our charts. Sometimes around one a.m., Bill would imitate a trumpet while I belted out "Hard Hearted Hannah." Those were the towns where we didn't get asked back.

In Green Bay, things were better organized, and between making pitches, singing, introducing local clog dancers and telling fans who called in that even for a ten-dollar pledge we could not give away the plot of *Days*, a lovely young mother and her daughter appeared in my line of sight. They wanted to say something to me, so we stepped out of the lights and away from the nearly musical band.

"I want to thank you, Julie. Remember when your face was so burned and you were afraid to have skin grafts? Afraid of the pain and that the grafts wouldn't work? My little girl had been burned, too, and when she saw that Julie got her courage up for the operations, my girl did, too. 'If Julie can do it, so can I.'"

As her mother told her story, the pretty little girl nodded and smiled shyly at me, her eyes all round with excitement. "I'm so glad I helped. And everything's okay again?" I asked.

"Yes, okay. And we just wanted to say thank you." I had to sit down and collect myself for a while. When you're doing a story line in the studio it's just a story. You have no idea if it is actually touching people's lives. You would be lucky in a lifetime's career to point to such a moment. That was mine. I took the credit because the mother wanted to give it to me, the visiting telethon hostess and familiar actress from her soap, but I was just the conduit for change when her child needed it. What power *Days* had to do good. These are the experiences that lead you to take soap operas seriously.

BILL

HOPE IN FARGO

Trying to bring hope to cerebral palsy victims in the winter of 1978–79, we went on the air at six p.m. Saturday, to begin a twenty-four-hour telethon.

Do not think Jerry's Kids, with multiple hosts reading pitches off teleprompters, interspersed with Elvis impersonators and tuxedoed performers singing with Vegas bands, thousands of volunteers writing up pledges in the millions. No, sir! Think Fargo, North Dakota, population 75,000, on one concerned local TV station.

They had built us a pretty little set and hired a pianist who could read music. Susan and I were flown in to be cohosts. But we also were—along with the local talent—to perform all the numbers we could, announce totals, interview patients and their families, and come up with endless pitches off the tops of our heads.

Minutes crept by. We had a small bank of telephones with local celebrities and volunteers, and when the phones didn't ring, we tried to whip up our TV audience to make that call. Twenty-four hours can be a long time to fill, and Susan and I began to whisper to each other the hours we had left to go. "The magic number is twenty-two!"

Some good folks called in, giving pledges. Others came by in person to dump cans of nickels, dimes and quarters, stacks of dollar bills, and personal checks into the big playpen. The pledge total inched up: $3,000, $5,000, $7,000, finally $10,000.

Then, while twelve cute little tap-dancers in gold-spangled leotards were doing their thing, the producer excitedly came to us and said, "Bob Hope has been watching the show and he says he'll be over in a little while to help."

We said, "Are you kidding? Bob Hope?" We thought it was somebody's cruel joke.

"Well, that's what he said."

Half an hour later, Susan and I were in the middle of our "Those Were the Days of Our Lives" piece of special material, when a red plaid sport coat walked past the camera and waved at us. We finished our number and, a bit nonplussed, rushed over to the main set to welcome him. It really was Bob Hope, ski nose and all.

He was in Fargo to do a concert at North Dakota State University on Sunday afternoon. Because of threatening weather he'd flown in on Saturday, had a bite of supper and turned on the TV, to see us pitching away. He'd found out where we were and came—at no pay, I might add—to see if he could help.

He immediately turned to the camera and did a pitch, and then said, "Anybody who pledges fifty dollars, I'll talk to them on the phone." And the phones began to ring. So, over he went to the phone bank, joshing and making small talk, urging callers to increase their pledges. He stayed on the phones for nearly two hours.

At the eleven p.m. station break he said, "I've got to go, kids. But after my concert tomorrow, I'll be back."

We pitched, we did our last scheduled interviews, Susan wrapped her pink boa around her shoulders and knocked out "Hard Hearted Hannah." Just before midnight I crooned "It Amazes Me," and then our pianist went home for the night. The next couple of hours we sat at the piano and sang songs of the "Shine On, Harvest Moon" and "For Me and My Gal" vintage. Sunday morning, a blue-robed choir from a nearby church was sardined onto the set and sang two peppy anthems.

Finally the magic number wore down to four. We were wearing down, too, but constantly bucking each other up. I did "I Remember You" and Susan did her dramatic reading of Anne Boleyn's last letter to Henry VIII. Our total climbed over $30,000.

And at four p.m., darned if that red plaid sport coat didn't come charging back into the studio, full of ginger from the reception at the university. We welcomed Hope back, he did a beautiful pitch, and then he said, "Anybody who calls in a pledge of twenty dollars, I'll talk to them." And, while I interviewed two youthful parents of a palsied child,

Bob Hope took Susan aside and said, "Susan, I love the way you put your soul into your work. You are a gutsy performer!"

During our final hours the total climbed steadily. We had alerted our producer that we had a plane to catch at seven, and that after we wrapped the telethon, we'd have to leave immediately for the airport.

Just as we were saying our good-byes, Bob Hope thanked us for the job we had done and then said to the camera, "Friends, we're going off the air now, but I'm going to stay here and answer the phones as long as you call in. I don't care how much you pledge. It's important!"

I shook his hand and said, "Thanks, Bob." Susan gave him a hug and a kiss, and he liked that, I could tell. Then we skedaddled. We put on our coats and walked out into a blinding blizzard that the North Dakota folks seemed to think was quite normal.

You never know.

SUSAN

THE ACTOR AND THE AUDIENCE

A new nurse popped her head through the door and told me it would be just a few minutes more before the doctor arrived. Once my medical questions had been settled, our conversation rambled. The slender, serious girl admitted to being a *Days* fan for many years. Then, unexpectedly, the nurse described a reunion scene Bill and I had played many thousands of episodes ago.

Doug and Julie were unhappily wed to other spouses, then thrown together by circumstances (a storm) in a picturesque setting (the Hessian Inn). The background of the scene doesn't matter much. The point was that two lovers, whose paths divided in the woods of mistake and mischance, come together for one night of passion and regret on a four-poster bed. The next morning the characters' muddle remains, but the audience has been between the sheets with them and shares all the sweet pain of a stolen moment that may never come again. Sex is the centerpiece, but the real theme is longing, expressed, fulfilled and returning.

This type of scene is the heart of soap and is constantly repeated with every cast on every show many times a year.

The girl in the doctor's office had never forgotten what Doug and Julie were feeling that day at the Hessian Inn. It was as vivid in memory to her as to me. I'd been on the set and received the kiss that sank me to the pillows, while she had been in front of a TV set watching, but that kiss was hers, too. Our connection was so clear, time had not dimmed the moment in her mind. What a gift she gave me. To meet a viewer who so keenly felt something that I had been a part of was a big reward.

Sometimes actors will say, shaking their heads, "I've worked in show business forty years and the two years I spent on [fill in any daytime drama] is what people still remember me for." Yes, exactly, buddy, and aren't you glad?

Time changes the executive guard on daytime dramas, and often writers who worked hard on other shows and never knew you before are now driving the cart your character is sitting in. So year by year your character is written over, written out, then written back in. For an actor it's a mistake to turn back and say, "That used to be me. Why can't I be that person again?" New characters get in the front seats, and your agent and friends advise you you're lucky to have a ticket to ride at all. Well-adjusted actors face forward with a smile and don't try to grab for the reins. Bill and I are adjusted. Time and temperament have left us "happy to be anywhere," as George Burns used to say.

My chance meeting with that nurse in the twenty-first century was life-affirming for me. It's wonderful to be remembered, like a song that makes you cry. Who cares where today's writers may take you? Who cares about appearances, ratings, plots or even pensions, when someone can prove that one day you did something so good in front of a camera that it hasn't been forgotten? For an actor, that stranger's recollection is your pride and your glory.

The soap opera viewer tunes in to have something to remember. This dynamic is quite apart from sitting on a sofa, passively receiving entertainment. Today plots are fast and furious, fabulous and fun. But it's still the moment when eyes lock and the soul opens that audiences

wait for. "The soap opera moment," Drake Hogestyn calls it, and, after twenty years of *Days*, he well knows. The moment may be silent or
scripted in a ream of dialogue. It's the revelation of life and is just as
much a work of art as Vermeer's *Girl with a Pearl Earring*. Quite similar, in fact.

Part Four

19

Behind Closed Doors

SUSAN

Loving couples on daytime soaps stay loving through tidal waves of natural disasters, villainous kidnappings, or the schemes of cunning little vixens trying to pull them apart. Drama in these relationships is inflicted from the outside.

Just stand back and regard Bo and Hope Brady, the hyperactive romantics of *Days*, still passionately in love yet constantly separated through no fault of their own. Bo gets preyed upon . . . Hope goes to search for him. Hope gets corralled in a hostage scenario . . . Bo goes to free her in the nick of time. When in danger, Bo reacts with immediate action, "pow right in the kisser" moments. Hope gets her blood up when thwarted and always takes too big a risk. These high-energy traits lead to endless drama.

Troubled couples in soaps are classically mis-mated, so things have to go awry. *Days'* well-meaning Lucas loves Sami the incorrigible. She doesn't grow older and wiser (if she did, where would the conflict be?). He gets hurt, perplexed and pushed around, but pines for her nonetheless. Sometimes Sami feels like a nut, sometimes she don't. Drama blossoms from her flawed seed and everybody suffers. It's a bad relationship that makes good television.

Would you truly want to be married to a Bo, a Hope, or a Sami? Maybe not, but viewers crave the emotional adventure of being near them. "What next?" Fans must shake despairing heads and groan across the wide airwaves, then press the ON button again.

In real American marriages it seems to me more danger comes from the dynamic interaction between husband and wife than from the villain plotting in his penthouse or the nympho stalking in the shrubbery. Genuine trials and tribulations are often made in our own hearts. And that's exactly where they must be arbitrated.

BILL

We have been married thirty years, so it's pretty well established that Susan and I get along. Most of our working life has been with each other—in the studio on *Days of our Lives*, onstage in theatrical productions, at the podium on shipboard, when we've done our enrichment lectures for Crystal Cruises. We plan dream trips and make many of them come true. We've seen memorable musicals and straight plays on Broadway and in London's West End theaters. You might say our life has been work-together-all-day and play-together-all-night.

So, the question arises: With all that being together, what disagreements have we experienced?

We come from starkly different backgrounds. I grew up near windy, gray Chicago, son of a Midwestern book salesman; Susan grew up in la-la-land, with its bougainvillea and the blue Pacific, daughter of a professional actress.

The day we married Susan was thirty-one, I was forty-nine. The age difference has never been a problem to us, but it does mean we grew up in different eras. I'm a product of the Great Depression, FDR and World War II; Susan grew up in the age of television with Eisenhower, Korea and the Kennedys.

We were molded differently and baked in different kilns. And on October 12, 1974, in our living room, when we said our I dos, we gave each other wedding gifts of traditions from our separate families and notions about how things ought to be done.

For one thing, Susan, who grew up with her mother and grandmother, surrounded by the outsiders in their rooming house, flourishes best in small groups. I grew up with two parents, two brothers, and dozens of grandparents, aunts, uncles and cousins, and feel perfectly at home with people crowded around a dinner table, massing in the kitchen, stepping over babies and card games on the floor. Susan always pleads for smaller groups. I instinctively plan large groups, and we do the best we can to accommodate each other's feelings.

The telephone is often an instrument of estrangement in our house. When the phone rings, Susan automatically does not want to answer. If it's for her and I say, "Yes, she's right here," she'll give me a remonstrative look meaning I should have known better.

Another way we differ comes from our psychological makeup. Example: Suppose somebody spills some ink. Susan is driven to say, though the person is already embarrassed and chagrined, "You spilled that ink!" I'm the opposite. I must find a positive, if at all possible. I might say, "Hey, it matches the color of the carpet!" So people think I'm a smiling idiot and that Susan is heavy-handed.

One of Susan's cute little traits that has me flummoxed is her preference for beauty over function. It's more than a preference, it's an obsession. An alarm clock in the bedroom is so unsightly it must be hidden behind a drape. The book I'm currently reading at bedtime *and* the glasses I use to read it must be stowed away in a cabinet. A telephone, that hideous object, is such an eyesore it must reside behind the vase of fresh-cut flowers.

I'm a saver, Susan is a thrower-outer. This sometimes causes disagreement. I certainly don't care if she wants to throw out something that is hers, but I reserve the right to keep what I want and throw out what I don't. Her inclination is to quickly toss unimportant mail, even mine. I prefer to decide for myself which mail is junky enough to be dumped. If we have any chocolate items in the house that sit for a couple of weeks, I need to hide them protectively or they'll be gone—into the garbage. Imagine: good chocolate! "It was beginning to look a little stale." Hmph.

I suppose what we disagree most about is my room (office). I keep more things in my room than I have space for, resulting in (the appearance of) serious clutter, which is perfectly fine with me. It's my room. Having to sit amid my clutter, however, is unnerving to sweetie pie. And when I see her casting her eyes about and biting her lips, I need to distract her with any odd item I can come up with. It's not easy to distract Susan, and sometimes I have to just lay it on the line to her: "Forget it, my love, don't even go there." My room has probably cost Susan many nights of sleep. I figure that's her problem.

SUSAN

My darling's office is indeed his private world, his sanctuary, because there is no room on the floor for a visitor to stand or space on the carpet for a chair to sit.

The shelves built to the ceiling are filled with books, guides, scripts, papers, music and photos. The walls are covered with eight-by-tens, a gold record, a paper rose, an American flag, paintings, photos of his barbershop quartet through the years, posters and pictures of the family.

The counters are piled three feet high with folders, albums, envelopes, awards, mementos, pens, bookends, copy machines, fax machines, frames, the computer, a water glass and small carry-on luggage. The desk is usually stacked two to three feet high as well with calendars, tickets, outgoing mail, incoming mail, lists of who called, receipts, yellow legal pads covered in bold handwriting, a phone, a pencil cup from Colonial Williamsburg in the form of a leather tankard, and—when he's taking a shower—his watch.

The floor cannot be seen because it's also stacked with trunks, a boom box, old fan mail, a forty-quart garbage can filled with small change and pennies, arrangements for thirty-piece orchestras, batteries, a box of tap shoes, 78RPM records, full five-gallon water bottles, empty five-gallon water bottles, Christmas gifts to be wrapped for next year, paintings that are not on the wall, genealogy texts, and a baseball bat in case of an intruder.

The afternoon sun pours over his computer while the rotating ceiling fan swishes slowly, so as not to set all the loose papers flying. He puts in hours there, so concentrated he forgets to open a window, have a glass of water or complain that dinner is late.

For Bill things are only as significant as the people connected with them. He loves his father's piano and his grandmother's copper teapot because he loved the lives that touched them. He's given me the rest of our home to dust or do whatever with. If I complain something's gotten in the way, a high-power reading lamp, say, he sweeps it into his office, smiling. "I'll put it away." It's not exactly away, but it's out of my way. He thinks I long to see those counters clear, the desktop clean, but no. I'm happy he has one place to spread his life around and be so happy all to himself. I have missed seeing the floor for ten years though.

BILL

Hair. Now there's a nondivisive topic, you say? Wrong! To me hair is a small potato, but to Susan it is big medicine. I combed my hair (the wet look, pompadour, slicked back) pretty much the same way from high school all the way into the late 1960s. Then I finally stopped using Vaseline Hair Tonic or Vitalis, let my hair become windblown and untethered, one nice result of the release from tradition of the sixties. When I joined the cast of *Days of our Lives*, Doug was a romantic rogue, and his hair always reflected that quality. But, in 1982, when Brian Frons became the new NBC head of daytime, the writing style on our show abruptly changed. Doug was no longer a free-spirited romantic, and his clothes have been coming off the conservative rack ever since.

Doug's hairstyle has been a point of conversation for Susan and me. And, since there is a short distance between Doug and the actor who portrays him, my own hairstyle has likewise come under scrutiny. To Susan, if my hair is not coiffed a certain way, if I don't make a real attempt to blow, fluff and swirl it just the right way, she believes I don't love her. (Sigh)

When I point out to her that others in my general age group— Newman, Eastwood, Connery, et al.—don't have theirs blown and fluffed, I'm talking to myself. To Susan your hair is your glory. Of course, now that I'm in my seventies I also have to deal with thinning hair, and glory is even more of a challenge.

SUSAN

Yes, Bill's hair is often on my mind because it is fine, wavy, and shines in the darkest room like a halo of platinum. My own hair is limp and dull and has never created comment beyond "What are we going to do with it?" Just being around Bill's hair gives me a lift. And speaking of grooming, have you ever noticed the ears of men over sixty? They begin to sprout hair. Now why would a wife let her husband walk around growing caterpillars of hair in his ears? Have these wives looked at their spouses for so long they no longer see them? Can't they spare the time for a little snip and pluck? Remember, "Esau was a hairy man." Well, my Bill is "a smooth man."

BILL

I've had to slow down my speed dramatically going up or down stairs. Susan's attack on everything else in life is quick-right-now-with-alacrity. But stairs are enigmatic obstacles to her. She and her mother trudged millions of stairs in their home in downtown Los Angeles—three floors plus basement—but Susan approaches every flight of stairs, up or down, as a consternation, if not a mystery. Each step must be studied and mastered individually. "Slowly" is the watchword.

SUSAN

Bill has probably never fallen on a stairway. I have. Back at 1353 I used to hurtle up and hurtle down. At Christmastime the ten-foot tree stood by the stairwell of our foyer, dripping with pre–World War II tinsel and fat colored lights. Every year some poor soul, distracted by the Tannenbaum and just trying to get to the first floor, would miss a step and crash bumbity-bump to the bottom. Stairs can trick you. Now that I wear industrial-strength bifocals, I can't just trust my eyes to show me where the steps are, so I feel for them with my feet. I'm cautious. Not slow, cautious.

When our Carrie and her husband, Greg, joined us for a week in Venice, Greg was intrigued that I kept falling up the steps of canal bridges. As it turned out I was using a three-pound telephoto lens on my camera, which kept coming unlocked and plopping out like an elephant's erection. The jerk of this phenomenon pulled me off balance and onto my knees. Today I have a new telephoto lens, small but powerful. My darling husband always grabs my elbow on the stairs now just in case. I love it.

BILL

We came to each other with scars from earlier entanglements. I was burned by Mary, Susan by Hal. We both learned how dismal life can be if feelings are disregarded by a partner. We know the importance of being allowed to have our own opinions, lifestyle, modus operandi. So we came to respect each other's different ways. Still do.

Perhaps the strongest differences stem from the simple fact that Susan is one hundred percent female and I am one hundred percent not. Like the heroine in every screenplay, Susan needs to have the words "I love you" spoken out loud, and, like every guy down the block, I've read the sports section every day since I was thirteen.

We have learned to keep lines of communication open. The lines of communication between me and Mary were out of service the last half of our marriage, and Susan's and my verbal prenup stressed the ongoing need for keeping those lines open.

Combine communication with truth and you have the basis of a relationship. If Susan does something that bothers me, we're actually both relieved if I bring it up and clear the air. And the reverse is true, of course. It may be unpleasant for the moment, but that blows away quickly. It's like keeping our eyes on the bigger picture. And what a wonderful feeling it is to have nothing festering in the craw!

A quiet, sincere apology is good salve for an interior wound. And what does "I'm sorry" cost? A little face, a little pride. Small price. I suppose we've apologized mostly for speaking curtly to each other. When Susan gets upset she starts speaking in negatives that have absolutely nothing to do with the question at hand. They're not related at all. When she comes out with, "Gas is very expensive and, besides, it's probably going to rain, and I didn't get to the cleaners today," in response to my asking her if she wants a banana, I know something is bothering her. And when she's tired she'll snap off a negative in a sharp, unpleasant way. Me, I'm like a mirror. My retort will come back in the same rude tone of voice. Then we're both hurt, and it takes a moment to realize neither of us meant for that to happen. We simmer a few minutes and then say, "I'm sorry, honey. I didn't mean that the way it sounded."

I know there will always be disagreements and differences between us. But that's no big thing. If our relationship is based on the right consideration and courteous treatment of each other, that *is* the big thing. As a long-married old Texan once told us, "You can be right . . . or you can be happy."

SUSAN

A pair of married friends from *Days* of yore got into a belittling battle in a Japanese restaurant one night. A party of six, including Hayes and Hayes, were out with them for a raw-fish nibble and a few laughs. Whatever was so bothersome about the wife, the husband threw down his chopsticks, chucked his wasabi and stormed out. She shrugged and ordered another eel roll. It shocked us to see tensions so unresolved that they could explode at a sushi bar. We had known and enjoyed these people for years, but a tantrum takes a toll on bystanders.

If you are in a state of marital misery, don't expect your friends to work things out on your behalf. Husband and wife must discover the core of a problem and examine it without violent, hurtful language, or the counsel of unlicensed and embarrassed friends who don't belong in the middle of the fight.

Our sushi-eating pals remain married, even renewing their vows with much fanfare and frequency. They are crazy about each other, too. I try to forget having seen the underbelly of their relationship and wish I never had. All's well that ends well. They may have just given up fish.

My own marriage to Bill has led me to develop some guidelines: If you get your own way, be grateful and say thank you. Never assume things are going according to God's infinite plan and that that plan mirrors your own. Your mate has made you the huge gift of cooperation, perhaps at some cost to what they wanted. Be aware and show it.

Stay in communication about the money, especially when there isn't any. Cash is never petty. What is his is yours, but visa versa, and that includes Visa. A delightful friend amazed me when I was redecorating her tiny home on the Malibu beach. We were on a peewee budget, and I hesitantly suggested buying a nifty screen, which she loved, for the bedroom. She said, "I'll just take some money out of my secret account, Ed will never know."

"Secret?" I said.

"Sure, most wives have accounts like that." News to me. I wonder how she got around her canny husband, who worked with the Rand Corporation think tank. (Maybe think tanks aren't all that deep.) But I digress. . . .

In our marriage we discuss exactly how we will use every check that flies over the transom or dribbles down the mail chute. I try to do this with material goods as well. "Honey, I would like to send these books to my friend Nancy in North Carolina, if that's okay?" I learned at the git-go not to give away our "stuff" without checking with Bill first.

Just because a box has been untouched for years and covered with dust doesn't mean it's not important anymore. Sometimes mementos are so precious you can't stand to look at them at all, because they remind you of the times they represent or the people you loved, now gone forever. Develop a touch of tenderness for each other's treasures.

BILL

WHAT CAN I DO FOR YOU?

One thing Susan does nearly every day that pretty much precludes disagreement is to say, "What can I do for you today?" When young people get married, I tell them to say that phrase to their new spouse every day. Not "What can you do for me?" but "What can I do for you?" Even if there is never anything to do! That's in the same league of importance as morning and nightly kisses.

Every once in a while you hear the old saw "Marriage is just plain hard work!" I don't buy that at all. Cultivating a crop is hard work. Parenting an autistic child is hard work. Coal mining is hard work. Marriage is just a mind-set that's different from when you're single. And maybe the hard work is the difficulty people have in changing the first-person pronouns from singular to plural. Changing I to we and mine to ours is a jolt to the system. After spending one's entire life being self-centered—through infancy, childhood, adolescence and young adulthood—grasping the concept of cooperation, consideration and sacrifice is life-changing. So, I guess "Marriage is hard work" actually translates to "It's hard to make that change."

I'm sure I was not considerate enough of the needs of Mary, the mother of my five. That fault probably contributed to the downfall of our relationship. There's no way I can change history, but I don't care to repeat the mistake with Susan. I hope I consider her needs every day and adjust my behavior accordingly. That's why "What can I do for you today?" is such an apt reminder. And if both partners are aiming to make the other's life better, they have a chance of making their marriage a happy, fulfilling experience.

SUSAN

Honor your darling's memories and life passages, even the ones you missed. Bill had lived a hell of a full life before I even met him. There are murals in his mind to recollect that I'll never know a thing about. But I can choose not to be jealous of the past, or be afraid of it, or be bored by it. If you respect your spouse today, respect his yesterdays. This includes the friends from ages ago, the old buddies who are so different from the person you love. They may not fit easily into the life you have together today, but make them welcome anyway. Old friends are a diminishing resource; don't waste a single one with neglect. Bill loves other people besides me. That's great. The more love in our personal universe the better.

BILL

Out of a hundred married couples, how many do you suppose have bedroom disagreements? My guess is the number is very high, probably over 50 percent. Fortunately, Susan and I have always been in the happy minority that gets along in the marital bed. Frosting on the wedding cake. And I love our morning and nightly rituals of hugs and kisses. Embraces to start and finish the day are good for the heart and soul. While I'm on the subject, in over thirty years Susan has never given me a cold kiss. Not one. And it's warm kisses that make life worthwhile.

SUSAN

That morning kiss from my darling sets a positive tone for my day, right through to the last embrace in the pillows each night. In between will be all the projects, distractions and people that make up most of a modern life. Whatever happens, at least we start and finish knowing our love is still in action, making us better and stronger than we would be alone. I say "I love you, Bill" every time he leaves my side, and he hears it, too. I just don't want to lose a single opportunity to tell him this life of ours is good. We may skirmish and scrap in any other part of the house, but battle in the bedroom? Never. For Hayes and Hayes each night has ended with the *yes* of love. We recommend it.

20

To Learn, Perchance to Think

SUSAN

"How do you learn all those lines?" people ask.

"How do we learn anything?" I ask myself. My learning Armegeddon took place in the second grade. Magnolia Avenue School was a mighty wooden building, two stories high, from the 1920s. Great purple jacaranda trees bloomed on the grounds, and ladies of the old school made up the teaching staff. At home I was used to banter and participation with adults, the only folks around. At school my verbal brightness was taken for endless sass, and one morning I got sent to the principal's office after not only putting down the class lumpkin but smacking him over the head with my workbook. With great sternness and sensitivity the principal, Miss Haskell, gave me an IQ test. It seemed I was clever but had no social skills and just refused to learn with my peers.

I was sent off to another area of Los Angeles to be enrolled in an "Opportunity Room," where all the bright and bewildering kids plowed through grades one through six together. Each day my grandmother drove me 174 blocks to and from this experiment in education at 87th Street School. The teaching was led by Miss Frances Emerick, who believed in inspiration. "Don't worry, one day she'll just pop," the loving and visionary woman would say.

How I longed to "just pop" into reading, writing and long division. I saw it work for some kids, but I'd stand at the board, chalk in hand, watching the little geniuses around me whip up and down columns of

figures two feet high, while I thoughtfully sucked my thumb and considered how many ways you could divide three. I shone at performance,
though, standing before the same roomful of tolerant misfits, singing in
a language of my own to tunes of my own composing. You could call it
speaking in tongues, if you are so inclined. I was certainly in the spirit.
We could all do pretty much as we pleased—draw pictures of dinosaurs,
chat about the good old Paleolithic days, or stage a class production of
Cinderella one afternoon for the hell of it. We were not cursed with a
planned curriculum. At last I was at ease in school, and not the strangest
person in the room by a long shot. But I had lost all ability to read and
write.

EXPOSED

This became startlingly clear the day I auditioned for the premiere of
Father Knows Best on radio. For auditions, Mother would always go over
the scenes out loud with me. While looking at the confusing symbols
on the script pages, I'd listen as if my life depended on it, and with one
hearing I'd remember what I was supposed to say. After "reading down"
dozens of eight-year-old actresses, I was about to be cast when my
mother's conscience kicked in and she whispered to the casting director
that actually my reading was poor.

"Nonsense, she's been reading all day."

"Try her on a new scene, something she's never seen before," Mother
suggested, well knowing that live radio meant spur-of-the-moment cuts
and changes and that my illiteracy could ruin a broadcast. Of course I
didn't know "cat" without coaching, and Mother and I were shown the
door.

That day Mother and Grammie gave up on modern education and
put me back with the real-world kids at Magnolia Avenue. Thank goodness. My canny third-grade teacher, Miss Trench, who wore her hair in
a crown of braids and let me follow her around the school yard at recess
like a puppy, taught me to read in about nine weeks by treating me like
a person and dropping me in the middle, not the bottom, of her class.
Oh, how I wanted to please her. I made such an effort that Miss Haskell,
still the principal, awarded me a Good Citizen badge.

Public schools were pretty tough in inner-city Los Angeles in the 1950s, or at least my family thought so. I should have stayed there and developed a thicker skin, but when middle school loomed, the ladies of 1353 found an affordable alternative.

ACADEMIC AT LAST

Hollywood Academy was a converted auto mechanic's garage on Western Avenue, smack in the middle of the small-business district. For twenty-five dollars a month you could enjoy half-day sessions and a full California curriculum. I doubt it was accredited. Dr. Strayer, a pixie-faced music teacher from Duke University in North Carolina, taught everything. He was the headmaster and there was no other. The student body numbered about twelve. Everybody had a story or a strange reason for being there, and who cared?

Dr. Strayer's method stressed individual "recitation." You sat slumped over your thick *History of Civilization*, starting at eight thirty every morning, pondering the same subject for four straight hours. Three times a day you got called up to Strayer's big square desk to discuss your readings with the wily old prof. "If Germany had come into nationhood earlier, would Bismarck have been less aggressive?" Talking to someone about what we were reading made us fearless at discussion and adept at organizing our thoughts. At recess we ran aimlessly around the asphalt yard and watched the Hollywood traffic through the fence. We sang from old songbooks and even painted with watercolors for an hour on Thursdays. These were the Mickey Mouse Club years, and sometimes we girls wore our ears to school. Best of all, it was over by one o'clock.

Dr. Strayer was a fussy gentleman who lived alone with his mother and may or may not have been light in his loafers. He certainly favored the boys, but even with points off for bad behavior I rose to the top of our funny little class. I loved him for expecting so much of us. He was always warning us that the future would be hard "when the baby days are over and no one will put up with your crap!" I believed him. Thus flew by six years behind a chain-link fence, seated against a set of Encyclopaedia Britannica, plotting how to get Jimmy Roebuck to give me my first kiss. Senior year I bought a used blue-and-white De Soto for six hundred dollars, from my acting earnings, and revved up for college on the cheap. Jimmy obliged me with a soulful lip-lock behind the stage curtains at the Christmas play and, wow, I was ready for higher education.

TOWARD THE HIGHER MIND

Los Angeles City College, a local junior college where the fees were twelve dollars a unit, was known for its excellent Theater Arts department. I enrolled as a TA major my freshman semester. Freshmen didn't get to perform, of course. They learned voice production, sewing and all manner of backstage slavey jobs. This was appropriate but boring, to me especially since I was having such a great time taking English and history classes.

A pivotal moment came when Jerry Blunt, the head of the Theater Arts department, personally interviewed me and verbally trashed my previous professional life as an actress. He accused me of being qualified only to sell toothpaste and incapable of acting at all unless I abandoned my Screen Actors Guild and Equity cards to become a full-time student. (This, without ever having seen me act.) I rushed home to share this upsetting Blunt evaluation. Mother got quite stirred up by my version of the meeting, and together we decided I should quit the department and change my major. Mr. Blunt never missed me. Instead of toothpaste, I immediately got a commercial for Mr. Clean.

This was my sixteenth year, and at LACC I met another product of an all-female household, my lifetime friend Barbara Wesson. She was a luscious African-American girl, just my age, trying her acting wings, too. We swapped stories of our experiences with men and art, just dripping with juicy details. She's a nationally known artist today, and I've always admired her power to invent herself and create an exciting life, because she wanted one. It took me decades to catch on that it was up to me to do the same for myself.

"DA DOCTAH"

Learning requires devotion to a goal as well as delight in study. I know this is true from watching Bill Hayes get his doctorate. In 1990, Bill was deep in the study and research of his family history, set off by a visit to nineteenth-century grave sites while we were working nearby at the West Virginia Public Theater. It seemed Lewis County was jammed with his kin, who had never left the old family stomping grounds. The director of the theater, Ron Iannone, was a curriculum adviser at West Virginia University, and he urged Bill to combine his enthusiastic research on his relatives with some practical education courses. The pedagogue's seduction set my husband on a path that took eight years to finish.

Bill became immersed in education theories for years, taking classes at UCLA and West Virginia University, while working at his usual musical, paternal, theatrical life. It was a whole new world, but he aced it all. Once the credits had piled up it was time for the dissertation. His proposals were refused six times by his committee. On Bill's seventh trip to the post they finally let him run. Two years of research and writing followed, then a triumphant defense of his dissertation to that same committee, and at last my sweetie was going to graduate a Doctor of Education.

The dissertation was written in scholarly, obfuscating language, but I'll let him boil it down for you.

BILL

FAMILY HISTORY

My (390-page) dissertation has an impressive ten-word title: *Family History Study Units in Secondary Schools: Their Educational Impact*, but the premise and what I set out to prove is very simple.

The study of family history is a crackerjack educator's tool—such a good one, in fact, it should be made a regular part of our nation's K–12 curriculum.

Imagine I'm a sophomore in high school today and my assignment is to write a five-page paper on someone over seventy, preferably a member of my own family.

I'm an average student and have never written a five-page paper on anything. But, since I've chosen to write about my grandpa, whom I adore, I think I'm actually going to enjoy this project. He's sixty years older than me and I know nothing about his life before 1995.

I make a date with Grandpa to interview him, and borrow my dad's little tape recorder. (I am self-motivated.) I ask my teacher what sort of things I might ask Grandpa. (I learn how to interview.) When I meet with Grandpa, I find out about World War II, when people were rationed on meat, sugar and gasoline, and no cars were being built, and nobody had television or computers. I am fascinated to learn that Grandpa's older brothers volunteered for service, one in the Army, one in the Navy. I didn't know anything about them before. I turn the tape over and find out about what TV was like in the fifties and sixties, about Civil Rights marches and the assassination of President Kennedy. (By making it all personal, I am learning a lot of nonfamily history.)

Grandpa asks me if I'd like to go to a ball game with him, and I say yes. (It brings generations together.)

I play the tape over and over and write down what Grandpa said. I have a lot more than five pages of material already. But I'm eager for more. (Joy of study.) Next I interview my aunt. She gives me some cool snapshots of when Grandpa was young and tells me when and where he was born. I can use that to start my paper. (Research skills.) Now I have to choose what to actually put in my paper. (I learn to organize.)

I get on the computer and write my paper, which is easier than I expected. I put down when and where Grandpa was born and what it was like during World War II. I make maps and indicate where Grandpa's brothers were in the war. I scan in the maps and snapshots. (History, geography, time line.) My aunt was so nice and cooperative, I take some of my own snapshots to show her. (Sense of family.) She and Grandpa both make me promise to make them a copy of my paper, and when other family members hear about it, they each want one, too. (Valuable family document.)

My paper turns out to be twenty-seven pages long! I put it on a disk so I can make a copy for whoever wants one. It makes me feel important that people want a copy of something I've written. (Self-awareness, self-esteem.) I get an A on my project, am very proud of it, and will keep the paper all my life. (Humanizes history, promotes self-motivated study, makes me a better all-around student.)

Sound far-fetched? No, that's the way it happens. I have dozens of actual reports on similar grandparent interviews. I've read the papers, full of excitement and pride.

In order to write my dissertation I studied two such projects at the Carolina Friends School in Durham. The assignments were challenging, the kids got inspired and produced sensational documents. Stepchildren and adopted children, studying whatever family was closest to them, found that the procedure gave them a new—more complete—sense of identity.

As to reenrolling in school at age sixty-five, I recommend it for everybody. I was introduced to a whole new library of authors. My studies forced me to think, analyze, and express opinions on many new topics. All good for the gray matter.

The repeated denial of my dissertation proposals was frustrating. I kept rewriting the proposal without changing my premise. Finally, one member of my doctoral committee said, "Bill, you can't just write an idea. You must prove your premise with research." Oh! It finally clicked in my head, and I knew what I had to do.

I wish auditioning for a job in a show was that easy. There you rarely get a second chance, let alone seven. Usually the disheartening comment is, "No, we're looking for a six-foot-two baritone who can sing Sanskrit while performing tricks on a skateboard."

SUSAN

In spring of 1998, with sons Tom and Bill beside me, I watched a handsome white-haired figure march with a class of three thousand into the athletic stadium of West Virginia University to the one-hundred-piece college orchestra's rendition of Aaron Copland's "Fanfare for the Common Man." Did we cheer? Did we cry? 'Deed we did! There was my darling, robed as a scholar. Not a costume, but the garment of merit he had earned fair and square.

When we visited England a few days later, our beloved friend Fred Shaughnessy (the writer of *Upstairs, Downstairs*) took pictures of Bill at Oxford to capture his scholastic glory at that ancient seat of learning.

My husband was the only person in sight wearing a mortarboard, and several tourists from Argentina snapped his photo, too. "We thought all the scholars would dress like that," they said and giggled. No, only my dear one. Barbara Wesson always calls him "da doctah" now. Mother commissioned a portrait of him in his robes that gazes wisely over our dining room table this very night. I admire my husband so: he learns, he thinks, he finishes what he starts. Boffo, socko, SRO.

Oh, yes, how do actors learn lines? Here's what I do. I visualize the page of a script. I repeat and repeat the dialogue in my head at all different times of day, and when I'm sure I know it I ask some human of generous character to run the damn things aloud. In short, drill till you drop, so you can relax when the time for performance comes. Alas, Dr. Strayer, they don't give prizes for recitation anymore.

21

Days of Soap and Glory

SUSAN

ONSTAGE

On the bottom of tomorrow's shooting schedule, which arrives by fax, is an asterisked message: "Note: There are three pages of items." An item is a scene, and the dreaded three pages means there are going to be more scenes to accomplish than usual. An average figure would be thirty-six, but the *Days* gang can knock down sixty-six in a working day, and often does.

This means "on your toes" is a permanent position for everybody. We have seen soap operas change a lot, from homespun fare to "No-Limits Productions presents." Under the reign of James Reilly, our head writer and producer, a stimulating fresh challenge has been given to the cast. Everybody has lots of lines and big speeches. Needless to say, we love it.

In the rearview mirror I see Salem family gatherings and crowd scenes where dozens of actors were called but few were chosen to speak. Though welcome, your salary felt more like a tip for standing by than payment for participating.

That was then. *Days* is an actor's Olympics now. Each and every character has a script with something to say, and dialogue generally is colorful, highly actable and important to the plot. And there's so much. Soap operas used to be mocked for being shows full of pauses. Well, that's over. And no more cue cards. I gasped when I heard this piece of news. Yes, the beloved cue-card guys are no more.

Behind the cameras, but in the light, two or three trusty men would stand, holding up big white cards with the scene handwritten in bold print. Before tape, as your nose got powdered, you could review the scene in a flash. In moments of mental meltdown a helpful finger might tap the key word you were forgetting: "Abe, I've come to see you about the, uh, uh . . . cracker." These guardians of our glibness developed strong arms and the ability to read minds. They could see the abyss of blankness opening before you fell in it. I believed the show couldn't go on without them. Again I was wrong.

It turned out everybody can memorize pages of dialogue and do an even better job without depending on the crutch of cards. We look in each other's eyes now, and the waves of excitement beam back and forth. It's more like live performance. If the first take is technically perfect, that's the one that gets printed. Knowing this, the actors pull out all the stops right away.

Getting it right the first time is what elevates soap actors head and shoulders above those fumbling folk in film, who take up hours "finding a moment." The gold-medal champion, always on her mark, set, and ready to go perfectly, is Deidre Hall, *Days'* slender, golden star. "Who do I work with Thursday? Deidre? Great, I'll be out by lunchtime, and the acting will be my best of the week."

So, picture the cast in production, keyed up and memorized. Three . . . two . . . one . . . action! We're pouring on the passion and delivering the lines at warp speed. Why so fast? Well, to get them on the air. If your pages run long, or you drop the tempo ball, you'll be cut. If you falter over that favorite speech you labored for three days to learn, it can get snipped down to one declarative sentence. So, in general, I follow the old rule they taught the cowboys at Warner Bros., "Wet your lips and come out acting." Lucky Kristian Alfonso, as Hope, can talk a blue streak and be tearfully tragic at the same moment.

The producers, "on the floor" or "in the booth," are ever present. They watch that clock with eagle eyes, but must make allowances for human frailty, too. When Hope was rescued from her "turret" a few years back, a big explosion was scheduled on the set, and half the cast was in the scene. Kristian could hardly wait for it, after playing cat and mouse with Stefano as her cell mate for weeks. She was happy, but the rest of us had seen stage directions in the script that described the rescuers: "The turret explodes and debris rains down, covering them all."

Steve Wyman, the producer, sensed trepidation in the ranks. Not mutiny, no sir, we'd already been through storm and fire scenes to get to this point, but those words "debris rains down" were causing worry. He called all hands on deck. We stood way back in the set while he addressed us from center stage. A wicked-looking contraption with a huge mouth was fixed high over Steve's head. "These are the stones of the turret," he explained, waving two fake rocks around. "They can't hurt you, but when the explosion comes, ladies and gentlemen, I suggest you fall to the ground and close your eyes. This is what's going to happen. . . ." *Bang*, and a cartload of crap dropped all over him. Wyman bounded to his feet. "See, I'm fine!" Well, he was. But the fine thing about it was seeing an executive put himself in an actor's place.

Another time, forty-five quarts of Technicolor blood were waiting in a bucket to drop on Thaao Penghlis, as Tony. He was in the middle of a circus set, dressed to be killed in the ringmaster's boots, cutaway coat and top hat. Thaao had a long speech before the dunking, and he rehearsed it full-out. There would be only one take and no stunt man. Just at the last moment, the special-effects coordinator whispered to Steve Wyman, "Is he going to wear that hat?"

Then on the loudspeaker, "Thaao, are you going to wear the hat?"

"Yes, I like it."

"But the weight from the blood on the hat will kill him," the coordinator hissed.

"Thaao, we really want you to lose the hat at the end of the speech."

"Oh, for God's sake, I'm trying to do the acting here."

The loudspeaker voice was cool but firm: "Lose the hat." On tape Thaao elegantly lifted the hat off his head. The bloody deluge fell. The actor dropped to his knees . . . and lived.

Every year Corday takes a cast picture to mark *Days'* place in daytime history. This is the only occasion when the whole mob is together in one room, and the moment is unique. The procedure for capturing Salemites on camera has changed through the ages. Originally, on the show's anniversary, someone just brought out a cake and a glass of champagne. After a few seasons it grew to a sheet cake, and we all cuddled around it. Then lunch—two choices of entrée—and a cake. Then the cake was dropped and it was just a picture on the set. Then a grand black-tie anniversary party at some posh hotel—and the picture. The picture finally became more important than the party and became a separate endeavor.

The publicity department runs the event. Where you stood was determined by history and plot importance. In short, rank. But, front row or back, glamour counted. The show's costumer, Richard Bloore, made the most of our natural beauties and masked our flaws forever, so it was no surprise that the crowd was always gorgeous. Putting forty-plus contract players and their egos together must have made him want to kill us all, but you'd never know it. The wardrobe crew steamed, pressed, pinned and dressed us for hours in advance, and by magic time they alone looked haggard.

One memorable year this century, Richard chose a fabulous picture frock for Julie. My place on the pecking-order chart for the photo was second row, left end. The whole team agreed a long black lace net over nude satin with a wide, low bodice, jet spangles, and a fishnet train would look just swell. The dress looked like a Marlene Dietrich costume from any of her old movies. This sold me. The train added a figure-shaping effect at my feet. Some life-threatening compression into a merry widow and, behold, the whore of Babylon.

When we got to the picture moment I realized the best laid plans of mice and character women oft times go awry. Joe Mascolo, as Stefano, was in front of me on the risers. He looked fine in his tux, but the mighty girth of Mascolo completely covered my spectacular dress. People had been getting primped for this all day, and now the snappy remarks began. At last the photographer yelled, "Quiet!" from behind the wide-angle lens. "Now, everybody, love each other," and we managed to do so for about fifty shots.

Legs numb, we carefully climbed down from the glee-club position and started to limp home. Bill and I had arrived at one p.m. for makeup, and the photo session wrapped at ten. When we saw the masterpiece later, printed on a key chain, we could just make out two little heads: Bill's pearly white and mine dishwater beige. As we hauled ass to the parking lot that night, John Aniston remarked, "I liked it better when we took the damn thing at the party, when everyone was half in the bag. It seemed more spontaneous then."

BILL

BONUS BABY

I didn't write a thank-you note at the time, but in 1983, *Days of our Lives* gave me a gift that keeps on giving. They presented this lovely girl one day and said, "Here, Bill. This is the new actress who'll be playing your daughter Hope. Her name is Kristian Alfonso."

Not only was she beautiful then, but the older she gets the prettier she gets. Not only was she an excellent actress in 1983, today she can play anything—funny, sad, dramatic, you name it—with reality and deep understanding. Not only was Kristian a person of character when she was a teenager, but twenty-two years later she has matured into a caring and thoughtful woman every bit as beautiful inside as out.

Her demeanor at work is inspiring. No matter how many tough scenes the writers throw at her, she shows up at the studio knowing her words and prepared to make every first take perfect. She comes in the door with an attitude that says, "I have a song in my heart," and she passes out smiling hellos to cast and crew alike. Kristian Alfonso is a day brightener.

I have come to love her as if she were my fourth daughter in real life. When she and I look at each other in the story, the feeling is like doing Doug-and-Julie scenes. I don't have to act that Julie is my wife, because she is. And I don't have to act that Hope is my daughter, because of the close rapport between Kristian and me.

When Doug was killed off and Hope demonstrated her affection, shock and loss, I cried. Doug was supposed to be stone dead, but if there had been less fog and more light you'd have seen the tears in my eyes.

My favorite scene between us was when Hope had a computerized chip in her brain telling her she was Princess Gina. We were all trying to help her remember her identity as Hope. As I sang to her "You Must Have Been a Beautiful Baby," and Hope began to flash back to earlier times, Kristian's face softened and her eyes blossomed with love. And, just as I sang the ending of the song, tears of happiness rolled down her cheeks.

If you're a viewer, I hope you saw that one. If you're Ken Corday, executive producer of *Days of our Lives*, please consider this a thank-you note.

SUSAN

OUR MOST INTIMATE FRIENDS

"DRESSED FOR SUCCESS" trumpets the banner line in a fan magazine each week, and below it a dozen or more soap actresses in beautiful outfits are pictured parading into galas or charity events. They look amazing. "*Days* designer Richard Bloore and I created this look together," a cast member gushes in the caption. "He is one of my dearest friends and soooo talented!"

The quote from the actress may sound phony, but I'm here to tell you she speaks truth.

When I joined the show to play Julie in 1968, William Hargate chose the clothes. He had one shopping option, The Broadway Hollywood, a nuts-and-bolts department store that customers were deserting; it would close its doors a few years later. The ebullient Hargate became our friend for life, and went on to design the entire run of *Murphy Brown*, among other great shows. But when we had him at our mercy, the budget was nil and choices were few. Frances Reid reduced him to tears one morning complaining about Alice's cloth coat. "Frances, I wish you would go down there and see what is available. I'm trying, Frances, I'm trying," he moaned.

This trait of taking an actor's desires and complaints seriously has been consistently present in the *Days* wardrobe gang all along.

They work in a cramped office, stuffed with clothes racks, trays of jewels, one mirror and the company supply of aspirin. The sign on the door reads, IF THIS DOOR IS LOCKED WE ARE FITTING. PLEASE KNOCK. So it's a place of privacy, where you can retire to have hysterics of the happy or sad kind. It is historically the intellectual center of *Days*, because our designers have been men of wit who read, traveled, saw every film, and shared their critiques. The only dictionary on the stage resides there, and gets used. Often a two-pound box of chocolates or a floral tribute sits on a desk, proof some actor was treated so beautifully a mere thank-you was not enough.

When you are behind that locked door, the atmosphere becomes very intimate. Being naked before Richard and Connie Sech (the second in command for decades) has always led me into garrulous confessions they never asked to hear but I poured out anyway.

The makeup staff also rides on the very wing edge of actors' feelings, and do their best to make the best of what we are. Working long hours with short breaks, the melancholy souls do not last. The self-starters with cheerful dispositions and a talent with the paintbrush are like perfume on the wind to me . . . proof that God just asks us to help each other. The good nature and infinite kindness of these people has kept many an actress afloat on days when scripts and schedules, struggles at home and inner demons might have stopped their personal production entirely.

Truly there is no adequate room to store *Days* at NBC. The main wardrobe department is where the tailors and alteration experts work. It looks roomy. If you take the NBC tour, you get to peek at them, clipping and fixing, through a big glass window. Upstairs over that space is a great locked storeroom where all the clothes we actually wear await, hidden under canvas sheets, the thousands of garments jammed in on racks tight enough to burst the walls. You must shove yourself down the aisle toward your character's space . . . and there hangs your career, in need of a good steam. I'll go up with Connie to try to recall the detail of a pantsuit I wore four years ago that she describes accurately. I draw a blank, but she forgets nothing. The old costumes hang in a state of cleanliness and are forbidden to leave the building with Elvis or you. The network believes the best things in life, after going out of style, go to resale.

Like the great craftsmen of centuries past, good wardrobe people carry huge inventories around in their heads, and without notes or computers put together thousands of items weekly. Then, unlike us mortals, they don't lose them. Laying out the clothes for the daily shoot starts about six thirty in the morning, with steaming and pressing, and wardrobe is the last to lock up when taping wraps. That is often after midnight. Richard stays for every scene in case a producer decides he hates a T-shirt or the stunt double rips his codpiece open. Excellence is in the details.

The clotheshorse people like Thaao Penghlis and Suzanne Rogers come in for fittings days before they work, because it's a preparation that diminishes anxiety. But most of the cast just take it for granted Richard will have something perfect waiting for them. I'm not sure that helps the staff much. Once selected, every outfit gets tailored, jewelry is supplied, and your underwear and shoes are delivered to your dressing room. Handbags and wraps are handed to you going onstage and removed thoughtfully as you leave. Real life is not like this.

From looking okay in some things, I've progressed into being a problem to fit. Those jelly rolls that hug my back and follow me out the door are troubling, and an incipient hammertoe has taken away my shoe options. Where I used to preen and pick at details in front of the mirror, now I'm happy if the fitting doesn't make us all laugh out loud. I've known Richard for over twenty-five years. The tall, talented darling is like a younger brother in a way. He knows all my secrets, but is too bored by them and too loyal to ever tell.

THE GIRLS IN THE MIRROR

Going into a beauty salon is always an eye-opener for me. Women on their own are such great talkers in the impersonal and cozy atmosphere. "The worst date I ever had" comes up a lot, or surviving-the-boyfriend stories of the "can you top this?" variety. Girls of the generations behind me will say anything out loud to a stranger. Can it be that good taste is something you find only on the food network?

Women, what do they want? Freud asked it, and the networks are mighty concerned with the answer. They stand by, ready to supply whatever it may be, if it will turn girls into loyal viewers. Corday Productions hands out free ice cream to cast and crew on Thursday afternoons of the weeks we win our demographic in the ratings. "Our demographic" is the young female, eighteen to thirty-five.

Back in the beauty salon, I sense the girls have brief attention spans, high expectations and short tempers. Something about modern life has certainly dropped a chip on their pretty tattooed shoulders. Prince Charming had better come up to the standards of Harry and William Windsor, to hear them talk. This is the potential audience we are telling stories for, acting for, and spinning dreams for. They are tougher little cookies today, but still sweet and hopeful. I know they can still fall for an actor, or a couple, and watch in a state of dreamlike content.

Some of the Salem High grads send shivers up my spine with tales of contemporary life. One afternoon our edgiest ingénue described a bar fight of two nights before that she had walked away from. It seemed her adventurous girlfriend had not been so lucky: beer was thrown and blows were exchanged. The next day the two of them drove up to the home of the punch thrower and began a fresh dispute in the street.

The beautiful little actress chattered on, snapping her gum and glossing her lips, oblivious to the quiet that had fallen over the makeup room we were all gathered in. She brings bravado to her role that comes from within. Off she flounced to nail her scenes. "What was she thinking?" we all whispered. "What if something had happened to her face?" Well, she's having a good time on her hours off, but I sincerely hope she never runs into a barfly that hates her character.

When our girlish audience gives its youthful love to newly minted actors, the young actors quickly take the adulation for granted as their due. 'Tis the old pitfall of popularity. Clever young soap actors, and there are some, get past the strutting-peacock period and into the acting.

Missy Reeves was a little beauty from New Jersey with clear green eyes and lots of hair. She's grown into a deep and spiritual actress who burns like a candle for the camera as Jennifer Horton. She enjoyed the fame and fun but gave her attention to the acting. When her matchup with Matt Ashford as Jack Deveraux was front page in the fan magazines, studio publicists booked them for extra photo layouts all over town after the workday finished in Salem. Bone weary from all the hoopla on top of heavy scripts, she'd say, "What do they think we're doing at NBC all day long, having a tea party? This is not a tea party." Reeves must have been haunted in her subconscious by missed tea parties. Now that she's a settled wife and mama she collects flowery cups and saucers. I've even added to her china cupboard from my own.

She's been in the fickle eye of the young audience, and has turned into more of a Horton devoted to family than a starlet devoted to herself. Between the story lines, the stresses, and a faith-based marriage, she's developed something of value for any woman. Inner grace.

Alison Sweeney has been playing Sami for ten years, since her start at sixteen. Obviously she wants to be a great actress and a major celebrity, too. She knows how to sing the song of self-promotion and make a loving audience shout, "Yes!"

I've watched many others, with less interest in the acting and too much in the celebrity, piss away the magnificent experience that ensemble acting can be. (A soap actor with a long run is a very demicelebrity, after all.) Each year the *Days* ensemble is spending longer hours making bigger shows, but with a schedule that compartmentalizes stories and actors. You may go for months without talking to the cast in other plots, so you miss out on the artistic exchanges and friendships that grow around rehearsal hours. For the junior cast that's a lot to miss.

The producers want things to go smoothly. They send out lots of memos. "Check with us before getting a [shudder] nose piercing," or "Your call time is not a suggestion, it's when we expect you to show up ready for work." You can tell which actors resent having their party plans intruded on by work. The last ingénue who lost her job just couldn't seem to make it in or even be reached on her cell phone. I'm always surprised. Everybody wants to be in show business. Don't they?

When just starting on *Days*, actors of any age are often shy and insecure, but some younger ones can get through a whole season ignoring the older cast completely. What concerns could a twenty-year-old have in common with a crone of Julie's age?

The crew and craftspeople, who are less self-absorbed and spend hundreds more hours a year on the big cold stages than actors do, chat with all the cast on the most intimate terms. Thank heavens. Our days would be lonely indeed without them. Behind-the-camera friends know we are in this Salem life together, but it takes years to learn that. Kids don't always see themselves in the mirror accurately, and thank goodness I don't see myself with clarity either.

For a spell there I lost all sense of real time. I walked onto these NBC stages as Julie and my inner clock stopped for years. I had make-believe adventures in the big dark studio with the same friends every day. I fell for my prince charming in Rehearsal Room 3 singing "Somebody Knows" together. When I left NBC and worked in other places, time whirled by, but back in Salem I was always Tom and Alice's grand-daughter. I'm a postmenopausal old bag now . . . but inside . . . I still feel some kind of daffy confidence because I'm a Horton girl, preserved in that perpetually-too-cold air conditioning and my own imagination.

So when the little chickies swap their outrageous stories in the beauty salon or the makeup room, I listen up and keep my mouth shut. Maybe the girls will survive their youth to become a character like me, rich in unnoticed experience. I just hope they like their work and enjoy the show . . . watching it or being on it.

Nobody asks about my private life in the olden days before my happy marriage. Who cares about ancient outrages? So I never mention the television personality I knew who loved to stand at the mirror and mas-turbate. It's old news anyway.

BILL

MY THEORY OF EVOLUTION

When Florence Henderson and I opened at New York's St. Regis Maison-ette, in 1958, we climaxed our operetta medley with "My Hero," from *The Chocolate Soldier*. In *Variety* speak, it drew big mitt.

NBC drew big mitt seven years later when they premiered *Days of our Lives*, with Dr. Tom Horton as its tent-pole character. Played by stage and film star Macdonald Carey, Dr. Tom was the prototype hero of early soaps.

Daytime serials had begun on radio in the 1930s, with fifteen-minute continuing stories, five days a week. Their audience was the housewife, chained in boredom to her washtub and ironing board. The characters were drawn from life, with plots that concerned real problems—broken dreams, illness in the family, romances with the wrong people. Villains were women with jobs and cavalier men who preyed on innocent ladies. Heroes were white-collar, wise doctors and lawyers who helped the downtrodden.

Those serial dramas, stories of and for housewives, were sponsored by soap products, then even produced by them. The nickname is still with us: "soap operas."

The writing emphasized emotional involvements. Live organ-music underscoring and naturalistic sound effects were added in the studio: footsteps, doorbells, matches striking, cup-and-saucer clinks, the sound of coffee pouring, an ice cube in a glass, thunder. Radio played to the imagination with virtuosity, holding for the gasps and sobs of the captive listener.

Soaps transitioned into television in 1952, beginning with the same fifteen-minute format. They still presented stories of housewives counseled by kindly old doctors, befriended by empathetic lawyers, and threatened by wild-card lovers (including yours truly).

So it's no surprise that the original producer, Ted Corday, created the Horton family, which included three doctors (Tom, Tommy and Bill), one attorney (Mickey), and a mother-housewife (Alice).

While the sixties and seventies transformed every fabric of our society, *Days of our Lives* hung on, doing people stories, until 1982, when we were forced to change. White-collar professionals seemed dull. Coffee chat became boring. Diagnosing ailments and pleading cases in court didn't kick up enough excitement for the younger audience.

We evolved. The staid old professions were discarded in favor of fresher, more glamorous ones: fashion design, magazine publishing. Instead of meeting at a restaurant like Doug's Place, characters hung out at the gym. Blue-collar working stiffs moved into town: enter the Brady family. To maximize the action, everyone seemed to be a cop (and/or a secret agent): Roman, Bo and Abe, Lexie, Hope and Billie, were all wearing badges. Working women and ladies' men were no longer villains. We now had *real* heavies: Alex Marshall, who was into S and M; Stephano, our very own Dr. Evil; Tony, who couldn't help being the crown prince of darkness; and Victor, the Titanically powerful crooked businessman.

Today's action films and prime-time action TV dramas are such a success that *Days* has instituted serial killings and cliff-hangers—with the cast actually hanging from cliffs. And our heroes are the hunks who can handle action. There's less call for shirts on the young studs, and the young women—a far cry from the drab housewife image—have to be gorgeous, built and active. These heroines of *Days* are strong leading ladies who personify the daydreams of our current "demographic."

Fans ask, "Why can't we have love stories like we used to?"

Well, lidded eyes over cocktails were exciting once upon a time, but our audience won't sit still long enough to watch them today. Today's love stories must be interlaced with high-speed adventures. Passion is thus heightened, putting very human stories right in the midst of de-monic possession, fake killings and real island captivity.

Jennifer, going into labor while hanging on for dear life over the chasm, was still reeling from the death of Jack and the relentless hostil-ity of her daughter Abby. Lexie deceived her husband, and Abe, with-out relinquishing his police duties, struggled for—and found—a way to forgive her, leaving their marriage stronger than before. And Bo, one of our all-out action heroes, would risk everything to save his wife, Hope, while still having feelings for Billie. When will *that* other shoe drop?

Days will always tell stories of love and heartache, but they will now be told at a pace that mirrors our current adrenaline-rush society. As Curly says in *Oklahoma!*, "Country's a-changin', got to change with it!"

So the dear old chocolate soldier, who looked so dashing in uniform but was a cipher on the battlefield, is a done deal, a relic, a memory. He's faded into the sunset, something we hope never to do.

SUSAN

Monday you have all the lines, Friday you have *three*. In daytime a star or supporting player looks just the same. These terrific actors were great friends, too.

JED

Jed Allan had a great run on *Days* as Don Craig, a Salem lawyer sexing it up with Deidre Hall, as Marlena, in her first big romantic story line. On NBC's *Santa Barbara* he was a master-of-the-universe character called CC Capwell. As of this moment he's working on *General Hospital*, playing another tower of power named Quartermaine.

Jed's silky charm is of the Rat Pack genre, a handsome guy who dresses sharp, smells really good, and always seems to get the great women. He could sing and harmonize with Bill of a morning, and it turned out they had both done automobile dealer shows as kids. We had stirring times together at work. His extraordinary wife, Toby, would crack us up at Robert Clary's dinner parties, with tales of her business, Rent-a-Yenta, an outfit that would arrange anything for anybody.

Jed's talent for comedy brought Deidre into focus as more than just a beautiful actress. He served and she volleyed until the audience realized they were the Tracy and Hepburn of daytime. Allan's enduring characteristic is self-confidence, giant even for an actor. To hear him tell it, he was born right as well as cute, which may well be the case.

On the *Days* variety-show episode of happy memory, we put Jed in a dress, playing Margaret Dumont in our Marx Brothers sketch. Jed worked up a fruity-tooty voice and looked ladylike, festooned with ropes of pearls. As Harpo, I chased him around, beeping my bicycle horn, with my eyes glued to his huge fake bust. Frances Reid played Groucho, but had refused to do any extra rehearsing of this taxing material, so her lines had a good many "uuuhhhhhs . . ." between jokes. Jed stayed imperiously in character, even when Robert Clary tap-danced by as Shirley Temple and Ken Corday pitched a wild one at his head and hit him with a rubber duck.

WESLEY

Back to Old Salem. Michael Horton was Laura's son by Bill Horton, conceived when she was married to Mickey Horton. John Clarke, who played the cuckold, got lots of fan mail explaining the situation to him, but his character lived on in ignorance. Whoever did the fathering, Mike Horton became a splendid juvenile role, played by Wesley Eure from 1974 to 1981.

Wesley is the kind of person to make a party out of a rainy afternoon. When Frances used to give her big holiday gatherings, he once brought her a tumbleweed he'd found on the highway and dressed it up as the Christmas tree. He's advised us on our nightclub act, our publicity pictures and, in 1998, urged us to organize our memories and start lecturing on soaps. An actor no more ("I'm so past that"), he's created game shows, cartoon serials, and books of jokes both tellable and utterly offensive. On our first anniversary he gave us a plant that lived for years, but our closeness outlasted it. Wesley put us together with the Crystal Cruise line, whose ships have taken us around the world, showing our tapes of "classic" television and speaking to the passengers as entertainment gurus.

I'm most grateful for one particular flourish Wesley accomplished at our dinner table. It was the last Thanksgiving Mother would spend in our home. She had survived her first bout of cancer and was in pretty fair shape. Bill and I had knocked ourselves out cleaning and cooking to make everything perfect. When we sat down to dinner, I was in my usual hostess state of slight sweat and relief to have finally dished up the dinner. Bill said a perfect grace, we "amened" and all lifted our forks, but before any guest could get the first bite across their lips Mother said, "I think we all should say what we are thankful for." Forks dropped and eyes began to well up. "My mother's life," I said. Suzanne Rogers's mom, Edna, said, "For my beautiful daughter sharing her home with me." Robert Clary was moved and serious for once. Bill's answer was loving and inclusive of all. Mom's suggestion had taken control of the table and the mood had gone from holiday happy, with stuffing and gravy, to gut-wrenching sobs in under ninety seconds, at least for me. The ball was in Wesley's court at last, and he bounced it up with a joke. Up to fun and back to life.

When I called to tell him my mother had died, he blurted out, "Oh, that wonderful brilliant crazy woman," and cried with all his heart.

SUZANNE

When we go out together faces light up, because my friend never steps out of her house without looking like an American Beauty rose. "Oh, you're Maggie Horton, I mean Suzanne Rogers, what a pleasure to meet you, and oh my, could I have an autograph?" As the sweetheart of Salem obliges, she'll nod toward me and say, "And this is Julie, you know." The excited Rogers fan will squint toward me with surprise, say, "Oh, yes, I remember you," then turn back to the main attraction, that adorable redhead.

Suzanne Rogers has been at the very pith of the Horton family on *Days* for thirty years. She's a fixture that lights up the stage. She's also a woman of powerful ability. Bill Bell created her crippled farm-girl character to entrance Mickey, then the rest of the Salem crew. She certainly made John Clarke's heart skip. He and Frances Reid, as Alice, depended on the steady hand of Suzanne to guide them through all those "family moments" of group celebration or personal crisis in the gray-green Horton living room.

We have been as close as podded peas from the start. Mother was so proud to have written the story line that made Suzanne an Emmy winner, and the belle from Virginia has always been grateful. Of all the cast she has always been the most charged up and committed to *Days*. She gets into the makeup chair before the artists who paint her have finished parking their cars. Still eager after all these years, with that whoopee curly hair and a smile on her face, she's irresistible.

When her character was murdered her heart bled inside. The remaining cast and crew felt absolutely horrible to lose her, for she had been the ruby in Corday's casting crown. Then head writer Jim Reilly told the world the mass deaths were all a trick, and the murder victims began popping out of their graves. I pictured Rogers cakewalking across the cemetery twirling two fire batons like the majorette she used to be.

Our birthdays are two days apart and we never miss a mutual congratulation at having survived another year. Maggie, her can-do character, isn't crazy, but Suzanne is, just a bit, and always ready with a bit of mischief or dripping with the latest gossip.

She married once, a handsome actor who looked very smart on her arm. I gave her a shower in our garden, and it was a happy day. The marriage didn't prove a good fit, and we all keep waiting for the right man to turn up worthy of her charms.

In Salem we attended another shower at Julie's house with much the same guest list. Only this time things began to go wrong. The set had a grand foyer with a great front door. I crossed to open it for Lanna Saunders, our Sister Marie Horton. The usually commanding actress took two steps across the set and fell flat on her ass. All the ladies in the cast whooped with laughter. The more we thought about it, the more we broke up. We were set to try another take when Suzanne gave way to an impulse and admitted, "I peed." We laughed so hard then we all wet our pants. Al Rabin stopped production entirely and talked about using the sequence for a spin-off.

THAAO

Thaao Penghlis is a lot like the French. You wonder why they are carrying on so. Then you go to Paris, see how glorious it is, and realize the French have a lot to be arrogant about. In the dark ages, when Tony DiMera, Thaao's character, was introduced, his first episode with Joe Mascolo had forty pages of dialogue, a veritable Everest of exposition. The actor was fine but frantic and stayed on the edge of breakdown for months. This nerviness, plus Thaao's beauty and talent, made Tony fascinating to watch. Sort of like Montgomery Clift, only with bigger eyes.

He was Greek and also Australian, worldly and chatty both. We both liked to have the last word, so there were little irritating clashes between us. Penghlis had already done a lot of world travel when I was just getting started, so his stories of distant lands sometimes provoked my negative side. "Why don't you go stuff a grape leaf?" I'd mutter to myself.

After months on the show, he went home to Australia to visit his parents and enjoy some cheering from the fans for their returning homeboy. As I've said, *Days* was hot in the antipodes. Passing in the hall of Stage 9, the returned Thaao said in his princely way, "Oh, hello . . . didn't see you . . . just got back from Australia." "Really?" I responded generously. "Didn't notice you were gone." "Cunt!" he yelled.

An hour later I faced him, my eyes flowing with tears. "No one ever called me that before," I said.

"I'm surprised," he coolly replied.

We've gotten way beyond all that and discovered Penghlis and Hayes love all the same things—art, travel, good books and the ever-dangerous witty remark. He writes, he thinks, he sees the sights of life with the judgment of great taste. I look forward to hearing about his journeys now, and he makes me believe I'm the friend who appreciates his insights. Well, I really do.

Thaao has never stopped going to acting class and consequently growing as an artist, refining his gold. All actors want to appear opposite gifted friends. Thaao's operatic theatrical style is so mesmerizing I'd like to duet together in a great scene someday, just to prove I've got more notes than a C.

MARY FRANN

Mary Frann was our friend. How exquisite that face, how warm that heart. She played Amanda on *Days* before her memorable years as the leading lady on *The Bob Newhart Show*. Mary gave me a real-life wedding shower when I married my sweetie pie. Everything around her was delicate and fine. In her kitchen stood an antique iron stove. Mary couldn't actually cook anything, so that stove was covered with cut-glass decanters and thin-stemmed wineglasses.

The day of my shower, when ribbons were flying and we girls were at our giddiest, a tall woman in a long lace dress with hat and fan to match showed up to congratulate the bride and guests. "Where did she come from?" Denise Alexander asked. "Brazil! Where the nuts come from!" the lady answered, flicking open her fan. It was Bill in his *Where's Charley?* costume. (Why he had kept it I didn't dare to ask, since we were already married.)

Suzanne was a redhead, I was brunette, and Mary Frann was a champagne-blonde. I used to think, when we three pals put our heads together, we looked like the label on a jar of Jergen's face cream.

When Josh Taylor played the Chris Kositchek character, Mary was his partner. The lady and the tough-guy couple. Josh fell hard for Mary

for a while, and those scenes were some of his best. Then she had a story
line with Peter Brown as Dr. Greg Peters. Peter once donned his lab
coat for a hospital scene and kept calling the EKG results the XKE stats.
Mary called him baby-cakes. Brown is an actor who discovers a prop
and enjoys playing with it creatively. One day a bowl of peanuts turned
up in their pivotal love scene. Peter grabbed for it. He threw a nut in the
air, said, "I love you, Amanda," and caught it in his mouth, "I really do,"
then fielded another salted red-skin and crunched down affectionately.
Later Mary described the scene with her hair bouncing and invisible
peanuts. She was fit to be tied.

Mary was a marvelous actress. She appears in my lecture reel about
soaps, and I always catch my breath when I see her, acting up a storm in
our scene together, saying lines about our friendship and how she wants
the best for me. She passed away in her sleep on the eve of her second
marriage. The priest cried at her funeral, praising her generosity, faith-
fulness and selfless love. When Death's Bright Angel came, I know he
lifted Mary straight to God.

SERENADE IN BLUE

"Try aquamarine eye shadow. I think that will work very well." I had
just asked Deidre Hall for some makeup suggestions as I faced an upcoming photo shoot for my current headshot. I had never used aquamarine around my eyes before. Well, it looked good. Swell, actually. I
went out to get jewelry to go with the makeup. Sweaters to go with the
jewelry. Scarves to go with all of it. Now I have two colors to look for
in stores: black, my idea of a can't-go-wrong safe choice, and aqua, the
suggestion of a pal who ought to know. Now when I stand on deck
during a cruise, I am dressed to be at one with the ocean. Of course, I
never say so out loud.

Maybe it was our fourth anniversary, but certainly an early one, when
we spent the evening having dinner with Deidre and Quinn Redeker,
the handsome actor-writer who played Alex Marshall on *Days*. Quinn
was smitten with Dee, but then, "All the men fell in love with her," as
Frances Reid said. It was only a question of degree. Bill continued to

love me while Hall was brightening up our lives at work, and I'm damn grateful.

This particular anniversary Deidre had sewn two old-fashioned long-sleeved nightgowns together for a gift. The one opening accommodated two heads and, when slipped on, each person had one arm in a sleeve with a free hand and one hidden inside the gown to tickle the other with.

The restaurant we dined at was Middle Eastern, so I must have requested it. Anyway, we had lots of laughs around the baba ghanoush, before going back to our Studio City home. Wearing the marital-bundling gift, we said good night at our door, put out the porch light and drifted into the bedroom. Then, from somewhere in the bushes outside our window, two voices burst into "The Anniversary Waltz." It was Quinn and Dee serenading us, singing the old melody with humor and love. Come to think of it, that nightgown had an aqua bow.

THE BIG SOPRANO

"It isn't over till the fat lady sings," the old saying goes. That bravura soprano stands for the final resolution—the end. She never appears on soap operas, because daytime is about tomorrow and tomorrow. Well, we're not ready to hear that fat lady. Not yet. Like any devoted fan, I want to know what happens next and next . . . no endings, please. Ken Corday is still watching over the show his parents created and nurtured and Bill and Susan still feel at home in Salem. I've never seen anyone actually die on our stages, but we've all felt like biting the big one in the course of a scene. I can imagine it.

If our luck holds, maybe we'll all be onstage together when that abundant soprano opens up . . . and we'll go on to glory . . . hearing "The Look of Love."

22

Lessons

SUSAN

GET A LIFE

All my life I've been short on time because I filled the hours with too many tasks. I've done housework with such a will, whole years of my life must be counted as hard time at the kitchen sink and laundry basket. Clean beats dirty, after all. Ever since my marriage, and long before, I squeezed the hours to make space for flea-market safaris and the study of color swatches. The beautification of my personal nest and the houses of friends was an obsession. I flipped through all the home magazines, clipping and remembering without a Martha to guide me or a budget to ground me.

Even in the years of high employment I wanted to do it all myself. I gave up church to push the vacuum cleaner around on a Sunday morning, sweating and rushing toward perfection.

I was both proud of never having a maid and distracted by never getting things completely clean. A dinner party required two days just to get the house in shape before I could face the cooking. Just who all this manic housework was for was a puzzle. Bill doesn't notice dust or ever complain about disorder. We have no permanent houseguests or children living at home. As for pets, our dog, Scraps, is imaginary, and only jumps up to bark with joy and knock things over when we return from long trips. He's quite clean, too, and sheds no hair.

For years on "garbage night" I've wrestled those overflowing cans out into the moonlight, then next morning by seven I'd be hanging around the curb to check the big green city truck as it lumbered down the street, lest it miss our particular trash. Sometimes the driver waved at me, the one woman on his route who had clearly lost her mind.

"Get a life," moderns advise. Of course, I have a life, a great one, and I've given too much of it to the spirit-sucking cause of "home improvement." When Bill and I travel, we call any hotel room or friend's spare room "home." For us, home means any place we are together. Four walls and a mailbox are really meaningless. The person in the house is more important and deserves more attention than the décor.

I decorated my mother's home top to bottom twice, and talked and worried about fabrics and flower arrangements a great part of the time we were together (generally achieving stalemates rather than decisions, I must add). I wouldn't do that now; I'd spend more time looking at her rather than the pictures hanging on the walls. She was the golden egg and her house was just its shell. The Mother Goose that set her in that nest has flown away for good. Now I have her house to paint and change around to my heart's content, but she isn't in it. The rooms are empty as hell.

I suspect that this was the lesson I needed to learn. Too late to make Mother happy, but not too late to improve my relationships with everyone else. Not too late to stop losing sleep over choosing the finish for a drawer pull and take a deep breath in the pleasure of my husband's company. For all my worry and shopping, fussing and mopping, not one room of our house is done and perfect. But are they ever? People don't live in decorator showrooms, after all. Why become agitated over a slipcover?

Our home is pretty enough—not perfect, but a huge blessing. It's time to relax and enjoy it. Let the next "improvement" go and just ease into the worn upholstery of a cozy chair. Pick up the phone and call the friend whose voice I miss so much. I want those kitchen-sink-swabbing, dust-mopping, lampshade-switching years back . . . but they aren't coming. Oblivion is coming, and the next pile of dust is going to be me. Time to take it easy.

BILL

I COULDA BEEN A CONTENDA

When I was a boy, I played baseball every day. The first time my dad took me to Wrigley Field in Chicago to see a professional game is still vivid in my memory: Jurges to Herman to Grimm, Kiki Cuyler, Riggs Stephenson, Gabby Hartnett.

I got so I could hit pretty well. I always related to Yogi Berra, who would swing at the ball wherever it was—high, outside, in the dirt. In the fields where we played we never had a backstop, and often not even a catcher, so we'd swing at anything so we wouldn't have to run to retrieve the ball after every pitch.

If I hadn't ruined my throwing-arm rotator-cuff wrestling in the Navy, I think I could have enjoyed playing baseball for many years. Except for one thing. I never learned to spit.

In those days we didn't have trainers like they do today. I tried for years, but the secondary glob always landed on my chin. I burned my lip one day trying out chewing tobacco, my jaws ached after a day of chomping on paraffin, and the day I choked on my bubble gum, I realized I was never going to end up in professional baseball.

I look at it now as one of life's lessons. You have to soldier on through life's disappointments. Sometimes you have to resign yourself to the fact that you're going to enjoy your life through the accomplishments of others, and try not to be envious. My daughter-in-law Bonnie, for instance, can spit a watermelon seed all the way to the pitcher's mound. I just swallow my pride and live through her.

SUSAN

GIVE AND TAKE

Once I had a chance to exchange voice lessons for acting lessons. My teacher was the wonderful Carlo Thomas, a fine singer and inspired coach who always gets good results. In one lesson I shimmered with improvement. Then we strolled out of the music room at Valley College to sit on the grass and begin my part of the bargain. I floundered, waffled, and quickly dried up. I simply could not structure what I know about the art of performing into helpful sentences. Fortunately Carlo is a basso with bounce and didn't dump me, but transitioned into that old conversation starter, "Well, what have you read lately?" When you're in a situation of having nothing to give of yourself, remember you can always give the name of a good book. One good book can change the life of a questing soul. It happened to me.

I picked up a copy of *Beyond Geography* by Fredrick Turner on a remainder table in the bookstore years ago. It is more or less a history of the west as an idea, beginning with Genesis in the Old Testament and ending with the death of Buffalo Bill. I went crazy over it. I wrote to Turner himself to get my hands on twenty copies. He complied, and was surprised and pleased at my reaction, writing to inform me that most of his family had never gotten through the thing. I gave copies to pals until just a few were left. Because of that book I was turned on to Mary Austin, Wallace Stegner, and Barry Lopez, great writers I might have never known existed in my little autodidact world.

One day in Dutton's Books, North Hollywood, a customer wandered in looking for *Beyond Geography*, but the shop had nary a one. Overhearing, I thrust my face into the conversation, saying, "I have a copy. Wait here," dashed home, rifled my stack, and returned in ten minutes to sell the book myself on the sidewalk out front. This event jazzed me considerably.

When I met Turner in person over lunch in Santa Fe a few years later, fan paralysis grabbed me by the throat. Bill and Fred carried the conversational ball, talking music and jazz while I stirred my tortilla soup and stared at my favorite living author, simply gaga. I've stood in line to get autographs from Gore Vidal and Larry McMurtry with the same voiceless reverence. To me a book is magic, a piece of the writer's mind to clutch in hand, and hold in your heart as well. Even if you never meet in the flesh, you and that writer are communing in consciousness.

BILL

GOLDEN LIGHT

Filmmakers often shoot their most meaningful scenes late in the afternoon, when shadows stretch out and the sun's rays pass through a cushion of mist just above the horizon. This effect, called "golden light," is actually the beginning of sunset. From then on, as shadows deepen, the golden light becomes tinged with orange and rose, nature's most vivid palette of warm colors.

When life's shadows lengthen toward the infinite, bright golden spotlights bathe our most memorable scenes, enhancing their importance. Lesser objects fade from sight, and what is left is of purest value, of rarest beauty.

What is golden light illuminating for me? People, always people. The treasure of my heart is my family. My children. And their families. The oval frames in my personal gallery contain the dear pictures of my parents and grandparents, my aunts and uncles and cousins and nephews and nieces and many friends as close as family. My sweetest memories are of the times we spent together.

My career has been six decades long. I've been happy with my moments of success and celebrity, the magnitude and flashes of stardom that I've tasted along the way. I've entertained and pleased a lot of people, and for that I am certainly proud.

Yet sharing the past thirty years with Susan is center stage in my golden spotlight. The rosy thread of affection that ties me to my children and my wife warms my heart more than any STANDING ROOM ONLY sign ever could.

SUSAN

GIVE ME A HUG

I miss "You're welcome." Remember that phrase? You would say "Thank you" for some little service or kindness, like being handed a purchase across a counter, and the person on the other side would smile and say, "You're welcome." It meant "The pleasure was mine" or "I'm glad we did this business together, you and I."

Now people say, "No problem." It's not the same. It means "It cost me nothing, taking care of you is of no consequence, and there's plenty left of me." No problem, no nothing. And forget the smile. Smiles shine in memory more than modern urban experience. Too bad. I suppose the coldness has crept in since more of us interface with electric screens than people to receive information.

We have a wonderful grandson who spoke little and listened well as a child. He looked at a multitude of screens. He's never cultivated the facial animation of an actor, so when he brooded or smiled you knew it was coming from deep inside. He's a master of the dot-com universe and drives a business empire. Most wonderful to me, since his recent happy marriage, he's learned to smile.

We attended a family wedding last month, where his little sister tied the knot beside a lake in Maine, with kilts and pipers and a Scottish groom. It was a golden day, with all the hundred and more guests standing around in generational clumps. As I ambled by this grandson, splendid in his plaid costume and beaming at his sister's happiness, he called out to me, "Give me a hug." Oh, I felt so much when he said that, surprised, connected, wanted . . . loved. I'm still hugging him in my prayers.

So, in addition to never storing tomatoes in the refrigerator, here's what I've learned in sixty years. Don't spare your smiles, the world is too hard to bear without them. Hug the person you yearn to, another chance may never come. Say "You're welcome" when someone thanks you for the sweet taste of life you've given them. Love the Lord. Learn your lines.

That's all I know for certain. I hope it's enough.

BILL

WE

And so I come back to where I started, the day Susan and I met in the *Days* office, April 1970. What a golden ride it's been from that day to this. Thirty-five years of work, dreams, and a genuinely shared life of love.

I love Susan a lot, and I know she loves me. And, with thanks in my heart, I will quote my grandfather's poem, written to his wife a hundred years ago.

> That I am I and you are you
> Would seem indubitably true;
> And without me can you deny
> There's something you would fain supply?
> And now the real truth I see—
> How fully you and I are we.

>> —W. Foster Hayes

SUSAN

HORIZONS

Today, when we lecture on cruise ships, the topics are from our career experiences in early television and soap opera, with tapes of old golden performances thrown in for nostalgia's sake. These "enrichment" programs are attended by people on vacation, having a wonderful time in the salty air and luxurious surroundings, who probably haven't given television a thought for years. Many are just looking for a cool spot out of the sun to sleep off a delicious lunch, some are early for the movie scheduled next in the theater space. A few are fans, and several folks recognize us but can't exactly pinpoint from where.

We set the scene, and run the tapes. The audience gets caught up in the stories and laughs, then cries. This surprised me at first, because Bill's classic shows are filled with comedy and wonderful music. A lady from New York explained, "It all takes me back to my childhood when the whole family was there gathered around the set to watch our shows together. I'm remembering my family, too." She was smiling at us through heartfelt tears.

I understand. For years I couldn't look at our tapes of days gone by, but now I think the present can only be enriched by staying in touch with the past. Bill and I have had wonderful long runs in life. We've shared many kinds of happiness. I'm sure, though, if we are remembered at all, it will be for being connected to a soap opera and each other.

This is what we tell the cruisers: "Most actors' turns are limited; the play closes, the movie wraps, the festival is finished. But with soaps the stories go on and on, and the prize for remembering them all is sharing with others, who just can't seem to forget. Here's the important part: If you have ever been a fan and felt a little foolish for loving an actor, a character, a dream, I assure you that the actor loved you back and for one shared moment . . . your dream came true."

On the ship we thank our lecture audience, and one by one they depart. We pack up our tapes and walk out on deck to face the endless blue arm in arm, wind ruffling our silver hairs. Bill gives me a kiss, and together we turn toward the far horizon. It's a happy ending.